SHADOW WAR

Untold Story of Jihad in South Asia

SHADOW WAR

Untold Story of Jihad in South Asia

Brig. M.N. Sarin (Retd.)

Gaurav Book Centre Pvt Ltd

Delhi

Publisher
GAURAV BOOK CENTRE PVT LTD
4832/24,Prahlad Lane,S-207 Ansari
Road, Daryaganj, Delhi-110002
Ph.: 43570976, 23278261
Email: gauravbookcentre@gmail.com

Edition: 2016

ISBN: 978-93-83316-23-6

Laser Typesetting
JEE-VEE Graphics, Delhi

Price: 1295/-

Printed
Vikas Computers, Delhi

Contents

Preface

Analysts have often cited Pakistan's support for Islamist militancy as strategically shortsighted. Islamabad has adhered to essentially the same strategy in pursuit of the same ends for most of its history, using non-state actors in an effort to alter territorial boundaries in South Asia without triggering a full-scale conventional conflict in the region.

From the viewpoint of the ISI, if the death of hundreds of soldiers may serve their interest, the price is not too high. The Swat valley is a critical issue because if the jihadists continue to gain ground, they will have a corridor linking Afghanistan and Kashmir. No army can then dislodge an alliance between jihadists, Taliban and members of al-Qaeda which has a sanctuary in that part of the Himalayas.

Another concept that deserves clarification due in the context of our discussion is that of "jihad". The exact meaning of "Jihad" is "effort". Thus, in Islam, "to carry out jihad" is "to show effort, to struggle". The Prophet Muhammad explained that "the greatest jihad is the one a person carries out against his lower soul". What is meant by "lower soul" here is selfish desires and ambitions.

This book is a modest attempt to discuss all these issues.

—Editor

1

Introduction to "Jihad"

Another concept that deserves clarification due in the context of our discussion is that of "jihad". The exact meaning of "Jihad" is "effort". Thus, in Islam, "to carry out jihad" is "to show effort, to struggle". The Prophet Muhammad explained that "the greatest jihad is the one a person carries out against his lower soul". What is meant by "lower soul" here is selfish desires and ambitions.

Assessed from the Qur'anic point of view, the word "jihad" can also mean a struggle carried out on intellectual grounds against those who oppress people, treat them unjustly, subject them to torture and cruelty and violate legitimate human rights. The purpose of this struggle is to bring about justice, peace and equality. Apart from these ideological and spiritual meanings, struggle in the physical sense is also considered as "jihad". However, as explained above, this has to be a struggle carried out solely for defensive purposes. The use of the concept of "jihad" for acts of aggression against innocent people, that is for terror, would be unjust and a great distortion of the true meaning of the term.

Killing Oneself, In Other Words Committing Suicide, is Forbidden in the Qur'an

Another important matter that arose in the wake of the latest terrorist assaults against the United States is that of suicide attacks. Some people who are ill-informed on Islam have made utterly erroneous statements to the effect that this religion of peace allows suicide attacks, whereas in Islam killing oneself and killing other people are both prohibited. In the words, "Do not kill yourselves."

(Qur'an, 4:29) God has declared suicide to be a sin. In Islam it is forbidden for anyone to kill himself or herself, for no matter what reason. The Prophet reveals suicide to be a sin in a parable, when he says that those who commit suicide will be punished:

> *Indeed, whoever (intentionally) kills himself, then certainly he will be punished in the Fire of Hell, wherein he shall dwell forever.*

As this makes clear, committing suicide, and thus carrying out suicide attacks, and causing the deaths of thousands of innocent people while doing so, is a total violation of Islamic morality. God says in the Qur'an that it is a sin to put an end to one's own life. For that reason, it is quite impossible for someone who believes in God and says he abides by the Qur'an to do such a thing. The only people who can do such things are those who have a very mistaken perception of religion, have no idea of true Qur'anic morality, fail to use their reason and conscience, are under the influence of atheist ideologies, and who have been brainwashed with feelings of hatred and revenge. Everybody must oppose such actions.

COMPASSION, TOLERANCE AND HUMANITY IN THE HISTORY OF ISLAM

To sum up the facts we have seen so far, we can say that the political doctrine of Islam (in other words, Islamic rules and principles regarding political matters) is exceedingly moderate and peace-loving. This truth is accepted by many non-Muslim historians and theologians. One of these is the British historian Karen Armstrong, a former nun and an expert on Middle East history. In her book Holy War, which examines the history of the three divine religions, she makes the following comments:

> *... The word 'Islam' comes from the same Arabic root as the word 'peace' and the Koran condemns war as an abnormal state of affairs opposed to God's will... Islam does not justify a total aggressive war of extermination... Islam recognises that war is inevitable and sometimes a positive duty in order to end oppression and suffering. The Koran teaches that war must be limited and be conducted in as humane a way as possible. Mohammad had to fight not only the Meccans but also the Jewish tribes in*

the area and Christian tribes in Syria who planned on offensive against him in alliance with the Jews. Yet this did not make Mohammed denounce the People of the Book. His Muslims were forced to defend themselves but they were not fighting a 'holy war' against the religion of their enemies. When Mohammad sent his freedman Zaid against the Christians at the head of a Muslim army, he told them to fight in the cause of God bravely but humanely. They must not molest priests, monks and nuns nor the weak and helpless people who were unable to fight. There must be no massacre of civilians nor should they cut down a single tree nor pull down any building.

After the death of the Prophet, the Caliphs who succeeded him were also very sensitive in exercising justice. In conquered countries, both the indigenous people and the newcomers led their lives in peace and security. Abu Bakr, the first Caliph, demanded his people adopt just and tolerant attitudes in these lands. All these attitudes were in compliance with the values of the Qur'an. Abu Bakr gave the following command to his army before the first Syrian expedition:

Stop, O people that I may give you ten rules to keep by heart: Do not commit treachery, nor depart from the right path. You must not mutilate, neither kill a child or aged man or woman. Do not destroy a palm tree, nor burn it with fire and do not cut any fruitful tree. You msut not slay any of the flock or herds or the camels, save for your subsistence. You are likely to pass by people who have devoted their lives to monastic services; leave them to that to which they have devoted their lives. You are likely, likewise, to find people who will present to you meals of many kinds. You may eat; but do no forget to mention the name of Allah.

Umar ibn al-Khattab, who succeeded Abu Bakr, was famous for the way he exercised justice and made contracts with the indigenous people of the conquered countries. Each one of these contracts proved to be an example of tolerance and justice. For instance, in his declaration granting protection to Christians in Jerusalem and Lod, he ensured that churches would not be demolished and guaranteed that Muslims would not worship in churches in groups. Umar granted the same conditions to the

Christians of Bethlehem. During the conquest of Medain, the declaration of protection given to the Nestorian Patriarch Yeshuyab III (650 - 660 AD) again guaranteed that churches would not be demolished and that no building would be converted into a house or a mosque. The letter written by the patriarch to the bishop of Fars (Persia) after the conquest is most striking, in the sense that it depicts the tolerance and compassion shown by Muslim rulers to the Book of People in the words of a Christian:

> *They [Abbasids] have not attacked the Christian religion, but rather they have commended our faith, honored our priests... and conferred benefits on churches and monasteries.*

All these are very important examples revealing the understanding of justice and tolerance of true believers. In a verse God commands the following:

> *God commands you to return to their owners the things you hold on trust and, when you judge between people, to judge with justice. How excellent is what God exhorts you to do! God is All-Hearing, All-Seeing. (Qur'an, 4:58)*

Canon Taylor, one of the mission leaders of the Anglican Church, expresses the beauty revealed by the Islamic morality in one of his speeches as follows:

> *It [Islam] brought out the fundamental dogmas of religion – the unity and greatness of God, that He is merciful and righteous, that He claims obedience to His will, resignation and faith. It proclaimed the responsibility of man, a future life, a Day of Judgment, and stern retribution to fall upon the wicked; and enforced the duties of prayer, almsgiving, fasting and benevolence. It thrust aside the artificial virtues, the religious frauds and follies, the perverted moral sentiments, and the verbal subtleties of theological disputants... It gave hope to the slave, brotherhood to mankind, and recognition to the fundamental facts of human nature.*

The false assertion that people in conquered countries converted to Islam under threat has also been disproved by Western researchers, and the justice and tolerant attitude of Muslims has been confirmed. L.Browne, a Western researcher, expresses this situation in the following words:

> *Incidentally these well-established facts dispose of the idea so widely fostered in Christian writings that the Muslims, wherever they went, forced people to accept Islam at the point of the sword.*

In his book The Prospects of Islam, Browne goes on to say that the real motive behind the Muslims' conquests was the brotherhood of Islam. The vast majority of Muslim administrators who have reigned over the Muslim lands throughout history continued to treat the members of other religions with the utmost tolerance and respect. Within the borders of all Islamic states, both Jews and Christians lived in safety and enjoyed freedom.

Georgetown University's Professor of Religion and International Relations John L. Esposito describes how Jews and Christians who came under the administration of Muslim states met with enormous tolerance:

> *Muslim armies proved to be formidable conquerors and effective rulers, builders rather than destroyers. They replaced the indigenous rulers and armies of the conquered countries, but preserved much of their government, bureaucracy, and culture. For many in the conquered territories, it was no more than an exchange of masters, one that brought peace to peoples demoralized and disaffected by the casualties and heavy taxation that resulted from the years of Byzantine-Persian warfare. Local communities were free to continue to follow their own way of life in internal, domestic affairs. In many ways, local populations found Muslim rule more flexible and tolerant than that of Byzantium and Persia. Religious communities were free to practise their faith-to worship and be governed by their religious leaders and laws in such areas marriage, divorce, and inheritance. In exchange, they were required to pay tribute, a poll tax (jizya) that entitled them to from Muslim protection from outside aggression and exempted them from military service. They were therefore called the "protected ones" (dhimmmi). In effect, this often meant lower taxes, grater local autonomy, rule by fellow Semites with closer linguistic and cultural ties than the hellenized, Greco-Roman elites of Byzantium, and greater religious freedom for Jews and indigenous Christians. Most of the Christian churches, such as the Nestorians, Monophysites,*

Jacobites, and Copts, had been persecuted as heretics and schismatics by Christian orthodoxy. For these reasons, some Jewish and Christian communities aided the invading armies, regarding them as less oppressive than their imperial masters. In many ways, the conquests brought a Pax Islamica to an embattled area.

Another "Pax Islamica" brought by Islam was to women, a segment of society that was tremendously abused in the pre-Islamic times. Professor Bernard Lewis, known to be one of the greatest Western experts on the Middle East, makes the following comment:

In general, the advent of Islam brought an enormous improvement in the position of women in ancient Arabia, endowing them with property and some other rights, and giving them a measure of protection against ill treatment by their husbands or owners. The killing of female infants, sanctioned by custom in Pagan Arabia, was outlawed by Islam. But the position of women remained poor, and worsened when, in this as in so many other respects, the original message of Islam lost its impetus and was modified under the influence of pre-existing attitudes and customs.

The reign of the Seljuk Turks and that of the Ottoman Empire were also marked by the just and tolerant outlook of Islam. In his book, *The Spread of Islam in the World,* Sir Thomas Arnold, the British researcher, explains the Christians' willingness to come under Seljuk rule because of this attitude:

This same sense of security of religious life under Muslim rule led many of the Christians of Asia Minor, also, about the same time, to welcome the advent of the Saljuq Turks as their deliverers... In the reign of Michael VIII (1261-1282), the Turks were often invited to take possession of the smaller towns in the interior of Asia Minor by the inhabitants, that they might escape from the tyranny of the empire; and both rich and poor often emigrated into Turkish dominions.

Malik Shah, the ruler of the Islamic Seljuk Empire during its brightest age, approached the people in the conquered lands with great tolerance and compassion and thus was remembered with respect and love by them. All objective historians refer to the justice and tolerance of Malik Shah in their works. His tolerance also kindled feelings of love towards him in the hearts of the People of the Book. For this reason, unprecedented in history, many cities came under Malik Shah's rule of their own free will. Sir Thomas Arnold also mentions Odo de Diogilo, a monk of St. Denis, who participated in the Second Crusade as the private chaplain of Louis VII, refers in his memoirs to the justice administered by Muslims regardless of the subjects' religious affiliation. Based on the graphic account of Odo de Diogilo, Sir Thomas Arnold writes:

> *The situation of the survivors would have been utterly hopeless, had not the sight of their misery melted the hearts of the Muhammadans to pity. They tended the sick and relieved the poor and starving with open-handed liberality. Some even bought up the French money which the Greeks had got out of the pilgrims by force or cunning, and lavishly distributed it among the needy. So great was the contrast between the kind treatment the pilgrims received from the unbelievers and the cruelty of their fellow-Christians, the Greeks, who imposed forced labour upon them, beat them, and robbed them of what little they had left, that many of them voluntarily embraced the faith of their deliverers. As the old chronicler [Odo de Diogilo] says: "Avoiding their co-religionists who had been so cruel to them, they went in safety among the infidels who had compassion upon them, and, as we heard, more than three thousand joined themselves to the Turks when they retired."*

These statements by historians reveal that Muslim administrators who truly adopted the morality of the Islam always ruled with tolerance, compassion and justice. Likewise, the history of the Ottoman Empire which ruled lands on three continents for centuries abounds with examples of tolerance.

The way the Jews settled in Ottoman lands during the time of Sultan Beyazid II, after being subjected to massacre and exile in the Catholic kingdoms of Spain and Portugal, is a fine example of the tolerance that Islamic morality brings with it.

The Catholic monarchs who ruled much of Spain at the time brought grave pressure to bear on the Jews who had formerly lived in peace under Muslim rule in Andalusia. While Muslims, Christians and Jews were able to live side by side in peace in Andalusia, the Catholic monarchs tried to force the whole country to become Christian, and declared war on the Muslims while oppressing the Jews. As a result, the last Muslim ruler in the Granada region of southern Spain was overthrown in 1492. Muslims were subjected to terrible slaughter, and those Jews who refused to change their religion were sent into exile.

One group of these Jews without a homeland sought shelter in the Ottoman Empire, and the state allowed them to do so. The Ottoman fleet, under the command of Kemal Reis, brought the exiled Jews, and those Muslims who had survived the slaughter, to the land of the Ottomans.

Sultan Beyazid II has gone down in history as a most pious believer, and in the spring of 1492 he settled these wronged Jews who had been expelled from Spain in certain parts of his empire, around Edirne, and Thessalonica in present-day Greece. Most of the 25,000 Turkish Jews living in Turkey today are the ancestors of those Spanish Jews. They have adapted their religion and customs, which they brought from Spain some 500 years ago, to the conditions in Turkey, and continue to live most comfortably with their own schools, hospitals, old people's homes, cultural associations and newspapers. In the same way that they have traders and businessmen, they also have representatives in numerous professions, from technical subjects to advertising, with increasingly developing intellectual circles. While Jewish communities in many countries in Europe have for centuries been exposed to the fear of anti-Semitic racist attacks, those in Turkey have lived in peace and security. This example alone is enough to demonstrate the tolerance that Islam brings with it and its understanding of justice.

The compassion and tolerance exhibited by Sultan Beyazid II applied to all the Ottoman sultans. When Sultan Mehmet the Conqueror captured Constantinople, he allowed the Christians and the Jews to live freely there. André Miquel, who is known for the valuable works he has written about the just and tolerant practices of Muslims and the world of Islam, says:

Christians lived under a very well-administered government which they were unable to find in the time of the Byzantine and Latin states. They at no time saw any systematic oppression. On the contrary, the empire, and Constantinople in particular, became a shelter for those Spanish Jews who had been tortured. There was no forced imposition of Islam anywhere.

As is clear from these facts, Muslims have at no time in history been oppressive. On the contrary, they have brought peace and security to all nations and beliefs wherever they have gone. They have abided by God's verse which says: "Worship God and do not associate anything with Him. Be good to your parents and relatives and to orphans and the very poor, and to neighbours who are related to you and neighbours who are not related to you, and to companions and travellers and your slaves. God does not love anyone vain or boastful." (Qur'an, 4:36) and have behaved well to all people. In short, friendship, brotherhood, peace and love are the bases of Qur'anic morality, and it is to these superior virtues that Muslims try to adhere.

WHAT IS ISLAMISM? HISTORY AND DEFINITION OF A CONCEPT

Once, Jacques Delors, the former president of the EU Commission, defined the European Union (EU) as a UPO (Unidentified Political Object). By this definition, he of course wanted to emphasise the particularity and the uniqueness of the EU as a new and unprecedented political and economical construction. The UPO metaphor may also be applied to Islamism, as a URO (Unidentified Religious Object), since scholars have not yet reached a consensus about the definition and the meaning of this concept. Since the nineteenth century, the concept 'Islamism' has been used quite differently by western orientalists, islamologists and political scientists. The situation is not much clearer within the Muslim world. Muslims are using various names and appellations to define themselves and their coreligionists, '*Islamiyyûn*' [Islamists] being one of them.

It is almost certain that the etiquette of 'Islamism' was used for the first time by French writers at the end of the seventeenth century. *Le Petit Robert* gives 1697 as the first reference to the word. The Enlightenment philosopher Voltaire is one of the first writers to use the term: 'this religion is called *islamism*'. In a work from 1838, Tocqueville found the 'root of *islamism* in Judaism'. Caussin de Perceval, Comte de Gobineau, Ernest Renan and Baron Bernard Carra de Vaux equally make use of the term, the latter characterising 'Islamism' as a 'spent religion'.

The above-mentioned writers use 'Islamism' as part of the title of their respective works, either of a book or a chapter. Caussin de Perceval places it in the title of his book *Essai sur l'histoire des Arabes avant l'Islamisme, pendant l'époque de Mahomet* (3 vols, 1847–9). This title leaves no doubt that, in the mind of the author, 'Islamism' means 'Islam', e.g. the religion founded by Muhammad. Comte de Gobineau has devoted Chapter II of his book on *Religions et philosophies dans l'Asie Centrale* to the study of *l'Islamisme persan*. He considers Islamism as a camouflaged mixture of religions prior to Islam. After this very short remark, Gobineau continues his fascinating analysis on Iranian and central Asian societies, although he does not concern himself to engage in a further analysis of 'Islamism'. It is very clear that Gobineau uses the term 'Islamism' only in the sense of 'Islam' without any specific political or ideological connation. Some years later, Ernest Renan, a compatriot of Gobineau, used the term 'Islamism', especially at the famous conference he held at the Sorbonne (Paris) on 29 March 1883. This conference became very famous, and still is, because of its highly polemical aspect. At that time, an enigmatic Muslim personage named Sayyid Jamal al-Afghani (1838–97) was agitating in Egypt, Persia and the Ottoman Turkey. He sojourned in Paris and engaged himself in a lively debate concerning the position of Islam towards modernity and science. It is in this context that Renan holds his speech on *Islamisme et la Science*. Renan, in perfect accordance with the intellectual context of his epoch, uses 'Islamism' as a parallel to 'Christianism' (the equivalent of 'Christianity' in English). By 'Islamism', Renan simply means 'Islam' as he uses 'Islam' and 'Islamism' as interchangeable terms.

'Islam' and 'Islamic' have become the most frequently used terms by western islamologists, orientalists and political scientists.

This replacement is very clear indeed among a huge number of western writers of multiple disciplines, from Ignaz Goldziher (1850–1921), Arnold Toynbee (1852–83), Max Weber (1864–1920), Oswald Spengler (1880–1936), Fernand Braudel (1902–85), Claude Cahen (1909– 1991), Ann K.S. Lambton (b. 1912), Henri Laoust (d. 1976) and William Montgomery Watt (1909–2006) to contemporary scholars such as Samuel Huntington and Francis Fukuyama. We do not find the word 'Islamism' in the index of their works. Prior to the Islamist revolution in Iran in 1978–79, the terms 'Islamism' and 'Islamists' are also practically absent from the vocabulary of newspaper reporters.

The change in the vocabulary happened with the outbreak of the Islamic revolution under the leadership of Ayatollah Khomeini, who preached a political Islam and established the first '*Islamist* government' in the twentieth century. This religious revolution made it imperative to find a new vocabulary in order to outline the specificity of this new phenomenon. Suddenly, the world witnessed a multitude of terms and formal rules destined to grasp the 'novelty' of the new era in the history of Islam. By way of example, frequently used terms were 'Islamic fundamentalism', 'radical Islam', 'Islamic revival' and 'political Islam'. These terms, which became titles of numerous books and multiple articles, were clear and ambivalent at the same time. They indicated that this kind of 'Islam' is quite different from other versions of 'Islam'. However, what precisely does this 'new' form of 'Islam' contain? The ambiguity remains almost complete. Surely, it has become evident that this particular form of Islam was (more) political, often violent and severely critical towards the West, and, last but not least, determined in its hostility towards established regimes in the Muslim world. Nevertheless, this list determining the main characteristics of 'Islamic fundamentalism', 'political Islam', 'Islamic radicalism' or 'radical Islamism' does not bring about a clear conceptualisation of the phenomenon.

We had to wait until the tragic events of 9/11 to witness the rise of the need for conceptual clarification. It is a fact that, since 9/11, the use of the word 'Islamism' has increased among politicians and journalists worldwide. It is equally observable that scholars have progressively focused their attention on the ideological contients of Islamism.

Diverging from the nineteenth-century definition, 'Islamism' is no longer an emulation of '*christianisme*', but a rather new and independent concept. This change is observable in scholars' works, and particularly so in books and articles posterior to 9/11. For example, two eminent French islamologists, Olivier Roy and Gilles Kepel, previously used both 'political Islam' and 'fundamentalist Islam' extensively whereas they now tend to use 'Islamism' more and more often.

The term appears neither alone nor besides 'neofundamentalism' or 'political Islam'. Actually, the latter term is not equivalent to 'Islamism' in Olivier Roy's terminology. 'Political Islam' designates a failed project in his works, whereas 'Islamism' denominates the new form of activist Islam.

Bruno Etienne, director of the *Observatoire du Religieux* at the Department of Political Science, University of Aix-en-Provence, has dedicated much of his time to the study of Islam and gives the following definition of 'radical Islamism': 'it proposes as a cure of all the evils of modernity/modernisation the return to political Islam's roots: the ideal City State of the *Rashîdun*, (the 'rightly guided' four Caliphs: 632–61)'.

In general, 'Islamism' is abundantly present in many other articles and books. Malise Ruthven's new book on *Fundamentalism* is another example. Despite the title, she extensively uses 'Islamism' in her analysis. Parallel to 'Islamism', some authors are also using 'radical Islamism' (William E. Shepard), 'Islamic Activism' (Quintan Wiktorowicz) or 'Mobilizing Islam' (Carrie R. Wickham). The above examples are only representative, tracing the general trend on this issue without being exhaustive.

How do Muslim authors designate themselves and their coreligionists? In Arabic, Muslim/Muslims are called *Muslîm* (singular masculine), *Muslima* (singular feminine), *Muslimûn* (plural masculin) or *Muslimât* (plural feminine). However, the Muslim equivalent to Islamists is *Islamiyyûn*; it is used only in this form (plural masculine) and therefore with a significantly limited and restricted use.

The Qur'an uses the terms *Muslimûn* along with *Mu'minûn* [Believers], never *Islamiyyûn*. Islamic classical works generally respect the Qur'anic terminology. Theologians from the four prevailing schools (Hanafi, Mâliki, Shâfi'i and Hanbali) use *Muslimûn* and *Muslim*, not *Islamiyyûn*.

The same can be noticed in the works of great medieval historians, jurists and thinkers such as Ibn Ishâq (d. 768), Ibn Hishâm (753–5), Bukhari (810–70), Farâbi (870–950), Mas'udi (d. 958), Mawardi (972–1058), Avicena (980–1037), Ghazâli (1058–1111), Averroes (1126–98) and Ibn Khaldun (1332–1406). The same tradition is observed and followed in modern times among Muslim authors of the eighteenth, nineteenth and twentieth centuries.

This trend is observed with authors such as Muhammad Ibn Abd al-Wahhab (1703–92, the founder of Wahhabi sect), Sayyid Jamal al-Afghani (1838–97), Muhammad Abduh (1849–1905) and Rashid Rida (1865–1935). Continuing our route forward, we observe that Muslim leaders who played a crucial role in the twentieth century did not use 'Islamism' in their abundant works. Hasan al-Banna (1906–48), in his famous work *Rasâ'il* [Tracts], extensively uses 'Muslims' and 'Muslim Brothers' especially when addressing his own disciples. When he investigated 'Islam', he sporadically used the term *'Islam al-shâmil'* [Self-sustained Islam] or *'Islam al-Hanif'* [the True Islam]. Neither the zealous ideologue of the Muslim Brotherhood Sayyid Qutb (1906–66) nor Mawdudi (1903–79), an eminent Islamist leader of Southwest Asia, used the term 'Islamism'. A last example would be Ayatollah Khomeini (1902–89), who brought political Islam from theory into reality. While being a Shi'a, he used the same terms as the Sunnis, e.g. *'Muslimîn'* or *'Musalmanân'* (Persian version of Muslims). However, a number of Muslim authors actually have used 'Islamism' [*Islamiyyûn*]. The Sudanese Hasan al-Turabi (b. 1932) is one of them. When he discusses different fractions among Muslims in his book *Al-Islam wal Hukm* [Islam and Government], he uses *Islamiyyûn* to designate 'political Muslims for whom Islam is the solution, Islam is religion and government and Islam is the Constitution and the law'.

Some (Muslim) lay authors increasingly use *Islamiyyûn*, as for example the Tunisian Salwa al-Sharafi, author of *Al-Islamiyyûn wal-Dimuqrâtiyya* [Islamists and Democracy]. We find a thorough analysis of Islamism in Larbi Sadiki's book *The Search for Arab Democracy*, where he presents a critical analysis on Islamist discourse and ideas, although not as an independent study, but as an appendix to the main issue of his book (democracy). The problem is that Sadiki, like western authors, deals with the terms 'Islamism' and 'Islamists' without providing a clear definition of these concepts.

Aziz al-Azmeh, the author of *Islams and Modernities*, labels contemporary Islamic movements 'political Islamism' and not, for instance, 'Islamic fundamen-talism'. William Shepard uses 'Islamic totalism' to describe 'the tendency to view Islam not merely as a "religion" in the narrow sense of theological belief, private prayer and ritual worship, but also as a total way of life with guidance for political, economic, and social behaviour'. Commonly, this takes the form of the claim that Muslims should have an 'Islamic state', 'that is, a state in which all law is based on the *Shari'a*'.

This is, in our view, a fairly precise definition of what 'Islamism' is. However, it is difficult to understand why Shepard constructs a neologism 'Islamic totalism' different from 'Islamism', which in his view is 'the tendency to view Islam as an ideology'.

Unfortunately, he does not elaborate further on the reason for this distinction between the two terms 'Islamic totalism' and 'Islamism'. Shepard's merits lie essentially in his conscious academic *démarche*, where he acknowledges the necessity of defining concepts that a scholar has the intention to use in his/her works. He points out that labels such as 'fundamentalist', 'modernist' and 'secularist' have 'undoubtedly often functioned as obstacles to understanding the actual people and tendencies involved, in part because they are frequently used without explicit definition'. It is equally interesting to observe how various Muslim groups address each other, whether in a friendly or an unfriendly manner. Let us mention some of the most noticeable and politically significant groups. At the very beginning of Islam's history, the first group which was distinguished in a negative way from the community of Muslims is the *Munafiqûn* [Hypocrites]. At the time of Muhammad's rule in Medina, they expressed views that differed from and even contradicted Muhammad's world vision. They built a mosque without his authorisation, which led him to qualify their mosque as *Masjid al-Zirar* [The Mosque of Dissension].

The Qur'an is particularly severe vis-à-vis this particular group. The second group is the *Khawârij*, who, under the Caliphate of Ali (656–61), disapproved of his decision to accept the arbitration between him and his rival Mu'awiya. Later in history, the immense Muslim empire has witnessed the emergence of a variety of concurrent groups and sects: Sunni (various schools) vs Shi'a (different sects), *Mujâhid* [Combatant] vs *Munâfiq* [Hypocrite], *Khâriji*, ['Excommunicated'], *Mu'tazili* ['Rationalists'], *Usûli* [Theological Fundamentalist] vs *Akhbâri* [believing that the tradition of the prophet provides sufficient guidance], and finally, in the Iranian context, *Khodi* [Insider] vs *Nâ khodi* [Outsider]. In fact, Iranian 'Islamists' of our day call themselves *'Usul gara'*, which literally means 'fundamentalist', but in a positive sense. It designates a 'person of principles' who is the 'true Muslim'. These Muslim authorities who are against Islamists often call them *Irhâbiyyûn* [Terrorists] or *Mutatarrifûn* [Extremists].

In the light of these considerations, it seems necessary to present a definition of 'Islamism'. This definition must satisfy two demands. First, it must encompass all or at least the most significant elements that are normally attributed to 'Islamism'. Second, it must exclude attributes that are alien to 'Islamism'.

AN IN-DEPTH ANALYSIS OF JIHADISM

Jihad is an Arabic word that literally means "combat" or "striving" and jihad is sometimes regarded along with allegiance to the Iman as the violent Sixth Pillar of Islam, although orthodox Islam only recognizes Five Pillars. The idea of jihad being the violent Sixth Pillar comes from the Khawarij sect, which was part of the fundamentalist Islamism movement that started in the early 20th Century.

The Khawarij sect is named after Dhul-Khuwaysarah, a man that Muhammad prophesied would have an overprotective love of religion. The Khawariji interpretation of the role of excommunication is completely the opposite of the Salafist interpretation of excommunication (*takfir*). Salafism is rather restricted about who should be declared an infidel and therefore excommunicated. Followers of the Khawariji interpretation, or Jihadists, see few if any restrictions on who can be declared an infidel, and therefore justify unrestricted warfare or terrorism against infidels. Even traditional Qur'anic interpretations hold that those who reject Islam reject God, and one of the principal characteristics of rejecting God (*kufr*) is the inclination toward violence and oppression, encapsulated by the broad concept *zulm*, which means transgression against one's own soul or human nature. Now, many if not most Muslims reject the duty to propagate Islam by force and limit jihad to self-defence (Hashmi 2006), but then again, there is no such thing as a pacifist movement in Islam, and most Muslims respect the necessity of a continuous tension between incessant warfare and peace.

There is some controversy in Islamic thought as to whether jihad can be declared before or after an enemy attacks, or in other words, in a pre-emptive strike or in self-defence. A strict and literal reading of the Qur'an says self-defence only, but Islamic law has always justified a first-strike position. Just saying that women ought to have a right to vote is a crime of violence against all of Islam, and this can trigger a Jihadist reaction against not only the person who said that, but against whomever they got that idea from — a kind of scorched earth policy or nipping things in the bud. The basis for most anti-Americanism among Muslim extremists is part of the notion that any country that would give women the right to vote, or all minorities equal rights, is probably a country populated by infidels who are attacking Islam with crimes of violence. It may be important to note the quite popular opinion in the Muslim world that it was under attack by America first. Jihad is also part of the name in at least two terrorist groups that make up the shadowy umbrella group called Islamic Jihad, which has millions of supporters throughout the Islamic world because these supporters agree with militaristic interpretations of jihad. The two main groups are the Egyptian Islamic Jihad and the Palestinian Islamic Jihad, both formed in the mid-1970s with origins going back to the 1928 Muslim Brotherhood.

Suicide bombings (a tactic that came into popularity around 1983) are a trademark of jihadists. The religious element involved is that believers think they will attain a heavenly reward for their sacrifice. The political element involved is that it sends a message of how desperate and passionate the believers are. Expert opinion is mixed on the effectiveness of suicide bombing as a strategy of asymmetric warfare. Experts also agree that it is difficult if not impossible to profile a suicide bomber. Some say it ultimately backfires by turning public opinion against the bombers and those who support them. Support often comes in the form of charitable donations to the family of suicide bombers. Many poor parents in the Arab world may be inclined to encourage their children to become suicide bombers. For its photogenic value in a globalized world of mass communication, suicide bombing is a weapon of genius.

The Guarantee of Heaven for Islamic Martyrs

Suicide, under orthodox Islam, is a sin. However, Jihadists consider the circumstances to cleanse the sin, making it the act of a holy martyr, not a suicide. The actual percentage of Muslims who agree with this interpretation is hotly disputed, as is the concept of martyrdom. A martyr is technically someone who dies for their religious faith, but the outcome also matters, in terms of who gets to write history. Martyrdom, therefore, is intimately tied up with Islamic arrogance that their goal of religious domination will be victorious in the end. The study of all things in the end is known by the religious term *eschatology*, and Islam contains strong elements of Zoroastrianism, the world's first religion to have a full-blown eschatology. Many experts believe that Zoroastrianism, a religion that existed from 1500 BC to 700 AD in Persia and still popular in parts of Iran and India, had a significant impact on Islam. In a nutshell, the basic idea that Zoraster had is that earth is a battlefield between good and evil, and that good is destined to win out over evil, and anyone who allies themselves with good is guaranteed to be part of this destiny. What Mohammed took from this is the idea that whoever martyrs themselves for the sake of good goes directly to a special place in heaven, or in a worst case scenario, goes to hell for a short time and then goes to heaven. Satan, as the embodiment of evil, also plays a big role, as a real entity who tempts people to renounce their faith, and the martyr with the most guarantee of a special place in heaven is the one who fights Satan.

Demonizing America as the "Great Satan" makes it a fitting opponent in the predestined war between good and evil. Heaven is more than a transcendental place to Muslims. Orthodox Islamic eschatology holds that the afterlife is physical; people are said to have bodies, and they will experience material pleasures, including unlimited food, drink and sex. Heaven is known to some Muslims as the Gardens of Paradise where unimaginable spiritual and sensual pleasures await. To other Muslims, the rewards are quite imaginable, such as the 72 virgins waiting to have sex with each martyr every day (their hymens miraculously regrow the next day). This account was popularized by the media in 2001 when a CBS reporter interviewed a Hamas recruiter who talked about it. According to one translation, the Koran 78:31 reads "*As for the righteous, they shall surely triumph. Theirs shall be gardens and vineyards, and high-bosomed virgins for companions.*" Some Islamic scholars argue this is a false translation, and that passages like that are referring to angels or heavenly beings. Other Islamic scholars argue it's only 70 virgins instead of 72, and that your wife is always one of them. Yet other Islamic scholars say the whole thing is intended to be taken in a transcendental way, the pleasures of heaven being so great it's like having an eternal erection or first-time sex all the time.

HISTORICAL EXAMPLES OF JIHAD

With the exception of the battle of Uhud in 625 and the battle of the ditch in 627, all the battles of the prophet of Islam were offensive. All jihad wars undertaken after his death were offensive expansive wars. The Persian and Byzantine empires bordering Arabia were not a threat to the Muslim Arabs. In the West, Islamic armies conquered the Levant, North Africa, and finished the conquest of most of Spain by 715. Christians completed the liberation of Spain in 1492. In the East, the Muslim invaders conquered the Persian Empire. By 1206, they had invaded the Punjab, Sindh, Delhi, and beyond. Muslims stopped waging large scale jihad wars after 1683 because the Islamic world had grown too weak. Examples of jihad wars and the atrocities associated with it abound in Islamic history. We cite a few of them herein.

Wherever the Islamic armies invaded, they caused massive destructions, countless systematic massacres of extermination, enslavement and exile of a great portion of the population, and great human suffering. Looting and pillaging the wealth of conquered lands, periodic ransoms, and the jizya tax impoverished and ruined the conquered populations. Economic decline and general impoverishment followed in the conquered territories. More blood has been shed for Islam than for any other cause in history. Some historians estimate that in India alone, more than 80 million people were massacred by the sword of Islam. In addition, 10 million Buddhists, 120 million Christians and African Animists, and many Zoroastrians in Persia were killed by marauding Islamic armies, both during their conquests and in the centuries that followed. The sword of Islam spread death, devastation and dark terror over many lands.

Examples of violent Islamic jihad in modern times are the civil wars in South Sudan, Afghanistan, Lebanon, the Russian war in the Caucasus, and the attacks in the West. To the Muslim fundamentalist, a Muslim terrorist who kills unarmed innocent non-Muslim men, women, and children in the predominantly non-Muslim West is a war hero. What the Islamists could not accomplish by military conquest in the world of today, they are attempting to accomplish peacefully by proclaiming the religion of Islam. The problem is that they do not tell the truth about Islam in their proclamations. Instead, they sugarcoat it in their attempts to sell it dishonestly to unwary Westerners.

The Early Islamic Era

Banu Qurayza, the last Jewish tribe in Medina, rejected Islam. They remained neutral in the battle of the trench (627). Muhammad, the prophet of Islam, questioned their loyalty, and besieged them. They surrendered. Muhammad appointed Sa'd ibn Muadh, one of his most fanatic followers, to decide their fate. Sa'd was wounded in the battle of the trench and lusted after revenge. He died soon after issuing his verdict. His verdict was that all the men of the tribe were to be killed, and the possessions of the tribe were to be divided among the Muslims. Muhammad ratified this unjust horrific judgment, and in order to justify the bloodbath, he claimed that his god sanctioned it (al-Ahzab 33: 26-27).

Muhammad ordered that a trench be dug in the night across the market place in Medina, and commanded that the male captives be brought forth to the trench in companies of five or six at a time, where they were beheaded and buried in the trench. This continued all day long into the evening till all the men of the tribe, numbering 800-900, were killed. Muhammad observed in person the horrific killings. If is important to stress that these tribesmen were not armed, and were not a threat to Muhammad and his followers. They were murdered in cold blood. Muhammad was responsible for the first Islamic massacre of 627 in the long bloody history of Islam.

The women and children of the tribe were sold into slavery, and its possessions were looted. Muhammad took for himself Rihana whose husband and all her male relatives had just perished in the massacre. Muhammad wanted to remove non-Muslims from Medina and Arabia by the sword, if necessary (Bukhari 4.52.288; 5.59.716; 4.53.392, 380). He started the process, and his followers completed it (Muslim 19.4366). In fact, till this day, it is illegal to build a church in Saudi Arabia. In addition, the religious police will raid a house where Christians are gathered to worship, will arrest the leader of the worship service and torture him in prison.

Muhammad warned the people who harassed him in the market place of Mecca saying that he would come back as slaughterer. The army that Muhammad led in his invasion of Mecca years later had a black flag signifying death with the word "punishment" written on it. Upon conquering Mecca, Muhammad ordered the killing of several persons for making satirical songs against him. In conquering Mecca, Muhammad brought to it death, not salvation. This contrasts with the peaceful triumphant entry of Jesus into Jerusalem riding a donkey, not bearing a sword and without an army.

After the death of Muhammad, the caliph Abu Bakr invaded Syria. During the campaign of 634, the entire region between Gaza and Caesarea was devastated. Four thousand Christian, Jewish and Samaritan peasants were massacred. During the military campaigns of caliph Umar ibn al-Khattab, the second guided caliph, in Mesopotamia between 635 and 642, monasteries were sacked, the monks were killed, and Christian Arabs executed or forced to convert.

In Elam, the population was put to the sword. The Arab invasion of the Middle East was not by any means a joyous liberating experience. It brought a great deal of death and destruction. The inhabitants of towns taken by storm were either killed or led into captivity, and their property was looted. Umar ibn al-Khattab was so brutal and despotic in his retaliation against the Persians for opposing Islam's spread that to this day the Iranians celebrate the anniversary of his assassination with great festivities.

Amr ibn al-As conquered Egypt in 639-642. As he advanced in it, he captured the town of Bahnesa near Fayum and put to the sword its inhabitants, including old men, women and children. He committed the same atrocities in other towns in Egypt. Similar atrocities occurred in North Africa. Tripoli was pillaged in 643. Carthage was razed to the ground and most of its inhabitants killed. The same pattern was followed in Anatolia, Syria, Iraq, and Iran.

Al-Hajjaj, the governor of Iraq (694-714), instructed his commander Muhammad ibn Qasim in 712 to invade India and destroy the unbelievers. After the capture of the port of Debal, the Muslim army took three days to slaughter many of its inhabitants. In the town of Brahminabad, the Muslim army killed more than 6000 men. In subsequent invasions, Islamic armies targeted the Hindu temples and monasteries in an orgy of pillage and arson. Those not killed were captured and sold as slaves. Mahmud of Ghazni (971-1030), the head of a Turco-Afghan dynasty, invaded India destroying, pillaging and massacring. He justified his actions by constantly referring to Qur'anic injunctions to kill the idolaters. At the battle of Somnah, the site of a celebrated Hindu temple, he killed about 50,000 inhabitants.

The Middle Ages

The Jews of North Africa and Spain suffered several massacres under the Islamic Arab rule, such as the massacre of more than 6000 Jews in the town of Fez (Morocco) in 1033, the massacres of Cordoba and other places in Spain in 1010-1013, the massacre of the entire Jewish community of about 4000 in Granada, Spain in 1066, etc.

The Muslim Berbers Almoravids (1056-1147) arrived in Spain in 1086, followed by the more fanatic and violent Almohad Muslim Berbers who arrived in Spain in 1146-47. Almoravids deported from Spain a large number of Christians to Morocco in 1106, 1126 and 1138. The Almohads (1130-1269) wreaked enormous persecution on both the Jewish and Christian populations in Spain and North Africa, including massacres, slavery and forced conversions.

The Muslim Seljuk Turks invaded Asia Minor over a period of four centuries from the middle of the eleventh century. These invasions were accompanied with extermination of local populations or their precipitate flight. Entire cities, and whole provinces fell into decay. Some fertile districts were laid waste. Impenetrable thickets sprang up in vast areas replacing fertile fields and pasture. This was followed by Ottoman jihad campaigns in the European Balkans. The Turks practiced wide-spread forced conversions which persisted throughout the sixteenth century.

In the fourteenth and early fifteenth centuries, Timur the Lame (known as Tamerlane) launched jihad wars against both non-Muslims and Muslims accusing the latter of lukewarmness towards Islam. He combined Mongol barbarity with Islamic fanaticism. He massacred in the thousands out of Qur'anic piety, as a duty and sacred mission. The following is a sampling of his massacres: his cold-blooded slaughter of 100,000 captive Indians near Delhi in December, 1398, his burying alive of 4000 Armenians in 1400-1, his erecting 20 towers of human skulls at Aleppo and Damascus in the same year, his massacre of 70,000 of the inhabitants of Isfahan in November 1387, etc.

The Wahhabis of Arabia condemned most non-Wahhabi Muslims as infidels, and waged jihad against them. In 1801 and

1802, the Saudi Wahhabis under the leadership of Abdul Aziz ibn Muhammad ibn Saud attacked and captured the holy Shia cities of Karbala and Najaf in Iraq, massacred parts of the Muslim population and destroyed the tombs of Husayn ibn Ali, the grandson of Muhammad, and Ali ibn abi-Talib.

The Armenian Genocide

In the nineteenth century, the Armenians demanded their equal rights and attempted to break out of their Ottoman Islamic dhimmitude peacefully. They sought reforms in the Turkish/ Ottoman system of government. As a result, the Armenian genocide began. The Muslim Ottoman Turks massacred more than 200,000 unarmed Armenian civilians in 1894-96 during the reign of sultan Abdul Hamid II (the Sassoun massacre). That was followed, under the young Turks regime, by the Adana massacres of 25,000 Armenians in 1909. This climaxed in the 1915 genocide when additional 600,000-800,000 unarmed Armenian civilians were massacred. The Muslim perpetrators who committed these bloody atrocities were guided by Islamic Sharia prescriptions providing that if the dhimmi requested his equal rights, and freedom from his bondage, he forfeited the protection of the caliph.

The genocide of the Armenian Christians in World War I was an ethnic cleansing of central Turkey by an Islamic jihad wherein Muslim Turks systematically murdered unarmed civilian Christian Armenian males over the age of twelve en masse in 1915. Women and children were deported from their centuries-old Armenian villages. Many of them died or were killed in their arduous journey. Others were given out as slaves, or forced to convert to Islam. The Armenian properties were looted. At the end, about one and a half million Armenian civilians died and were killed in those atrocities. Turkish Armenia ceased to exist. The four elements of the Armenian liquidation in central Turkey—deportation, enslavement, forced conversion, and massacre—reproduced the historic conditions of Islamic jihad carried out from the seventh century on. Successive Turkish governments have consistently refused to acknowledge the historic fact of the Armenian genocide, and to pay compensations to the Armenians.

The Sudanese Genocide

During the brutal civil war between the Muslim Arab North of the Sudan, and the Christian and animist black South (1955-72, 1983-2005), Sudan was the site of the most vicious anti-Christian persecution raging in the world. The Islamist government of the Sudan committed genocide in the South and the Nubba mountains, including massacres, rape, looting, and slavery. Hundreds of Christian villages were razed to the ground. The end result was a devastated economy, a divided country, the death of approximately two million people, and the displacement of over five million people. South Sudan seceded from the Sudan, and became an independent state on July 9, 2011.

Despite the relentless cruel Islamic persecution, the Sudanese Church grew very fast in that period. Many Muslims and animists came to Christ in the Sudan than anywhere else in the world. In twenty years, Christians grew from 5% to over 20% of the Sudanese population (and 80% of South Sudan). South Sudan is the Christian bulwark against the southward advance of radical Islam into central Africa.

In the late nineteenth century, the British General Charles Gordon succeeded in breaking the back of the slave trade in the Sudan. However, the Muslim Sudanese Mahdi, Muhammad ibn Abdullah, that succeeded him in 1885 declared jihad warfare, and restored the slave trade in the Sudan. During the civil war, the soldiers of the Islamic government of the Sudan and the Arab militias armed by the government attacked African villages, kidnapped and sold as slaves tens of thousands of Sudanese Christian and animist men, women and children. There is no doubt that slavery is still widespread in the Sudan, including exporting slaves to Muslim countries in the Persian Gulf.

Jihad Atrocity in the U.S.A.

On Sept. 11, 2001, the Islamist organization of al-Qaeda attacked the U.S.A. this resulted in the death of about 3000 innocent civilians. None of the leading Islamic clerics in the Muslim world condemned the 9/11 atrocities. In fact, some praised it?! Misguided Muslim crowds celebrated it in the streets of the Middle East.

Muslim governments, who call for tolerance of Muslims in the West, have never apologized for 9/11 atrocities. The U.S. military was able to locate the leadership of al-Qaeda and destroy it.

VARIANT FORMS OF JIHAD

The variant forms of jihad contain two modes of operation: violent and non-violent. The goal of both is identical: to subjugate he non–Muslim population to the Islamic rule of Sharia. The violent mode includes assassinations, devshirme, vigilante justice, torture, etc. Islamists call the non-violent mode "civilization jihad," more appropriately called "stealth jihad." It is a pre-violent jihad. It includes infiltrating the legal system, and the educational, financial, government, intelligence, and military institutions of the West.

Assassinations

Muhammad, the prophet of Islam, was the one who started in the seventh century the trail of blood of Islamic atrocities in Arabia. Muhammad urged his Muslim followers to kill his critics for him in order of silence them, and praised them for doing it afterwards. This led to the assassination of Asma' bint Marawan while she was nursing her baby home (A. Guilaune, The Life of Muhammad, pp. 675-676), 120-year-old Abu Afak (Ibn-Sa'd, Kitab al-Tabaqat al-Kabir, vol. 2, Trans. S. Moinul, p. 31), Kaab ibn al-Ashraf (Buchari 5.59.369; Muslim 19.4436), Abu Rafi Salaam (Bukhari 5.59.371), etc. That practice has been codified in Sharia. Blasphemy, criticizing or defaming Islam, its prophet, the Islamic god, the Qur'an, the Hadith or Sharia are punishable by death in all the schools of Sharia.

In the West, we can critically study Christianity and Judaism. In Islamic countries, Islamist writers attack Christianity. However, Christians are not allowed to criticize and refute Islam objectively. Intimidation and censorship express lack of confidence and weakness in the Islamic religion and its teachings. It cannot defend itself by reason. Therefore, Islamists resort to violence to protect it. Respect should be earned, not forced by intimidation. Islam forbids anything critical about Muhammad or his god, and condemns any one that originates the criticism, such as Salman Rushdie—the author of a 1988 book on the Satanic Verses of the Qur'an, the Danish cartoonists depicting Muhammad with a bomb in his bonnet (2005-2006) that precipitated mob violence in Islamic countries resulting in destruction and deaths, Theo Van Gogh who was murdered on Nov. 2, 2004 for producing a short documentary on the oppression of women under Islam, the anti-Islam Dutch politician Geert Wilders who has made a truthful 15-minute documentary on the violence in Islam and the Qur'an, etc. Islamist restraints on criticism of Islam are not directed only to states, but also against individuals.

Devshirme

Abduction of children in late antiquity was a routine practice of tribes in conflict. These children were released after their relatives paid ransom. Those not ransomed, were sold as slaves.

The abduction of Jewish and Christian Dhimmi children also represented a form of forced conversion. Although illegal, there is substantial evidence that it occurred throughout the course of history, either sporadically — ransoming, supplying harems or as a contribution to the tribute — or in an institutionalized way, as in the devshirme system that functioned over three centuries in the Balkans for Christian children (Bat Ye'or, The Decline of Eastern Christianity under Islam, p. 91).

The Ottoman sultan Orkhan (1326-59) introduced the practice of devshirme in 1330. It was a regular tribute (blood tax) of a fifth of the 7-15 year-old Christian children from conquered Balkan regions exacted every about four years initially. This periodic tribute eventually became an annual tribute. The cruel Muslim Ottoman soldiers literally wrenched the children from their weeping mothers' arms. Those who refused to surrender their sons were put to death on the spot by hanging. Those children were sent in the thousands to remote areas to discourage their escape. They were forcibly converted to Islam and given military training in the janissary corps. The heartless recruiters used to take a surplus of children in the hope of selling them back to their families. If their families were too poor to redeem them, they remained slaves.

The devshirme system enslaved and forcibly converted to Islam an estimated five hundred thousand to one million primarily Balkan Christian adolescent boys. The janissaries became the Muslim power's elite troops, the cruelest soldiers against Christianity and their own people because of the fanaticism taught to them, and the cruelty they lived through.

This regular bloodletting from the conquered peoples increased the Muslim population and correspondingly reduced that of the Christians. The devshirme was theoretically abolished in 1656, but recruitment of ichoghlani continued until the mid-eighteenth century (Bat Ye'or, The Decline of Eastern Christianity under Islam, p. 115).

Vigilante Justice

Islamic Sharia encourages vigilante justice under certain conditions, because a Muslim is not only required to follow the laws of the Islamic god, but is also entrusted to enforce them on earth without needing authorization from the state. Examples on that abound: the 1994 Islamist attempt in Egypt to assassinate Dr. Nagib Mahfouz, a moderate Muslim, who won the 1988 Nobel Laureate in literature for his novel of "Children of Gebelawi" which islamists considered blasphemous; killing Dr. Farag Foda, a liberal Muslim Egyptian professor, in 1992 in Egypt by Islamist fundamentalists; the death fatwa of Ayatollah Khomeini of Iran against the Indian writer Salman Rushdi for his 1988 novel on the Satanic Verses of the Qur'an supported with a million-dollar reward (doubled in 1997) for his death; the killing of the Dutch film maker Theo van Gogh in Amsterdam by an Islamist for producing a twelve-minute film called Submission decrying the mistreatment of Muslim women; etc.

Every Muslim is required to correct the conduct of his fellow Muslims. A killer of an apostate who left Islam, a robber, or an adulterer is forgiven and exempted from punishment for murder under Sharia law. Muslims who commit genocide are spared from punishment if they repent. Individual fatwas issued by Islamic clerics for killing apostates, while not binding on the Islamic state, can be acted upon by any Islamist without getting punished for his crime. Radical Islamists brand all who disagree with them as enemies of Islam and apostates. The violators of Sharia fear vigilante justice by the Islamist public, such as their friends, neighbors, relatives, parents, brothers, or sisters.

Vigilante justice has no restraints and is bound to be abused. It results in relationships between Muslims based on fear and arrogance. It leads to a chaotic society. Death squads or street mobs take justice into their own hands. Mobs stone women accused of adultery. Boys throw acid at girls because they do not like their dress, etc. Muslims are turned against each other. They have to watch their backs. Many of the accusations of apostasy and blasphemy are the result of personal grudges borne by the accusers against the defendants to settle personal scores, or are tools for Islamic governments to silence opposition. Deep-seated distrust plagues Islamic society. Vigilante justice is where Islam gets its power. It is not the power of conviction, but the power of fear.

Many Muslim converts to Christianity in Europe live in hiding fearing for their lives from Islamist violence. However, some European ex-Muslims are summoning the courage to stand up in defense of their rights. They have formed organizations of ex-Muslims in Germany, Britain, Finland, Denmark, Norway, Sweden, and the Netherlands. They no longer tolerate the intolerance of Islam. Mr. Ehsan Jami, the founder of the Netherlands Central Committee for Ex-Muslims (9/11/07) was violently attacked by Muslim fundamentalists on three separate occasions between May 2007 and Aug. 2007. This forced him into hiding.

The Islamists launched a campaign of intimidation including threats of destructive bloody Islamic riots in an attempt to prevent the anti-Islam Dutch politician Geert Wilders from releasing his 15-minute documentary, Fitna, which presented some hate verses of the Qur'an, followed by destructive actions in accord with them carried out by Islamists in the West in recent years. However, Wilders was strong enough not to succumb to pressure, and published his documentary. After 3.6 million visitors had viewed his film on the British website LiveLeak.com, the company announced that "Following threats to our staff of a very serious nature, LiveLeak has been left with no other choice but to remove

Fitna from our servers." However, Two days later, LiveLeak posted the film again. Wilders has been living for years under state-provided round-the-clock police protection, because of Islamist threats.

Legal Jihad

Islamist organizations call for censorship of any criticism of Islam on the grounds of being insulted. This is a common trick of totalitarian movements and governments. They label any objective truthful critique as an insult, and attempt to punish its source. Totalitarian tyrants and movements must not be appeased. Islamic organizations in the West attempt to intimidate people who speak out objectively against Islam by threats of lawsuits in order to silence them. They are well funded by petrodollars. Should the voices of anti-Islamist researchers and activists be silenced, the criticism of radical Islam may end within this generation. This poses a serious threat to the liberty and security of the West. It is becoming rather common in the West that a citizen be dragged to court for his negative views about Islam and Islamists.

Controlling the Educational System

Before the newly found oil wealth in Arabia, Islam around the globe was in a state of depression. The discovery of oil in Arabia animated the sleeping giant. Using their vast oil wealth, the Arabs of Arabia are funding mosques, Islamic schools, libraries, and academic centers worldwide. They are attempting to make their extreme version of Islam, Wahhabism, the Islamic norm that will eventually dominate the world. Wahhabism calls for enforcing the extreme cruel measures of Islamic Sharia, such as the killing of Islamic heretics and apostates, amputation of limbs, stoning, and decapitation.

An American survey conducted early 2012 by Faith Communities Today (affiliated with the Hartford Seminary) shows that the number of mosques in the United States has grown by 74% in the past eleven years, from 1209 in 2001 to 2106 in 2011. The Greater New City area ranked No. 1 with 192 mosques. According to a Barnabas Fund report, as of 2006, 210 Saudi-funded large mosques and Islamic centers have been built in the key cities of the world, including Washington D.C., New York, Los Angeles, London, Brussels, Geneva, Paris, Bonn, and Rome. It is believed that about half of America's small and large Islamic centers and mosques and six schools of Islamic higher learning have been built, at least in part, with petrodollars. In addition, 1500 small mosques, 202 colleges and about 2000 Islamic schools have been built in the West with petrodollars. In 2007, the university of Michigan installed ritual foot baths to accommodate the Islamic beliefs of the Sharia-adherent Muslims. A publicly-funded charter school in Minnesota was sued by the ACLU on the grounds that it promotes Islam.

The Saudis are buying campus presence by funding programs of Islamic studies and establishing Islamic academic chairs in prestigious academic centers and universities in the West, such as the universities of Georgetown, Harvard, Duke, Berkeley, California, Cambridge, London, Moscow, and Edinburgh. This is creating bastions of non-critical pro-Islamic scholarship within Western academia. In order to retain its Saudi funding, these academic Islamic studies centers are under pressure not to maintain its academic impartiality and integrity of scholarship. That is how the Islamists attempt to control the Western intellect and soul.

Saudi petrodollars provide scholarships for thousands of non-Muslims from the West to study at Islamic universities in Saudi Arabia. The obvious goal is to introduce the Islamic faith to prospective converts.

The American Textbook Council and The Textbook League have reviewed the top-selling textbooks used by thousands of American public schools to teach about Islam.These two highly respected American organizations found those textbooks severely distorted and compromised in their discussion of Islam and Islamic history. They blatantly glorify and promote Islam, while demonize Christianity. They white-wash the violent bloody history of Islam by omitting the fact that it spread out of Arabia primarily through the military conquests of jihad (holy war). They decouple Islam and Islamist terrorism.

They present Islamic beliefs as facts instead of religious beliefs. And they deny the fact that Islam oppresses and subordinates women. In addition, homework assignments involve exercises that make the students act as if they were already Muslims. This amounts to proselytizing 12-year-old Americans to convert them to Islam stealthily.

Islamic propagandists operating in America influence public school textbooks by threatening charges of racism and xenophobia against textbook publishers. Revising history and leaving out important facts are thought-control brainwashing techniques that were used by the Nazis and the communists in their quest for world dominion. These techniques are used today extensively in the Islamic world.

Financial Jihad

Islamic finance and banking is called financial jihad—jihad with money instead of violence. It is going after the lifeblood of the economy of the West. The oil rich Islamic Arab countries are attempting to take control of the American economy through buying real estate and stocks of American corporations. As of 2008, Sharia finance sector managed assets of more than $800 billion. Standard and Poor estimated that this sector could reach $4 trillion before long. The probable locations for future expansion are Saudi Arabia, United Arab Emirates, Indonesia, Turkey, Singapore, and some Western countries. Britain has a bigger Sharia finance sector than the Islamic countries of Egypt and Pakistan. At least, twenty-two financial institutions offer Sharia-compliant services in Britain, compared with nine in the United States. The British Prime Minister Gordon Brown declared in 2006 that London was going to be the Islamic banking capital of the world.

Some U.S. financial institutions and businesses are engaging in Sharia-compliant financing by accommodating Sharia law (Islamic law) in order to attract Islamic investments and tap into petrodollars. They structure investments and transactions that comply with Sharia requirements that prohibit financial transactions involving interest, excessive risk, or certain assets such as alcohol, tobacco, pork, gambling, or non-Muslim religious entities. In order to conform to the Sharia (Islamic law) requirements, Western financial companies must submit to "Sharia advisers." Almost all of those advisers are Islamists dedicated to the destruction of the West.

Those advisers certify that the subject financial products have been modified to comply with Sharia requirements. Supporters of Sharia-compliant finance see a golden opportunity for expansion in an economic downturn.

Oil rich Arab Islamists have bought into financially troubled banks, and then demanded that an approved Muslim Imam be installed on their boards of directors to assure that financial products offered to Muslims are "halal"—kosher. Halal finances provide preferential treatment to Muslims, including interest free loans and credit cards.

Sharia finance is an extension of Islamic law. It is a tool of political Islam to control global economies, and to fund violent jihad. Embracing Sharia finance leads to the eventual enforcement of the brutal oppressive Sharia law. Islamic financial institutions are involved in funding Islamist terrorism worldwide. From 1988 to 2001, Bank al-Taqwa (registered in the Bahamas) transferred tens of millions of dollars to the Islamist terrorist organizations of Hamas, al-Qaeda, the Taliban, and others. Bank Meli of Iran is under U.S. and EU sanctions for facilitating Iran's support of Hamas and Hesbollah and funding Iran's Uranium enrichment program. In fact, as of 2010, Iran had six of the ten biggest Sharia-compliant financial institutions.

Miscellaneous

Other forms of jihad include suppression of freedom of religion and speech, the Islamic taqiyya, torture, breaking oaths and treaties, the higher Islamic fertility rates, Islamic immigration into Christian lands, etc.

2

Jihad: Islamic Holy War

Two variant forms of jihad are distinguished in Islam: a spiritual mode (inner struggle), and a violent mode of striving in holy war to spread Islam and expand the Islamic state domain by force. Only 2% of the Bukhari hadiths that relate to jihad refer to the spiritual mode. The other 98% of the hadiths devoted to jihad claim that the violent mode of jihad is the supreme Islamic religious act. The small marginalized heretical Sufi sect adheres to the first mode of jihad. However, the paramount mainstream understanding and usage of Islamic jihad throughout fourteen centuries of Islamic history has been striving in offensive military conflict to expand the territory of Islam, conquer new populations for Islam, and establish Islamic law (Sharia). This is the classic primary meaning of jihad codified in Islamic law (Sharia) and attested in Islamic history. Contemporary Islamists are striving to impose Sharia globally and restore the totalitarian Islamic caliphate which Kemal Ataturk, the father of modern Turkey, abolished in 1924 in order to modernize Turkey.

There is no doubt from the historical record of Muhammad, the prophet of Islam, and his followers that he meant the jihad verses in the Qur'an to be understood literally, not spiritually (an-Nisa' 4: 95; al-Anfal 8: 65; etc). In fact, the Islamic scholarly consensus on the definition of jihad as aggressive warfare against non-Muslims was achieved over a thousand years ago. Muhammad was born into a culture of tribal conflict and bloodshed. Instead of improving it, he incorporated it into Islam through the concept of violent jihad. He retained the tribal warring culture as the basis for Islamic survival. Jihad warfare is a central doctrine of Islam. It helped define Islam from its very dawn. Islam was born as an ideology of totalitarian terror.

While wars are the exception to the norm in the history of any civilization, it is the norm in the Islamic civilization in dar-al-harb (the house of war), which is the territory of the non-Muslim populations. Jihad warfare is an Islamic institution, not a mere isolated event in Islamic history. The long bloody history of Islam reflects these teachings. It is rife with continuous harassment, persecution, subjugation and killing of non-Muslim infidels. All the battles of Muhammad were offensive except for the battles of Uhud (625 AD) and the ditch (627 AD) which were defensive.

Although Muhammad proclaimed in the Qur'an, al-Baqarah 2: 256 and al-Kafirun 109: 6 that there is no compulsion in religion, he abrogated that concept in al-Baqarah 2: 193; Al-'Imran 3: 83, 85; an-Nisa' 4: 89, 101-102; al-Anfal 8: 9, 12-13; al-Tawbah 9: 5, 29; Muhammad 47: 4; al-Hashr 59: 7; etc. In fact, the verse of the sword (al-Tawbah 9: 5) commanding Muslims to fight all who choose not to convert to Islam, whether they are inside or outside Arabia, abrogated at least 124 verses in the Qur'an that speak about love, peace, and forgiveness.

Muhammad taught and practiced persecution, military conquest, subjugation, coercion and killing of non-Muslims. While Islam prohibits Muslims from paying or charging interest, it permits them to extort money from infidels and suppress them with usury to gain the upper hand.

At the end of his life, Muhammad, the prophet of Islam, said: "... I have been made victorious with terror, and while I was sleeping, the keys of the treasures of the world were brought to me and put in my hand ..." (Bukhari 4.52.220). On his deathbed, he commanded his followers to purge Arabia of non-Muslims (Bukhari 4.52.288; 5.59.716; 4.53.392, 380). He started the process (Muslim 19.4366), and his followers completed it (Bukhari 3.39.531; Muslim 10.3763). In fact, till this day, it is illegal to build a church in Saudi Arabia. In addition, the religious police will raid a house where Christians are gathered to worship, will arrest the leader of the worship service and torture him in prison.

CRITICISM OF ISLAMIC TERRORIST IDEOLOGY

Although "Islamic" terrorism is commonly associated with the Salafis (or "Wahhabis"), the scholars of the group have constantly attributed this association to ignorance, misunderstanding and sometimes insincere research and deliberate misleading by rival groups.

Following the September 11 attacks, Abdul-Azeez ibn Abdullaah Aal ash-Shaikh, the Grand Mufti of the Kingdom of Saudi Arabia, made an official statement that "the Islamic Sharee'ah (legislation) does not sanction" such actions. A Salafi Committee of Major Scholars"in Saudi Arabia has declared that "Islamic" terrorism, such as the May 2003 bombing in Riyadh, are in violation of Sharia law and aiding the enemies of Islam.

Criticism of Islamic terrorism on Islamic grounds has also been made by Abdal-Hakim Murad (Timothy Winter):

> *Certainly, neither bin Laden nor his principal associate, Ayman al-Zawahiri, are graduates of Islamic universities. And so their proclamations ignore 14 centuries of Muslim scholarship, and instead take the form of lists of anti-American grievances and of Koranic quotations referring to early Muslim wars against Arab idolaters. These are followed by the conclusion that all Americans, civilian and military, are to be wiped off the face of the Earth. All this amounts to an odd and extreme violation of the normal methods of Islamic scholarship. Had the authors of such fatwâs followed the norms of their religion, they would have had to acknowledge that no school of mainstream Islam allows the targeting of civilians. An insurrectionist who kills non-combatants is guilty of baghy, "armed aggression," a capital offense in Islamic law.*

Colonel Eikmeier points out the "questionable religious credentials" of many Islamist theorists, or "Qutbists," which can be a "means to discredit them and their message":

> *With the exception of Abul Ala Maududi and Abdullah Yusuf Azzam, none of Qutbism's main theoreticians trained at Islam's recognized centers of learning. Although a devout Muslim, Hassan al-Banna was a teacher and community activist. Sayyid Qutb was a literary critic. Muhammad Abd al-Salam Faraj was*

an electrician. Ayman al-Zawahiri is a physician. Osama bin Laden trained to be a businessman.

Fethullah Gülen, a prominent Turkish Islamic scholar, has claimed that "a real Muslim," who understood Islam in every aspect, could not be a terrorist.

There are many other people with similar points of view such as Karen Armstrong, Prof. Ahmet Akgunduz, Harun Yahya and Muhammad Tahir-ul-Qadri. Huston Smith, an author on comparative religion, noted that extremists have hijacked Islam, just as has occurred periodically in Christianity, Hinduism and other religions throughout history. He added that the real problem is that extremists do not know their own faith.

Ali Gomaa, former Grand Mufti of Egypt, stated not only for the Islam but in general: "Terrorism cannot be born of religion. Terrorism is the product of corrupt minds, hardened hearts, and arrogant egos, and corruption, destruction, and arrogance are unknown to the heart attached to the divine."

Identity-based Frameworks for Analyzing Islamist-based Terrorism

Islamist-based fundamentalist terrorism against Western nations and the U.S. in particular, has numerous motivations and takes place the larger context of a complex and tense relationship between the 'West' and the Arab and Muslim 'world,' which is highlighted in the previous section on motivations and Islamic terrorism. Identity-based theoretical frameworks including theories of social identity, social categorization theory, and psychodynamics are used to explain the reasons terrorism occurs.

Social identity is explained by Karina Korostelina as a "feeling of belonging to a social group, as a strong connection with social category, and as an important part of our mind that affects our social perceptions and behavior" This definition can be applied to the case of Osama bin Laden, who, according to this theory, had a highly salient perception of his social identity as a Muslim, a strong connection to the social category of the Muslim Ummah or 'community,' which affect his social perceptions and behaviors. Bin Laden's ideology and interpretation of Islam led to the creation of al-Qaeda in response to perceived threats against the Muslim community by the Soviet Union, the U.S. in particular due to its troop presence in Saudi Arabia, and American support for Israel. The Islamist terrorist group al-Qaeda has a group identity, which includes "shared experiences, attitudes, beliefs, and interests of ingroup members," and is "described through the achievement of a collective aim for which this group has been created," which in this case is to achieve "a complete break from the foreign influences in Muslim countries, and the creation of a new Islamic caliphate."

Social categorization theory has been discussed as a three-stage process of identification, where "individuals define themselves as members of a social group, learn the stereotypes and norms of the group, and group categories influence the perception and understanding of all situations in a particular context" This definition can be applied to the U.S.-led war on terror, in which conflict features such as the phenomenon of Anti-Americanism and the phenomenon of non-Arab countries like Iran and Afghanistanlending support to Islamist-based terrorism by funding or harboring terrorist groups such as Hezbollah and al-Qaeda against Western nations, particularly Israel and theUnited States are, according to social categorization theory, influenced by a three-stage process of identification.

In this three-stage process of identification, the Arab and Muslim world(s) are the social group(s), in which their members learn stereotypes and norms which categorize their social group vis-à-vis the West. This social categorization process creates feelings of high-level in-group support and allegiance among Arabs and Muslims and the particular context within which members of the Arab and Muslim world(s) social group(s) understand all situations that involve the West. Social categorization theory as a framework for analysis indicates causal relationships between group identification processes and features of conflict situations.

ISLAMIST MILITANCY

Islamist militancy is showing new signs of life in Bangladesh despite crackdowns. According to a Christian Science Monitor [CSM] report, terrorist groups are showing a persistence and resilience that has left local authorities worried. However, the CSM says that militancy in Bangladesh is not on the scale or tone that exists in Pakistan or Afghanistan, but has shown a frightening persistence in recent years.

It says that in 2006, police and paramilitary forces systematically targeted and took down the top terrorist organization, Jamat'ul Mujahideen Bangladesh, or JMB. Seven of JMB's leaders were hung in 2007. One estimate suggested there were about 12,000 cadres actively operating in the country, mostly madrassa [Islamic seminary] teachers, students and clerics of mosques.

In April of this year, Bangladesh intelligence agencies declared that the Islamist terrorist groups are reorganizing with the aim of making a deadly comeback.

Bangladesh's teeming cities and rugged countryside have proven an unlikely safe haven for some of the jihadi world's most hardened operatives. In September 2009, police in Dhaka [capital city of Bangladesh] arrested an Afghan war veteran with ties to Lashkar-e-Taiba, the banned Pakistani terrorist organization held responsible for the Mumbai attacks in November 2008. The Christian Science Monitor reported in June that Bangladesh was becoming a hideout for South Asia's terrorists: Bangladeshi police in June uncovered a plot that used Bangladesh to funnel thousands of weapons to an Indian separatist group.

The police also arrested an operative working for notorious South Asian terrorist Daud Ibrahim, who is alleged to have ties to Al Qaeeda. The operative disclosed that 150 of Daud Ibrahim's operatives are stationed in Bangladesh.

Religious Extremism in Bangladesh

Definition of political parties has changed for some from the time of Edmund Burke as "an organized assembly of men, united for working together for national interest" to one that may not accept members from the minority community and is insistent on establishing Islamic rule or Khilafat. Indeed the head of the Hizb-Ut-Tehrir [HuT], Hizbut Towhid [HT], Khelafat Majlish [KM] as did few other Islamist parties publicly announced that "we always want to oust all governments in all Muslim countries in the world to establish Khilafat states". The world is already mired in the militant activities of al-Qaeda operatives, their latest victims being the carnage at Mumbai [India] and the Marriot Hotel in Islamabad [Pakistan]. In recent months, although Dhaka is governed by a political party having secularist ideology, notorious Islamist militancy group named Hizbut Towhid is allowed to openly publish and sell books and DVDs pronouncing Jews and Christians as 'enemies of Islam' and instigating the Muslims in waging 'holy war' against them. Hizbut Towhid denounces democracy and promotes Caliphate Rule in Bangladesh and other nations in the world. Leaders of this extremist group consider notorious terrorists like Osama Bin Laden as 'hero of Islam'. It was already reported in local and international media that Hizbut Towhid has expanded its activities in a number of Asian nations as well 'successfully' created its base in some Western countries.

After Afghanistan, Islamic fundamentalism went global with its appeal to a section of Muslim society based on moral, cultural and political grounds. The Islamists argue that western culture particularly the one practiced by western women is essentially degenerative and incompatible with Quranic literalism. They argue that the values propagated by the West threaten Islamic "purity" and hence their advance is to be thwarted at any cost. Political argument is by far the easiest to sell to the wayward Muslim population who despite declaration of piety could have nursed in the darkest corner of their heart a desire to commit the original sin. The Islamists argue that the reasons for economic backwardness, political repression and societal dysfunction were caused by Western, particularly American assistance given to the repressive regimes in the Muslim world. The situation in Bangladesh is no exception. Under the embrella of "Organization for welfare of the reptariate soldiers from Afghanistan and Palestine", militancy and anti-Semitic notions are planted in the minds of people. It was clearly proved that several terror patron nations, including Iran, is continuing to finance such activities. Later, a large number of people belonging to Organization for welfare of the reptariate soldiers from Afghanistan and Palestine, entered Harkat-Ul-Mujahedin Bangladesh, Harkatul Jihad [Huji] and other ferrocious Islamist militancy outfits. There are also evidences that a number of Islamist political parties in Bangladesh, as well as some 'secularist' forces have openly or secretly joined hands with such extremist Islamist groups either with ulterior political motive or for expanding their vote banks.

Democracy and Islam

An inconclusive debate remains about the incompatibility of democracy with monotheistic religions. Robert Dahl in his classic book 'Polyarchy' had set eight essential requirements for democracy: right to form and join organizations; freedom of expression; right to vote; eligibility for public office; right of political leaders to compete for support for vote; and institutions for making government policies dependant on vote and other expressions of preference. Other political scientists have added that democracy must also have a constitution that by itself is democratic in that it respects fundamental liberties and offers protection to minorities. Additionally democratically elected governments must rule within the confines of their constitutions, be bound by law and be accountable. From historical observations it has been found that religions place inherent obstacles in the way of democracy. Philosopher John Rawls found it particularly difficult in a pluralistic society in which citizens hold a variety of socially embedded, reasonable yet deeply opposed comprehensive doctrines to arrive at an overlapping consensus. In the case of Islam some western scholars have found that because of its Prophet's fusion of military and spiritual authority and because Quranic laws are deemed to be final the space for democratic debate for the formation of secular laws does not exist in Muslim societies. Some other scholars however have found that appropriation of political Islam by Islamic fundamentalists is untenable and millions of Muslims living outside the Arab world live in intermittent democracies and they may not become victims of so-called Islamic Free Election Trap in which fundamentalists use democratic means to get to power only to abolish democratic practices through legislation.

Democracy is a dynamic process and "a state's raison d'etre does not lie in the protection of equal individual rights but in the guarantee of an inclusive process of opinion and will formation in which free and equal citizens reach an under standing on which goals and norms lie in the equal interest of all". Clearly then an ethical question would arise as perceived by Italian political scientist Luigi Bonante while discussing the difference between the individual and the state. He argues that while the state has sufficient tools to defend its rights and reject its duties; for the individual as recipient it is much harder to elude his duties than to achieve his freedom.

This kind of asymmetry of power during the BNP-Jamaat [2001-2006] rule in Bangladesh provides strong argument for the protection of human rights. The Orwellian tyranny of the majority was further compounded by increasing activism of Islamists who wish to recreate a truly Islamic society not simply by imposing the Sharia but by establishing an Islamic state where religious edicts will be integrated into all aspects of society.

ISLAMIC MILITANCY AS PRETEXT

During the recent Awami League rule (1996-2001), India began a propaganda war which claims Islamic terrorists are becoming active in Bangladesh. A section of Dhaka-based dailies frequently made reports about the existence of the militancy in Bangladesh. They repeatedly alleged that the Muslim terrorists were being trained deep in the jungle of Chittagong Hill Tracts, or Sundarbans or different madrashas of the country. Security forces instantly rushed to those spots mentioned in the dailies, but found the reports fake and baseless. To provoke the America-led western power India deliberately launched media campaign that Bangladesh has become a safe base of al-Quada and Taliban terrorists. To promote the idea of the existence of the Islamic militant groups in Bangladesh, the government even officially published booklets on the eve of the US President Bill Clinton's visit to Bangladesh. American government, however, still officially claims that there is no real Islamic militancy in Bangladesh, rather Bangladesh is a moderate Muslim democratic country.

During its rule, AL government arrested a number of madrasha teachers and students and Imams of the mosques branding them either as terrorists or their godfathers and claimed that some of them were trained in Afghanistan or Kashmir. But the court failed to prove the allegation and they were released. But neither India nor AL stopped their fake propagation and their followers or hired columnists stopped their campaign. India and its allies in Bangladesh were cock sure about the existence of such extremist groups in the country, as they fueled them. It is unfortunate that our ministry of Home Affairs failed earlier about India's hand in floating a number of India-sponsored outwardly Islamic terrorist outfits that clandestinely served in the interest of India in justifying the allegation of India and its Bangladeshi allies.

India's constant aggressive designs to create disturbances in her neighbouring countries ventilates her expansionist as well as jealous attitude against her peace loving and innocent neighbours is known to all. But India is particularly intolerant towards her neighbouring Muslim countries, Bangladesh and Pakistan, as they were curved out of British India. India, after 58 years of the partition of the subcontinent, unfortunately failed to forget the spirit of two-nation theory. She applies this theory in dealing with the Muslims inside her own territory and beyond.

The recent bomb attacks on some NGO installations and cultural soirees and the subsequent arrest of some terrorists under the guise of so-called Islamic militants and their gangleaders unveiled India's involvement. A number of Bangladeshi dailies on February 25, 2005, quoting the interrogation of the arrested informed, that the recently banned so-called Muslim outfits-JMTB (Jagrata Muslim Janata Bangladesh) and Jamaatul Mujahiden-were the brainchildren of Indian intelligence agency-RAW. The outward and instant aim of floating these outfits was to justify Indian allegation that Bangladesh is a haven of the Islamic terrors and provoke the government to take stern action against the madrashas, their teachers and students. Such step will make the government unpopular among the people that will deter the possibility of returning to power of the alliance government and pave the way to install a puppet government in Dhaka. The long-term design is to invite American-led anti-terror invasion or get American permission to invade Bangladesh so that either the invaders or their puppets in Dhaka gradually can close down the madrashas and crush the Islamic scholars, intellectuals, and even the pro-nationalist forces and ultimately make Bangladesh a vassal state of India.

Now the question arises why India is inimical to madarasha education in Bangladesh. Historically, India believes in the unification of the pre-1947 map of the British India, which means destruction of independent Bangladesh. Indian policy makers believe that madrashas and madrasha education are main sources of inspiration of pro-nationalist forces. So long these institutions exist in Bangladesh, it will not be possible to control and keep Bangladesh under her occupation if she invades and captures it eve in remote future. Indians are aware that the maulanas, mulllahs, imams, pirs, darvishs, in brief the Muslim religious leaders, organised and led all the anti-British movements and struggles in the subcontinent when the Hindus extended their unconditional support to British occupation and exploitation.

So the real resistance in Bangladesh will come from the madashas, whenever India bids to capture it. On the other hand, this education keeps the candle of Muslim identity alive in Bangladesh, which is the main bar of the reunification of the British India. For this reason madrasha as well as madrasha education has become the prime target of India. After the emergence of Bangladesh in 1971, India tried its best to ban madrasha and Islamic education in Bangladesh alleging that all the teachers and students of madrashas were collaborators and they should be tried and given exemplary punishment.

But the then government paid no heed to pressure of Indian government, though madrahas remained closed for certain period of time. But India did not lose heart; rather worked vigorously over the years to defame the madrahas and their teachers and students branding them anti-liberation forces. Madrassas were termed as the producers of 'rajakars' and anti-liberation forces. Demand was raised from the pro-India elements to close down madrashs and madrasha education. During the immediate past AL rule, madrasha teachers and students passed hard days and many of them were the victims of harassment and persecution and thrown into jail under fake allegations. Pro-Indian print media branded the madrashas as Taliban training centres. Same of the madrashas were closed down during the AL regime (1996-2001). Moreover, all the governments were directly and indirectly influenced to change the curriculum and syllabus of the madrasha education in the name of modernisation and reformation, so that the students and teachers are gradually diverted to secularism, which is the road to the unification of dreamy 'Akhand Bharat.' Above all, the debacle of AL in the general election of 2001 scared India of and it came to this conclusion that religious parties played the vital role in installing a nationalist government in Bangladesh.

Indian intelligence are confirmed that the ruling alliance will come out victorious in the coming election scheduled to be held in 2006. Though the government adopts soft policy in dealing with India, it does not respond positively in allowing transit or port facilities to India or allow her forces to use Bangladesh territory to fight against the militants of her northeastern states. Moreover, the relatively independent foreign policy of the alliance government, its internal success stories, above all its 'look east' policy scared Indians strategists that Bangladesh would get out of Indian fold if the alliance is allowed to form government again. For all these reason, India took hard line against the alliance government. Other than disturbing the government in hundreds of ways, Indian agencies clandestinely recruited agents from those who are outwardly seen and known as religious and have relations with madrashas. This is how India now uses the card of the presence of the Islamic militancy in Bangladesh in order to crush religious education and brand Bangladesh a terror-infested country and isolate it from the international community and install a puppet government to turn it into a secular vassal state and annex it to India in course of time when Muslim identity will be replaced by secular spirit.

Quoting intelligence agencies a number of Bangladeshi dailies said, both the recently banned outfits were floated, financed and guided by RAW to carryout disruptive and subversive activities. 'The Inqilab, "The Manbjamin," The Amar Desh,' 'The Naya Diganta,' other dailies of Dhaka on February 25, 2005, unearthed how RAW floated a number of socalled Islamic militant outfits, JMJB (Jagrata Muslim Janata Bangladesh), Jamaatul Mujahideens, etc., to implement Indian design and controlled and guided their activities from across the border. Police recovered some vouchers from the house of Mantazar Rahman, which show that some unnamed persons used to come from and go to India through the Hilly Border. The arrested cadres confessed that an assembly of learning the holy Quran used to hold at Jaypurhat residence of Jamaatul Mujahideen Commander Mantazar Rahman and others on every Sunday and Tuesday. In those gatherings vegetables were served instead of beef during dinner or launch, but in Bangladesh, beef is the main item of such occasion. The intelligence agencies believe that the avoidance of beef indicates that some Hindus used to attend in those outwardly Islamic gatherings to brief the leaders and cadres of the outfits.

Other than briefing on subversive activities, other major task of these outfits, were to award erroneous 'fatwa' (Islamic Judicial decree). The main task of these RAW-financed organisations is to derail and crush the real pro-nationalist Islamic movement in Bangladesh. Indian RAW pours huge amount of money to expand these outfits and keeps them active. No worker of Jamaatul Mujahideen knows who was the real leader of the outfit and from which source money comes.

It is learnt that a group of Rajshahi-based lawyers belonging to Awami League (AL) and a section of anti-government dailies assisted these groups in earning prominence and spreading activities of Shahadat-e-Al Hikma, another outfit. Its Amir, Syed Kaowsar Houssain was a half-educated Maulana. He was admitted into Rajshahi College in 1999, but could no sit for HSC examination due to financial crisis. Kaowsar does not have the financial or educational ability to run such a militant organisation. So the question arises, how he could gain financial ability to run the outfit. One pro-AL lawyer, Rashidul Islam of Rajshahi Bar assisted and financed Kaowsar in drafting the constitution and leaflets, posters and other publications of his outfit. Rashidul Islam also provided him legal assistance when he was arrested along with his party worker. Sanjib Roy, the President of Hindu-Buddhist-Christian Okkiya Parishad, accompanied Kaowsar on a tour to India. Kaowsar was introduced in India with an Indian citizen

Ashim Kumar who later took him to a hotel and arranged his appointment with such a person who claimed himself that he was Mafia godfather Daud Ibrahim. It is suspected that he was high-ranking RAW official.

On the other hand, Jamaatul Mujahideen headed by Dr. Ghalib Rajshahi University (RU) was floated in 1998 during Awami League rule. Most the leaders and workers of this organisation are the followers of Ahale Hadith. Abdur Rahman, who once acted as the Amir of Jammatul Mujahideen, is the husband of the sister of Mirja Azam MP of Jamalpur-3 constituency belonging to AL. Using his relationship with an AL MP Abdur Rahman procured the dealership of fertiliser and earned a lot of money during AL rule. On the other hand, Dr. Ghalib of RU who now heads the outfit maintains warm relation with some influential political leaders of different parties.

On the other hand, concealing his real profession and identity secret during AL period, Dr. Ghalib using a business passport went to India and stayed there for 11 days. When this forgery came to light, the then Register of RU Prof. Mohammad Younus served showcause notice on him and took disciplinary measures against him. But the initiative deterred and foiled due to the interference of the then Home Minister Mohmmad Nasim and the Mayor of Dhaka City Corporation Mohammad Hanif. Both belong to AL. During interrogation, the arrested persons informed that an Indian prominent religious leader used to come to Bangladesh and inspired them to work for Islamic revolution. A number of Bangladeshis got huge amount of money, arms, explosives and Other materials through this Indian religious leader. As a result, the activities of these groups suddenly expanded in bordering districts like Satkhira, Chapai Nawabganj, Rajshahi, etc.

It is learnt that Indian RAW tried to brand Bangladesh as a terrorist country using these elements The coal of raisine outwardly Islamic outfits was to throw the government to an awkward position-internally and internationally. When the government would take punitive measures against the outwardly Islamic militants, the common Bangladeshis will go against it. On the other hand, if the government remain mum, it will be isolated from the international community. In that case, India will get chance to prove that the government nurses the militants. India will also try to persuade the western powers to impose punitive measures against Bangladesh, including trade embargo, economic blockade, even military invasion. Its short-term goal is to unseat the present government, while its long-term goal is to isolate Bangladesh from the international community and finally invade her.

The international community should evaluate India's historical design and evaluate its involvement in imposing terrorism in her neighbouring countries, particularly in Bangladesh. If a giant country constantly designs to undo a tiny neighbour, it can neither wipe out terrorism, nor survive. India is well aware of this evil theory and deliberately creates terrorists in different sectors to meet her ulterior goal. India is the architect of terrorism in Bangladesh. Under this situation, international community before blaming Bangladesh for all sorts of terrorist activities, should identify the real sponsor of terrorism, that let loose the terrorists not only in Bangladesh, but also in other South Asian countries and ask her to refrain from such heinous misdeeds.

PAKISTAN'S UNHOLY ALLIANCE THE MILITANTS

The heavily guarded, high-walled concrete structure right in the heart of Islamabad has no signboard. But everyone in the capital knows that the sprawling compound surrounded by barbed wire houses the Directorate for Inter-Services Intelligence (ISI). The spy agency has been the country's big brother. It is powerful, ubiquitous and has functioned with so much autonomy from the central government that it has almost become a state within a state. It is not only responsible for intelligence gathering, but also acts as a determinant of Pakistan's foreign policy and a vehicle for its implementation.

For every civilian and military government, control of the ISI was seen as crucial to maintaining a firm grip on power. The agency had been so powerful for so long that it played by its own rules. Its various heads had contrasting profiles, but emerged among the most powerful figures in the country's establishment.

For years they ran semi-independent operations in Afghanistan and Kashmir and helped to form and topple civilian governments.

For more than two decades the ISI had sponsored Islamic militancy to carry out its secret wars. It was a crucial partner in the CIA's biggest covert operation ever, one that forced the Soviet Union to pull out of Afghanistan and served as a catalyst to the disintegration of the communist superpower. In Afghanistan, as well as Kashmir, the agency discovered the effectiveness of covert warfare as a method of bleeding a stronger adversary, while maintaining the element of plausible deniability. The ISI falls directly within Pakistan's military chain of command and had also served as an instrument for promoting the military's domestic political agenda and the guardian of its self-professed 'ideological frontiers' of the country. Almost all ISI officers are regular military personnel, who are rotated in and out for a fixed tenure. However, there have been some exceptions. The export of jihad sponsored by the ISI had its blowback. It had allowed the Islamists a huge space for their activities. State patronage, in the form of an 'unholy alliance' between the military and the mullahs, resulted in an unprecedented rise of radical Islam. The ISI had helped to create much of the Islamic militancy and religious extremism that Musharraf was confronted with. That unholy alliance had been a major factor in the country's drift to Islamic fundamentalism. Founded in 1948 by a British army officer, Major-General R. Cawthome, then Deputy Chief of Army Staff in Pakistan, the agency was initially charged with performing all intelligence tasks at home and abroad. Its scope of operation extended to all areas related to national security. Until the 1960s, the ISI largely remained an obscure organization that confined itself to playing its specified role. But in the mid 1970s its scope was expanded to domestic politics. Ironically, it was a civilian leader, Zulfikar Ali Bhutto who created the ISI's internal wing which played a critical role in the ousting of his government a few years later. It was to cast its heavy shadow over the country's politics in later years.

A charismatic and populist leader, Bhutto took over a humiliated military and a brutally truncated Pakistan in search of a new identity, following the Indian-supported secession of East

Pakistan (now Bangladesh), in 1971. The country had been dismembered by civil war and Indian military action. It was no longer the country created by Mohammed Ali Jinnah. The Pakistan that emerged from the ashes of defeat required a different geopolitical orientation. A revolt by young Turks in the army in the aftermath of a humiliating defeat in the war had forced the military ruler, General Yahya Khan, 3 to hand over power to Bhutto. His legitimacy was rooted in the country's first democratically held elections in 1970. Bhutto's socialist Pakistan People's Party had swept the fateful polls in the western wing of then-united Pakistan, trouncing the right-wing Islamic parties.

The scion of a feudal family of Sindh and a former foreign minister, Bhutto was seen as the savior of the new Pakistan. He successfully negotiated with India the release of 90,000 troops taken prisoner by Indian forces. He had come to power with the largest support base of any Pakistani leader since the inception of the country in 1947.

But he failed to sustain the confidence of the nation. Bhutto was ideally placed to put into practice the objective of social democracy and develop secular ideas and institutions. But it did not happen. Bhutto's strategy was to bring the disparate elements of this divided society together through a kind of Islamic nationalism, which was then supposed to create the cohesion and stability necessary for socialist economic reforms, but unfortunately all Bhutto succeeded in doing was to rehabilitate religious extremism. Under pressure from the religious parties whose cooperation they were courting, Bhutto's government increased the religious content in school syllabuses and, succumbing to pressure from Saudi Arabia as well as to the demands of religious parties, declared the Ahmedis, an Islamic sect, to be non-Muslim. This apparently minor action had long-term implications for the country as it fuelled Islamic zealotry and sharpened the sectarian divide. Bhutto's attempt to co-opt religious elements merely emboldened them, and eventually the clergy joined hands with their traditional ally, the military, to plot the overthrow of his government. Bhutto's attempt to establish an authoritarian rule led him to rely more and more on the coercive apparatus of the state and the intelligence agencies. Bhutto did little to strengthen democratic institutions and to make the process of democratic reform irreversible. Instead, his entire effort was aimed at promoting a personalized rule. He did not trust anyone. Given his overwhelming paranoia and insecurity, Bhutto geared up the ISI to keep surveillance not only on his opponents, but also on his own party men and cabinet ministers. The agency kept dossiers on politicians, bureaucrats, judges and anyone else considered important. The collapse of democratic institutions and the Constitution's loss of sanctity created a vacuum of authority that provided a favourable condition for the Bonapartist generals. Bhutto's use of the army to crush the uprising in Pakistan's western province of Balochistan provided an opportunity to the military to reassert itself in the country's politics. Bhutto's politics of expediency and attempts to appease the country's religious lobby allowed the Islamists, who were routed in the 1971 elections, to revive themselves. A nationwide agitation, led by right wing Islamic parties in the aftermath of the controversial elections in 1977, shook his government. In a desperate attempt to appease the Islamists, Bhutto prohibited the sale and use of alcoholic beverages, banned gambling and closed down nightclubs. But the die had already been cast.

Bhutto had handpicked General Zia ul-Haq, a lesser-known officer, for the post of army chief in 1976 over the heads of half a dozen senior officers, believing he did not have any personal ambitions. General Zia was a devout Muslim and Bhutto thought he would never betray his trust. Once elevated to the top position, the General did not take much time to develop secret contacts with hardline religious groups and conspired with them to overthrow his benefactor. On 5 July 1977, a bloodless military coup brought an end to Bhutto's six-and-a-half-year civilian rule. There was a complete convergence of interests between the Islamists and the military leadership which had ousted the Bhutto government. Several accounts of Bhutto's last days in power revealed that Major-General Ghulam Jilani, Bhutto's handpicked chief of the ISI, played a key role in the coup plan. Two years later, in April 1979, Bhutto was hanged after a dubious trial on charges of murdering a political rival. A secularist, elected with an overwhelming mandate in 1970, Bhutto probably had the best chance of any leader of taking on the Islamists and winning. His inglorious demise can only fill Pakistan's current leader, attempting a similar task, with foreboding.

Bhutto's usurper, General Zia, came from a humble lowermiddle-class background. His father, a religious man, held a clerical government post during British rule in India. Despite his poverty, he provided his son with a decent education. Zia was educated at Delhi's most prestigious St Stephen's College before getting a commission in the Royal Indian Army in 1942. He was a captain at the time of the creation of Pakistan in 1947. He was a hard-working officer, but lacked brilliance. Many of his colleagues believed he was lucky to be promoted beyond Colonel. From a young age, Zia was actively involved with the popular religious movement, Tablighi Jamaat, 6 one of the most influential grassroots Islamic movements in the South Asian subcontinent, which had hardline traditionalist views on the role of Islam in modern society.

A short man with a thick moustache, Zia bore a strong resemblance to the British comedian, Terry-Thomas. But he was by no means a fool. He was shrewd enough to know how to make his way up. He convinced Bhutto of his absolute loyalty and more importantly of his incapacity to be otherwise. Zia was not only an authoritarian; he also aspired to turn Pakistan into an ideological state ruled by strict Islamic sharia laws. He was an unpopular and controversial leader, whose survival in power largely owed to the external factors that emerged after the invasion by Soviet forces of Pakistan's northern neighbour, Afghanistan, in 1979. Pakistan became a frontline state and a bulwark in the West's war against communism.

General Zia brought in his close confidant, Lt.-General Akhter Abdur Rehman, to head the ISI in 1979, as the spy agency became a crucial cog in the resistance against the Soviet forces. Its tentacles started to spread far and wide. An artillery officer, General Rehman 'had a cold, reserved personality, almost inscrutable, always secretive, with no intimates except his family.' His officers remembered him as a hard man to serve due to his brusque manner and reputation as a strict disciplinarian. 'That made him an ideal man for the job,' said Brigadier Mohammed Yousuf, a former ISI officer who served under him. General Rehman ran the organization until 1987. He was not a radical Islamist, but a staunch Muslim nationalist. Under General Rehman, the ISI, in partnership with the CIA, conducted the biggest covert operation in modern history. The two organizations had secretly collaborated for years, yet General Zia was not prepared to give a free hand to the CIA. He laid down strict rules to ensure that the ISI would maintain control over contacts with Afghan mujahidin groups. No CIA operatives would be allowed to cross the border into Afghanistan. Distribution of weapons to the Afghan commanders would be handled only by the ISI. All training of mujahidin would be the sole responsibility of the ISI. While the CIA supplied money and weapons, it was the ISI that moved them into Afghanistan. The Americans relied almost entirely on the Pakistani service to allocate weapons to the mujahidin groups. The framework provided the Pakistani spy agency with almost total control over the covert operation inside Afghanistan. The decade-long secret war raised the organization's profile and gave it huge clout. With the active help of the CIA and Saudi Arabia, the ISI turned the Afghan resistance into Islam's holy war.

The decade-long conflict in Afghanistan gave the Islamic extremists a rallying point and a training field. Young Muslims around the world flocked to Afghanistan to fight against a foreign invader. Some 35,000 holy warriors joined the Afghan war from 1979 to 1989. The largest number came from the Middle East. Some were Saudis, among whom was a young man called Osama bin Laden.

The 23-year-old son of a wealthy construction magnate said he arrived in Peshawar for the first time in 1980. He was a very shy person who had no experience of war and, as a fresh graduate from the King Abdul Aziz University, bin Laden had left the luxury of his home to help the mujahidin fighting jihad in Afghanistan. It was the beginning of his long association with Afghan and Pakistani Islamic radicals. By 1984 he was spending most of his time in Peshawar, sometimes with Abdullah Azzam, a Palestinian Islamic scholar and an ideologue who inspired the rush of foreign Muslims to fight in Afghanistan. It was also during this period that he developed links with the ISI, which had become the main conduit for arms and training for the Islamic warriors. The Afghan war placed enormous resources at the agency's disposal. Weapons provided by the CIA were channelled to Afghan fighters through the ISI. By the mid 1980s, every dollar given by the CIA was matched by another from Saudi Arabia. The funds, running into several million dollars a year, were transferred by the CIA to the ISI's special accounts in Pakistan. The backing of the CIA and the funnelling of massive amounts of US military aid helped the ISI develop into 'a parallel structure wielding enormous power over all aspects of government.' It became all-pervasive and there was an unprecedented expansion in the surveillance of political opponents.

Even those in the army were not spared. According to a former senior intelligence officer, part of the ISI's function was to keep a careful watch on the generals and ensure their loyalty to the regime. In the words of Brigadier Yousaf, 'So powerful had the ISI become that apprehension, even fear, of what the ISI could do, was real.' The Afghan war provided the agency with the public profile that it did not have before. Former ISI officials point out that the general expansion the agency underwent as a consequence of its Afghan role had a bearing on its overall functioning. While its role in supervising a successful covert operation in Afghanistan won the ISI international acclaim, at home it was a dreaded name.

The Afghan resistance was projected as part of the global jihad against communism. The ISI's training of guerrillas was integrated with the teaching of Islam. The prominent theme was that Islam was a complete socio-political ideology under threat from atheistic communists. The Afghan war produced a new radical Islamic movement. Besides the holy warriors from Islamic countries, thousands more joined madrasas set up with funding from Saudi Arabia and some other Muslim countries. More than 100,000 foreign Muslim radicals were directly influenced by the Afghan jihad. The military's involvement in the politics of religion, however, had started long before the Afghan jihad. General Zia not only ushered Pakistan into its longest period of military rule, but also tried to turn the country into an ideological state. He extended the army's role in domestic politics much further than defined by earlier military rulers. Previously, the military was seen as the ultimate guarantor of the country's territorial integrity and internal security. But Zia expanded its role as the defender of Pakistan's ideological frontiers as well.

Addressing army officers, Zia argued that, as Pakistan was created on the basis of the two-nation theory and Islamic ideology, it was the duty of the 'soldiers of Islam to safeguard its security, integrity and sovereignty at all costs, both from internal turmoil and external aggression'. He claimed the state was created exclusively to provide its people with the opportunity to follow 'the Islamic way of life.' Preservation of the country's Islamic character was seen to be as important as the security of the country's geographical frontiers. Zia's military rule differed by its very serious attempt to create an ideological basis for all areas of activities of the state and society. General Zia cleverly used Islam to consolidate his power and legitimize his military rule. The Islamization process became the most important feature of his eleven- year rule and its raison d'e^tre. For General Zia, Pakistan was an Islamic ideological state and therefore politics could not be separated from religion. He believed that he had a divine obligation to establish an Islamic society ruled in accordance with the Qur'an and sharia. Afraid to face a free electorate and having no mandate to govern, the General turned to Allah. He introduced a rigid interpretation of Islamic sharia, thus empowering the clergy. The move to Islamize the state found ready allies among the religious parties, many of which already had close ties with the military. The Jamaat-i-Islami and other Islamic groups were co-opted by the government. For the first time in Pakistan's history, the Islamists occupied important government positions. Being in power helped Jamaat-i-Islami, the most influential and organized mainstream religious party, penetrate state institutions. Thousands of party activists and sympathizers were given jobs in the judiciary, the civil service and educational institutions. These appointments strengthened the hold of the Islamists on crucial state apparatuses for many years to come.

The process of the Islamization of the state and society took place on two levels. Firstly, changes were instituted in the legal system. Sharia courts were established to try cases under Islamic laws. For the first time, the government assumed the role of the collector of religious taxes. Secondly, Islamization was promoted through the print media, radio, television and mosques. Through a series of religious decrees, the government moved to Islamize the civil service, the armed forces and the education system. School textbooks were overhauled to ensure their ideological purity. Books deemed un-Islamic were removed from syllabuses and university libraries. It was made compulsory for civil servants to pray five times a day. Confidential reports of government officials included a section in which the staff were given marks for regularly attending prayers and for having a good knowledge of Islam. General Zia's move to Islamize the army carried the most critical implications. Pakistan's army, carved out of the British Indian army, inherited British traditions and remained a secular organization until General Zia tried to give it a new Islamic orientation. Islam was incorporated into the army's organizational fabric. For the first time Islamic teachings were introduced into the Pakistan Military Academy.

Islamic training and philosophy were made a part of the curriculum at the Command and Staff College. A Directorate of Religious Instruction was instituted to educate the officer corps on Islam. Islamic education also became a part of the promotion exams. The officers were required to read The Quranic Concept of War, a book written by a serving officer, Brigadier S. K. Malik. The officers were taught to be not just professional soldiers, but also soldiers of Islam. In his foreword to the book, General Zia wrote: 'The professional soldier in a Muslim army, pursuing the goals of a Muslim State, cannot become "professional" if in all his activities he does not take on "the colour of Allah".' To gain promotion an officer was required to be a devout Muslim. Scores of highly professional and secular officers were sidelined for not meeting the criterion of a 'good Muslim'. As a consequence of this policy, many conservative officers reached the senior command level. Radical Islamist ideology permeated the army with the free flow of religious political literature in the armed forces training institutions. Friday prayers at regimental mosques, a matter of individual choice in the past, became obligatory. Mullahs belonging to the Deobandi sect were appointed to work among the troops.

They were supposed to be the bridge for officers between the westernized profession and the faith. Units were required to take noncombatant mullahs with them to the front line. Soldiers were encouraged to attend 'Tablighi' gatherings. The purpose was to indoctrinate cadets and young officers with an obscurantist interpretation of Islam. Many of those cadets later rose to positions of power and took control of sensitive institutions, including the ISI. The change in the social composition of the officer corps also led to the ideological reorientation of Pakistan's army in the 1980s. The army officer corps, till the 1970s, was elitist in character and composition. But the trend changed. In the past, members of the upper class or the rural aristocracy had largely dominated the army ranks; now the new officers mostly came from the lower and middle social strata. The rank and file of junior officers since the 1970s had come, not from prosperous central Punjab, but from the impoverished and relatively backward northern districts where a fundamentalist religious ethos prevailed. Unlike their predecessors, the new officers did not come from elite English-language schools, but were the product of modest state-run educational institutions. The spirit of liberalism, common in the 'old' army, was practically unknown to them. They were products of a social class that, by its very nature, was conservative and easily influenced by Islamic fundamentalism. They were distinctively less westernized.

Their narrow nationalist orientation and education, professional training and culture made them very receptive to the influence of Islamic groups, particularly to the Jamaat-i-Islami (JI), which freely carried out propaganda work among the officers and circulated Islamic literature. Most importantly, the JI's propaganda among vast numbers of troops was officially sanctioned by commanding officers on the battalion level and above. That led to the evolution of a long-lasting alliance between the military and the mosque. The main objective of the JI was to penetrate the army and use it to seize state power. The practice introduced by General Zia of sending combat officers to universities in Pakistan, in which the JI often had pervasive influence, facilitated the party's objective. The influence of the JI was particularly visible among officers from rural and semi-urban backgrounds. They had a high level of religious intolerance and held extremist views regarding 'external enemies' and the threat to Islam.

The number of officers sporting beards for religious reasons had visibly risen. These young officers constituted the main base for General Zia's regime. According to a retired general, 25 to 30 per cent of the officers had Islamic fundamentalist leanings. Many of them regularly attended 'Tablighi' groups that propagated the faith. They would take time off to join missionary bands preaching a return to purist Islamic values and recruiting other Muslim men to join them. Thousands of soldiers and army officers would join the annual gathering of the TJ at Raiwind on the outskirts of Lahore. More than one million faithful from across the country and abroad attend this Muslim congregation, the largest after the Haj in Mecca. Even the liberals adopted the philosophy on issues like jihad and support for militancy in Kashmir. The humiliating military defeat by the Indian army in the 1971 war, coupled with the disintegration of the country, also had a very deep impact on the psyche of army officers. Many young officers turned to religion for solace and became born-again Muslims. Given this situation, it was not surprising that radical Islamic officers made unsuccessful coup attempts in the mid 1980s. They wanted to bring about an Islamic revolution and establish a theocratic state. The fact that the attempts were crushed and the rebel officers were charged with treason indicated that, notwithstanding its Islamization, the state was not prepared to tolerate a theocratic rule.

The situation in Afghanistan provided inspiration to a whole generation of Pakistani Islamic radicals who considered it their religious duty to fight the oppression of Muslims anywhere in the world. It gave a new dimension to the idea of jihad, which till then had only been employed by the Pakistani state in the context of mobilizing the population against the arch rival – India. The Afghan war saw the privatization of the concept of jihad. Militant groups emerged from the ranks of traditional religious movements, who took the path of an armed struggle for the cause of Islam. The ISI's active role in the Afghan jihad brought Pakistani army officers into direct contact with the radical Islamists.

The handling of jihad also indoctrinated the military and intelligence officers. At least two former ISI chiefs – General Hamid Gul and General Javed Nasir – remained actively involved with Islamic radical movements. Both promoted pan-Islamism and strove for an Islamic revolution that would free Pakistan from perceived western, and particularly American, cultural and political influences. General Gul, who liked to call himself a 'Muslim visionary', succeeded General Rehman in 1987 when the Afghan resistance had entered its most critical juncture. The most charismatic of the ISI chiefs, he openly aligned himself with the hardline Afghan mujahidin leader, Gulbuddin Hekmatyar, and right-wing Pakistani Islamic parties. He would later take credit for dismantling the Soviet Union. General Gul had worked closely with the CIA, but turned anti-American after the Geneva Accord in 1987, which paved the way for the withdrawal of Soviet forces from Afghanistan. The Accord was signed by the Pakistani civilian government led by Prime Minister Mohammed Khan Junejo against the wishes of President Zia, who believed it deprived the Afghan mujahidin of the opportunity to take over Kabul. Resentment among the military and ISI officers deepened in 1990, just one year after the Soviets pulled out of Afghanistan and the US administration imposed sanctions on Pakistan for its nuclear programme. The CIA ended its support for the Afghan rebels and its links with the ISI went cold. It was a sudden end to the strong link between the two agencies. The military leadership accused the United States of dumping Pakistan after the collapse of the Soviet Union. Long before the Afghan war was over, General Gul had started organizing a new jihad front in Kashmir. 'It is the years of our work that has realized the armed uprising against the Indian forces in Kashmir,' he told me in early 1990 when he was commanding the country's elite armoured corps.

The death of General Zia ul-Haq in a mysterious air crash in August 1988 brought an end to Pakistan's longest-serving military government. It left the generals with the choice of either imposing martial law again or holding elections and transferring power to a democratically elected civilian government. They went for the second option, realizing that a perpetuation of military rule might provoke public resistance and exacerbate the turmoil in an already highly polarised society. However, the generals were not prepared to pull out completely and leave the political field solely to the politicians, particularly to the daughter of Zulfikar Ali Bhutto, Benazir Bhutto, who now led the Pakistan People's Party, which was certain to sweep the polls. To contain Benazir, the military cobbled together the Islamic Democratic Alliance (IDA), uniting all the right-wing parties under the leadership of Nawaz Sharif. General Aslam Beg, then Chief of Army Staff, and General Gul justified the move by saying it was necessary for the viable functioning of a democratic system.

The main objective, however, was to ensure the military's continued role in the new system, overseen by the generals. By creating a counterbalance in the form of the IDA, the generals constrained the new government of a political party that had led the resistance against military hegemony for ten years. The military-sponsored alliance comprised a mix of traditional power brokers, religious parties and politicians who had emerged on the scene during the 1980s under military patronage. General Zia's regime, needing a measure of legitimacy and a social base of support, had co-opted segments of Punjab's dominant socio-economic strata: influential landlords, industrialists and emerging commercial groups. The new leadership of the Pakistan Muslim League thus largely consisted of politicians who owed their political rise to the military's backing. The other important components of the alliance were the right-wing Islamic groups, including the Jamaat-i-Islami, which had been involved in the Afghan jihad against the Soviet forces and the separatist war in Indian-controlled Kashmir.

While the IDA, which carried General Zia's legacy, could not achieve any significant electoral gains in the 1988 elections in the three smaller provinces, it did relatively well in Punjab and prevented the PPP from winning an absolute majority in the National Assembly. The military reluctantly handed over power to Benazir at the centre, but prevented her party from forming the government in Punjab, the biggest and most important of Pakistan's four provinces, which was being ruled by Nawaz Sharif. Political manipulation by the ISI helped Sharif retain power in the province with the support of independent members. Benazir Bhutto's assumption of power, touted at the time as the dawn of a new democratic era, was in fact a transition from direct to indirect military rule. The formal restoration of civilian rule in 1988 did not reduce the ISI's clout. A return to the barracks did not mean that the military's structure of control and manipulation had been dismantled. The ISI still kept a close watch on civilian rulers. The strains in civil and military relationships remained the biggest obstacle to democracy taking root in Pakistan.

AUTONOMY MOVEMENT OR ISLAMIC MILITANCY

The Kashmir problem is quite different. It existed since the time of independence and is essentially an autonomy movement. That those spearheading this movement are Muslim is incidental to the whole issue. The political, social and legal factors that have been responsible for the present situation in Jammu and Kashmir deserve separate discussion and the paper does not allow presenting it here in details. However, it must be noted here that Kashmir where nearly 80 per cent of the population was Muslim remained under Dogra rulers (Hindus) from Maharaja Gulab Singh to Maharaja Hari Singh for 106 years from 1846 and 1952, yet there never arose a communal conflict.

It was these Kashmiris who rejected the two nation theory of Jinnah in 1947 and took up arms to resist Pakistani sponsored armed infiltrators, sang national anthem on every platform of Kashmir and supported the State's accession to the Union of India signed by Maharaja Hari Singh on October 26, 1947. They lived in peace and harmony for 40 years, supported the secular fabric of the state and opposed any and every communal move of a microscopic section of Jamat-e-Islami in the Valley. The foremost Kashmiri Muslim's leader, Sheikh Mohammed Abdullah, had to change the name of his 'Muslim Conference' to 'National Conference' because of public pressure as the Kashmiris, both Hindus and Muslims had grown together under the spirit of the Kashmiriyat.

It must be noted here that the nature of Islam in Kashmir is very different from some other parts of India. The *rishi* tradition has predominantly shaped religious and public life in Kashmir for centuries and is the basis of their self-identity as Kashmiris. Some people held Islam responsible for the uprising of militancy in the valley which shows intellectual felony.

Though we can not completely deny the existence of fundamentalist strain in the present Kashmiri movement, but the fundamental question here is, whether it is religion which instigate them to fight or the situation so develops that they feel inclined to take resort to religion as instrument to easily mobilize the people?

As pointed out by Engineer, though Islam was always there in the Kashmir and it could have inspired them anytime during all these years, but why extremists appeared on the scene so late, in fact only at the end of 80s.

The mistake lies with the Indian government who never kept the promise of granting autonomy and special powers to Kashmiris under Article 370. Not only that special powers promised to Kashmiris remained in the paper, but there was attempt by the Indian government to curtail the existing freedom and autonomy. Mandate of the people were hardly respected and democratically elected governments invariably were overthrown. The only fair election held was in 1977 during the Janata Government in the Centre.

The movement for regional autonomy remained non-violent for four decades after independence. But when the democratic space to voice their demands shrank, people had no option but to take to arms to demand their rights which were long overdue. This provided opportunity to Pakistan to play with the heightened emotion of the people and it started providing support in the form of weapons and money to the Kashmiris to fight against the Indian government. Thus the nature of the entire movement changed form one of an indigenous movement to demand autonomy, to political aimed at destabilizing Indian government. In the light of above discussion the case of Kashmir thus can not be regarded as Islamic militancy.

Is there Possibility of Islamic Militancy in India?

The rise of Hindu communalism has gathered wide acceptance in today's environment which would have been unacceptable only a few years back. The fact that a right wing political party, BJP is ruling at the centre and in many of the states has given fillip to the Hindutva forces to impose their agenda on the national mainstream. There is an increasing tendency on the part of Hindu right-wing groups to present Muslims as the 'other' in order to unite Hindus against the Muslim so as to consolidate their hold over the power structure of the state. The rise of Hindutva forces has led many commentators to say that it will give rise to Islamic militancy in India (Narula; Kamal Chenoy; Sunil Khilnani; 2003)4. In order to deal with the issue it must be noted here that Muslim constitute largest minority in India that is 11.6 (around 120 million) per cent of total population according to 1991 census of India. Thus India is the home to the second largest Muslim population after Indonesia. This makes the issue of Islamic militancy more critical in India.

The rise of Hindutva forces in India has already resulted in some devastating consequences. In February and March 2002, over 2000 people were killed in state-supported violence against Muslims in the western state of Gujarat, led by the Hindu nationalist BJP that also heads a coalition government at the center. The attacks were carried out with impunity by members of the BJP, the Rashtriya Swayamsevak Sangh ("RSS," National Volunteer Corps), the Vishwa Hindu Parishad ("VHP," World Hindu Council), and the Bajrang Dal (the militant youth wing of the VHP) (Narula 2003).5 Collectively, these groups are known as the *sangh parivar*, or family of Hindu nationalist organizations. Police and state officials were directly implicated in many of the attacks.

Nationwide violence against India's Muslim community in 1992 and 1993 and against India's Christian community since 1998, including in the state of Gujarat, has also stemmed from the violent activities and hate propaganda of these groups. The Indian government continues to exploit rhetoric surrounding the global war on terror to silence political dissent while the sangh parivar invokes the threat of Islamic militancy in the aftermath of September

11 to justify the persecution of Muslims. Operating under the guise of patriotism, the proponents of Hindu nationalism are achieving mainstream credibility. The promotion of Hindu nationalism as a legitimate political and cultural force has consequences beyond its impact on the lives of India's religious minorities.

Attacks on Muslims in India have their corresponding effect on Hindus in Bangladesh and Pakistan. If the activities of these groups remain unchecked, violence may percolate to other parts of the South Asian region. When compounded with the growing political influence of the Islamic right and the military in Pakistan and Bangladesh, Hindu militarization may destabilize the region as a whole. The process of modernization and democratization which has been undergoing in India have also helped in the creation of minority consciousness and enabled minorities to organize them politically. They are not only determined to preserve their cultural identity, which has been threatened because of the rise of Hindutva concepts of national identity and secular state, but they also seek to grab the share in the development and prosperity resulting from ongoing process of modernization and liberalisation of the country. It must be noted here that the process of modernization has resulted in the increasing number of educated and underemployed youth within all religious communities. Further, the influx of uneducated or undereducated migrants from rural into metropolitan areas in search of jobs and better opportunities creates groups of rootless people having no ties with neighbourhood and not held together by kinship bonds. Such alienated and atomized individuals are readily available to be moblised by militant organsiations that play on their emotions (Malik and Vajpeyi 1989). Even in the face of these developments militancy within Indian Muslim community has not found widespread expression. This is not to deny that there are radical Muslim groups in India, but they have failed so far to earn wide public acceptance. The radical Muslim groups situated in the peripheral regions like Assam in the north east and Malabar region in Kerala can not be said to inspire to fight for religion. Rather their anger needs to be understood in the context of marginalization and economic deprivation which always engulf peripheral region.

Their anger against the state is manifested by targeting specific groups.

Thus their struggle is to achieve political gain rather than to earn religious merit. Islamic militancy is not possible in India because of India's adoption of liberal-democratic framework after independence. India's success as a democracy lies in its successful handling of minority problems. Indian constitution like other democratic country incorporates a number of provisions which aim at safeguarding the interests of minorities and allow them to maintain their own identity through cultural and educational rights and provided special safeguards to protect their interests. However, the fruits of these special measures could not help much, especially to the Muslim minority, to achieve economic prosperity. But they could feel a sense of security. But this sense of security has been gradually, especially in the 90s, shattered owing to rise of Hindutva forces. This poses a serious question for Indian democracy; whether this will give rise to Islamic militancy? There is no any concrete answer to this question and much will depend upon the nature of Indian state, whether it will be able to maintain its democratic and secular credentials or will it allow it to be maneuvered by the right wing forces. However, since independence the political balance of power has undergone a significant change and the politico-legal system does not allow any operative system for the rise of militant Islam in India. Indian Muslims have had never in a position to give a militant response for their grievances as in such situation they are the principal sufferers. Because of the above reason and the growing power of the Indian Muslim middle class, militancy can not take root among the community. Faced with grievances, they would rather prefer to resolve it through democratic means rather than taking to arms.

Unlike migrant Islam in Europe, Indian Islam is historical Islam and there exists a very close proximity between Indian Muslim and Indian Hindu across cultural lines, which also makes Islamic militancy a distant possibility in India. As put by Assayag, 'the continuous process of integrative and antagonistic acculturation has allowed each tradition to preserve its peculiarities and maintain a demarcating line between Hindus and Muslims'.

'This is obvious because Hinduism and Islam, as they were practiced until recently, continue to show a great deal of flexibility and a spirit of accommodation in their mutual relations.

In fact, they display an understanding that is infinitely richer than the limited sectarian approach adopted by dogmatic, fundamentalist and neotraditionalist circles on both sides' (Assayag 2004).

MILITANT ISLAM AND AL QAEDA

For years, in a number of South Asian nations, Islamic militancy is continuing to gain strength, thus finally leaving potential threat to regional as well as global security and peace. On the other hand, Jihad and terrorism is being preached in Madrassas, not only in Muslim nations but also in several non-Muslim countries. Jihadist notions are also planted in the minds of people through 'Dawah' promoted by Tablighi Jamaat. First of all, it is essential to understand the latest situation of Madrassa education in Muslim and non-Muslim countries.

Madrassas in Pakistan and Bangladesh

The madrassas in today's Pakistan and Bangladesh, as in India, represent the legacy of the spectacular resurgence of Islamic religious education in India during the late nineteenth century, beginning with the establishment of the Deoband Madrassa in 1867. In most of the madrassas there are no formal admission procedures and legitimacy to the respective madrassas. Major policy decisions regarding doctrinal preferences, curriculum, and selection of teachers and students remain the exclusive prerogative of the ulema. Unlike Pakistan, Bangladesh has two kinds of madrassas: Quomi madrassas—estimated at more than 57,000 at the secondary, intermediate, and higher levels with about 5,762,000 students and 400,000 teachers. The Quomi madrassas are private, receive no financial support from the government, and are supported by local and foreign donations, mostly from the Middle East.

According to the latest data [2007–08) available to the madrassa education board, there are 6,906 non-government Alia madrassas in Bangladesh with the largest number, 12,740, at the dakhil level. The total number of students at all levels in the Alia system is 3,786,500. The number of teachers in these madrassas is 312,898. Unlike the graduates of Quomi madrassas, whose degrees are not recognized by the government and who pursue their careers in religious establishments and private businesses, the majority of the graduates of Alia madrassas merge into the general stream of education by continuing their education in colleges and universities. It is no wonder that a recent survey found that 32 percent of Bangladesh university teachers in the humanities and social sciences were graduates of Alia madrassas.

There are also elementary level madrassas known as maktabs, or ibtedai madrassas, first formally approved by Bangladesh's the then President Ziaur Rahman in 1978. The Madrassa Education Board has approved 9,320 of all independent ibtedai madrassas, with 45,300 teachers and 689,865 students. But in reality there are more than 38,000 ibtedai madrassas with 130,000 teachers and close to four million students. This latter figure is supported by Bangladeshi Ministry of Education estimate made in 1992 which shows the total number of ibtedai madrassa at 17,279. More than 50 percent of students in Quomi madrassas and more than 70 percent of students in Alia madrassas come from an ibtedai background. In Pakistan, the number of secondary and higher madrassas 12,000; Senior and graduate level madrassas 7,446; Deobandi madrassas 5,120; Barelvi madrassas 3,765; Ahl-i-Hadith madrassas 400; Shia madrassas 280; Number of all students Pakistani students in madrassas 15,765 and Afghan students 61,876. There are a few thousand madrassas in Pakistan which are not registered with the government. And, while in 1947, there was only 137 Madrassas in Pakistan, in 2001, the figure went upto 4,345.

There are approximately eighteen million students in various Madrassas in Pakistan, Bangladesh and India. Majority of these students come from poor families. In Pakistan, the majority of madrassa students belong to the rural areas of the North West Frontier Province [NWFP], Pakistani part of Kashmir, and Punjab. They are mostly drawn from the low strata of society. In a survey conducted in 1976, more than 80 percent of the madrassa students in Peshawar, Multan, and Gujranwala were found to be sons of small or landless peasants, rural artisans, or clergies of the village mosques. They remaining 20 percent came from families of small shopkeepers and rural laborers. A survey, conducted in 2000, found that 55 percent of madrassa students came from peasant families and petty traders. The interesting thing to note is that the number of students whose fathers were employed in lower level private sector jobs rose from 5 percent in 1976 to 35 percent in 2000. Only 3 percent of students in the 2000 survey said their fathers were imams [clergies] of the mosques. The majority of students come from large but low-income families. The 2000 survey found that 63 percent of madrassa students had five or more siblings, and 28 percent of them had seven or more brothers and sisters. In the case of Bangladesh, an overwhelming majority of Quomi madrassa students [82 percent] come from poor families of rural areas and small towns. Sylhet, Chittagong, Comilla, Noakhali and some northern districts have traditionally been the main base of recruitment for the Quomi madrassas.

Madrassas are Breeding Ground of Jihadists

Several reports on internationa media including CNN, BBC etc, as well as Jessica Stern's article in Foreign Affairs and Jeffrey Goldberg's article in the New York Times Magazine, besides several dozen columns of Thomas Friedman, have suggested that the madrassas in Pakistan have become a hotbed of Islamic extremism and the breeding ground of terrorism. They have been variously described as dens of terror, Jihad universities, Jihad factories, and, as the then Indian Prime Minister Atal Behari Vajpayee described them, factories of terror.

There is no doubt that Madrassas have become actibely linked to terrorism and terrorist training camps. Many journalists and commentators have suggested that these madrassas teach Jihadist literature in their course of studies and that their entire curriculum is intended to produce holy warriors. It has also been suggested by many Western scholars that there is an inherent relationship between what is taught in the madrassas on the one hand and religious extremism, Talibanism, militancy, anti-Americanism, anti-Semitism and terrorism, on the other. Madrassa students, through their reading of religious texts, become soldiers of Allah [God] and engage in militant activities against those they consider enemies of Islam [Clergies and teachers in Madrassas teach the students to hate Jews and Christians and term them as enemies of Islam, thus giving provocations of Jihad, alluring heaven and 72-virgins, if anyone would become martyr.

Understandably the US Congress keeps itself informed of the madrasa education in South Asia. A report by the Congressional Research Service [International Terrorism in South Asia] states that among the approximately ten thousand madrasas in Pakistan some that have been implicated in teaching militant anti-western, anti-American and anti-Hindu values. Many of these madrasas are financed and operated by Pakistani Islamist political parties and foreign entities. Foremost US analyst on South Asia Stephen Cohen states that the largest Islamic sects with the greatest control over religious schools are the Deobandis, who are among the most militant in their demand for Pakistan to become truly Islamic. Incidentally Deobandi groups were in the forefront of declaring Ahmadiyyas as non-Muslim in Pakistan. In Bangladesh, anti-Ahmadiyya activities started under the patronization of some Islamist clergies as well as some Islamist leaders thus finally causing series of attacks on Ahmadiyya mosques in various parts of the country under the leadership of Mufti Noor Hussain Noorani and Moulana Momtaji.

Radical Islam and Madrassa

The Iranian Revolution and the Soviet occupation of Afghanistan, both in 1979, inspired a profound shift in the Muslim world—and in the madrasas. Iran's mullahs had managed to overthrow the Shah and take power, undermining the idea that religious education was useless in worldly matters. Although Iranians belong to the minority Shiite sect of Islam, and their madrasas have always had a more political character than Sunni seminaries, the image of men in turbans and robes running a country provided a powerful demonstration effect and politicized madrasas everywhere.

Ayatollah Khomeini's revolutionary regime promised to export its revolutionary Shiite ideas to other Muslim states. Khomeini invited teachers and students from madrasas in other countries to Tehran for conferences and parades, and he offered money and military training to radical Islamic movements. Iranians argued that the corrupt Arab monarchies must be overthrown just as Iranians had overthrown the Shah. Iran's Arab rivals decided to fight revolutionary Shiite fundamentalism with their own version of Sunni fundamentalism. Saudi Arabia and other gulf countries began to pour money into Sunni madrasas that rejected the Shiite theology of Iran, fund ulema who declared the Shiite Iranian model unacceptable to Sunnis, and call for a fight against Western decadence rather than Muslim rulers.

When Awatollah Khomeini captured power in Tehran, he stared funding anti-West and anti-Semitic groups under the umbrella of 'Al Quds Society' and Iranian embassies in various countries openly or secretly continued to fund such activities. Even in the official newsletter published by the Iranian embassies in a number of countries, extreme propaganda against United States, Israel, Jews and Christians are continuing in the name of re-capturing the Al Aqsa [Temple Mount] by the Muslims through Jihad. Leaders and ministers in Khomeini's regime even visited several Muslim and non-Muslim nations to deliver cash to the Islamist groups promoting Tehran's theology. Unites of Hezbollah were created in several Muslim nations and were assigned to recruit members mostly from the madrassas.

In the midst of this conflict, and the madrasa boom it spawned, the United States helped create an Islamic resistance to communism in Afghanistan, encouraging Saudi Arabia and other oil-rich states to fund the Afghan resistance and its supporters throughout the Muslim world. Pakistan's military ruler at the time, Gen. Mohammed Zia ul-Haq, decided to establish madrasas instead of modern schools in Afghan refugee camps, where 5 million displaced Afghans provided a natural supply of recruits for the resistance. The refugees needed schools; the resistance needed mujahideen. Madrasas would provide an education of sorts, but they would also serve as a center of indoctrination and motivation.

General Zia's model spread throughout the Muslim world. Maulana Samiul Haq, headmaster of the Haqqania Madrasa, is a firebrand orator who led anti-U.S. demonstrations soon after the beginning of the war in Afghanistan. When asked if he thought it appropriate to involve his 5 and 6-year-old charges in political demonstrations, Haq remarked, "No one is too young to do the right thing." Later, he added, "Young minds are not for thinking. We catch them for the madrasas when they are young, and by the time they are old enough to think, they know what to think." The 'success' of General Zia's experiment led to the creation of similar free schools in places as diverse as Morocco, Algeria, Indonesia, and the Philippines. Muslim immigrants in Europe and North America established madrasas alongside their mosques, ostensibly to teach religion to their children. Islam requires Muslims to set aside 2.5 percent of their annual savings as zakat [charity], and religious education is one area on which zakat can be spent. Madrasas do not need huge funds to run, though. Teachers' salaries are low, the schools need no funding for research, and books are handed down from one generation to the next.

Madrasas have proliferated with zakat and financial assistance from the gulf states. [Some classrooms at Haqqania Madrassa in Pakistan have a small inscription informing visitors that Saudi Arabia donated the building materials for the classroom]. Modern technology has also played a role, whether by creating international financing networks or new methods of spreading the message, such as through online madrasas. Pakistan had 244 madrasas in 1956. By the end of 2004, the number had risen to 10,000. As many as 1 million students study in madrasas in Pakistan, compared with primary-school enrollment of 1.9 million. Most Muslim countries allocate insignificant portions of their budgets for education, leaving large segments of their growing populations without schooling. Madrasas fill that gap, especially for the poor. The poorest countries, such as Pakistan, Bangladesh, Somalia, Yemen, and Indonesia, boast the largest madrasa enrollment.

3

Pakistani Jihadists and the Kashmir Jihad

The Islamic Revolution in Iran in 1979, followed by the jihad in Afghanistan (1979-89) against the Soviet occupation soon turned Pakistan into what one commentator termed as 'the original staging ground of Jihad as an international movement'. Large sums of money and huge quantities of arms now began pouring into Pakistan from various sources, particularly from the USA and Saudi Arabia, apprehensive as both of them were of Soviet expansionism and the Iranian-style anti-monarchical and anti-Western Islamic radicalism in the region.

From the early 1980s, Pakistan emerged as the major launching pad for numerous militant Islamist groups fighting in Afghanistan, with large numbers of activists flocking there not only from Afghanistan, but also from the Arab world and from Muslim communities in the West, fired by an irrepressible zeal for the cause of the jihad against the godless Soviets. Several Pakistani Islamic parties, particularly the Jama'at-i Islami, the Jami'at-i 'Ulama-i-Islam and the Jami'at-i 'Ulama-i-Pakistan were also drawn into the jihad, and set up or sponsored their own militant wings. Numerous Islamic seminaries (madrasas) sprang up all over the country, lavishly patronized by the Pakistani military dictator Zia ul-Haq and the Saudis, almost all based on sectarian affiliation, to train their students for the jihad.

The consequent spread of what has been called the 'gun-culture' in Pakistan was a major consequence of all these factors.

Thus, with arms and funds easily available, Pakistan was rapidly faced with widespread internal conflict, which took several forms—ethnic, between Mohajirs and Pathans in Karachi; and sectarian, between Sunnis and minority Shi'as and, among Sunnis themselves, between Deobandis and Barelwis.

Besides the Soviet presence at Pakistan's very doorstep, several internal factors were responsible for Zia's patronage of radical jihadist outfits. Having captured power through a military coup in 1977, and lacking legitimacy for his rule, he sought to win support for his regime through appeals to Islam, introducing cosmetic changes in the law, such as Islamic punishments, in the name of Islamization, for which he won the warm support of Islamist groups such as the Jama'at-i Islami. Linked to the Islamization project that Zia and Pakistani rulers after him sought to pursue at home was Pakistan's Kashmir policy. To begin with, Pakistan is believed to have extended armed support to the JKLF, arranging for training some of its fighters in the wake of the beginning of the armed uprising in Kashmir in 1989. Soon, however, it was clear to the Pakistani establishment that the JKLF, with its agenda of a free, democratic Kashmir, would not only not toe its line but also pose a threat to its own strategic interests. Hence, from the early 1990s began a policy of deliberate marginalization of the Kashmiri nationalists by the Pakistani establishment, alongside with the cultivation of Pakistani Islamists, who had emerged in the years of the Afghan war, to enter the Kashmir jihad, coupled with lavish patronage extended to Kashmiri Islamist groups such as the JIJK and the HM.

As a result of this change in Pakistan's Kashmir policy from the early 1990s onwards, particularly since the mujahidin victory in Afghanistan in 1992, numerous jihadist outfits in Pakistan began turning their attention towards Kashmir. By the late 1990s, these Pakistani jihadists were playing a key role in the fighting in Kashmir, eclipsing even local Kashmiri groups. Thus, a report brought out by the Indian army in 2000 highlighted the fact that almost all the militant groups active in Kashmir were pro-Pakistan or Pakistan-based, and that the JKLF, the only non-Islamist group included in its list, was 'presently on a low profile'. It estimated that there were some 2750 pro-Pakistan Islamist militants active in Kashmir, while it put the number of JKLF militants at only 60. The groups to whom these Islamists belonged groups were actively assisted by the Pakistani establishment, in particular by its ISI.

With increasing Western criticism of the Pakistani state's role in sponsoring what some have termed as 'Islamic terrorism', an increasing 'privitization of jihad' has occurred. Thus, Pakistan-based organizations that claim to be autonomous of the Pakistani establishment, but are, of course, still dependent on it for patronage, have taken up the task of spearheading the jihad. What is particularly striking about most of these groups is the relatively small Kashmiri presence in both the leadership as well as cadre levels, with almost all their leaders being Pakistani and most of their fighters being Pakistani nationals as well as some Afghans, Arabs and others. Apparently, it is felt that Pakistani strategic interests can be secured only if the leadership and even the rank-and-file of the jihadists remain in Pakistani hands. It has also been argued that the failure or the unwillingness of Kashmiri militant groups to engineer large-scale killings of non-Muslims in Jammu and Kashmir so as to reduce the Hindu population has been an important factor in the promotion of Pakistani-based groups, who have little such compunctions, to take over the armed struggle.

Jihadist Discourse: The Markaz Da'wat ul-Irshad and the Lashkar-i Tayyeba

If the JIJK seeks to seriously question the legitimacy of the discursive framework of the Kashmiri nationalists by seeking to present the Kashmiri armed struggle as a jihad between Islam and disbelief, a further radicalization of the jihadist discourse is clearly evident in the writings and statements of the several Pakistan-based Islamist organizations actively involved in fighting in Kashmir. The most prominent of these groups are the Harkat ul-Ansar, also known as the Harkat-ul Jihad-i Islami, al-Badr, Jami'at ul-Mujahidin, al-Jihad and, probably the most influential of them all, the Lashkar-i Tayyeba ('The Army of the Pure'). All these groups share a common Islamist ideology and advocate the merger of Kashmir with Pakistan.

The Pakistan-based Islamist groups actively involved in the Kashmir conflict are thus today central players in the Kashmiri armed struggle. One of the consequences of their emergence and growing influence has been the further radicalization of the terms of discourse within which the JIJK has sought to portray the Kashmiri armed struggle, arguing against the claims of the Kashmiri nationalists and further developing certain themes that are only vaguely touched upon in Gilani's writings. The jihad is no longer limited to liberating Kashmir from India, but goes far beyond, as we shall see. This is strikingly illustrated in the publications and statements of the Lashkar-i Tayyeba, the 'new masters of Kashmir', and said to be 'the largest jihadi organization in Pakistan'.

The Lashkar is the military wing of an organization called the Markaz Da'wat ul- Irshad ('The Centre for Preaching and Guidance'), set up in 1986 by two Pakistani university professors, Hafiz Muhammad Sa'eed and Zafar Iqbal. Its headquarters are located in a sprawling 160-acre campus at Muridke, a small town in the Gujranwala district of Pakistani Punjab, some thirty kilometres from Lahore. The Markaz is affiliated to the Ahl-i Hadith school, known for its fierce opposition to Sufism and to the established schools of Islamic jurisprudence, insisting that Muslims must go back to the original sources of inspiration—the Qur'an and the Hadith. It seeks to refashion the worldwide Muslim community in the mould of the Companions of the Prophet. It sees itself as the inheritor of the legacy of the first major jihadist movement in modern times in India, the movement launched by Sayyed Ahmad Barelwi and his band of followers, who, in the early nineteenth century, attempted to set up an Islamic state in the Pathan borderlands and launched an abortive jihad against the Sikhs. The Markaz is believed to be closely linked to the Pakistani establishment as well as to the Jama'at-i Islami of Pakistan.

The Markaz, like many other Pakistani Islamist outfits, was originally designed to serve as a training base for Pakistani militants involved in the Afghan jihad against the Soviets. In 1987, a year after its founding, it set up a training centre inside Afghanistan itself, at Jaji in the Patkia province, and then, shortly after, another in the Kunnar province. It claims that the warriors produced at these centres 'performed outstanding operations' against the Russians. In Afghanistan it carried out its jihad in league with an Afghan outfit, the Jama'at al-Da'wat il al-Qur'an. As the Markaz's activities rapidly grew, it was decided to divide its work into two separate but related sections: the educational and the jihadist. Thus, in 1993, the Markaz established its separate 'jihadic and warfare' wing, the Lashkar. The Lashkar later established four training centres in Pakistan and Afghanistan, where, 'thousands of mujahidin from all over the world are being trained'. Markaz authorities claim that militants produced at these centres have played a leading role in the armed struggles in Afghanistan, Bosnia, Chechenya, Kosovo, the southern Philippines, Kashmir and 'in other areas where Muslims are fighting for freedom'. According to one report, in recent years the spread of the Markaz in Pakistan has 'been phenomenal', and today it has some five hundred offices all over the country, most of them in Punjab, which operate as recruitment centres for would-be mujahidin.

At its Muridke headquarters, the Markaz runs an Islamic school and university, most of whose students are local Pakistanis, with some from Pakistan-administered Kashmir, a few Kashmiris from the Indian-ruled part of the state, and several Afghans and Arabs. Besides, the Markaz has established a network of over seventy schools, mainly in Punjab, where Islamic and modern education are imparted. Young boys of the age of eight are taken in and are given a twelve-year training. A strict military atmosphere is enforced, students must wear military uniforms, abide by military discipline and 'properly assimilate the commandments of their theologians and military instructors that their future profession—as mujahidin—will be in great demand in the Muslim world on the threshold of the new millennium'. At its four training centres, would-be mujahidin are given rigorous military training. This is of two kinds. Firstly, a short twenty-one day course, the daura-i 'ama ('general course'). Secondly, a three month intensive course, the daura-i khasa ('special course'), geared to guerrilla warfare, in which trainees learn how to handle small arms as well as survival and ambush techniques. These courses, it is claimed, 'change the course of life' of the trainees completely', and a sign of this is said to be that they 'no longer shave' and 'wear their shalwars above their ankles, as enjoined by the Prophet Muhammad'.

As in the case of the other Pakistan-based militant groups active in Kashmir today, the Markaz's direct participation in the Kashmir conflict dates to the end of the Afghan war in 1992, in which an estimated 1600 of its militants are said to have participated. After the Soviet withdrawal from Afghanistan, it shifted its attention to Kashmir to 'help the oppressed and innocent Kashmiris who were undergoing Indian aggression for the past fifty years'. In this, they were assisted by the Jama'at-i Islami of Pakistan and the Pakistani intelligence agency, the ISI, key players in the Afghan jihad. The Lashkar is said to have first entered Kashmir in 1990, and then to have 'upgraded' its jihad there in 1993, when its militants attacked an Indian army base in Poonch. In 1994 it began sending large numbers of its fighters into Kashmir, most of them non-Kashmiris. From 1995 it claims that its fighters have been 'engaged properly and striving hard' against the Indian forces. 1996 witnessed a major shift in the Lashkar's Kashmir strategy, with greater attention being paid to the border districts of Jammu, particularly Rajouri and Poonch, as well as Doda. Reports suggest that some of the mass killings of Hindu villagers in these areas have been the work of the Lashkar, with the aim of causing an exodus of the Hindu population of these areas so as to make their task easier. By 1998, it was estimated that the Lashkar had some 350 mujahidin present in Indian-controlled Kashmir. Its fighters are considered by the Indian armed forces to be the best trained among all the militant groups in the region.

In mid-1999 India and Pakistan almost came to war after Pakistan-based militants, believed to be backed by the Pakistani army, occupied certain strategic heights in the Kargil sector in the Ladakh province in the remote northern part of Indian-controlled Kashmir. The four principal militant groups taking part in this operation, all Islamist and manned almost entirely by non-Kashmiris, were the Harkat ul-Mujahidin, the Tahrik-i Jihad, al-Badr and the Lashkar. These groups together formed a joint military command to co-ordinate their military operations against the Indian army. The Lashkar contingent consisted, among others, of several students from its college at Muridke, led by one 'Abdur Rahman 'Abid, a graduate of Medina University. They were joined by some two hundred militants from the Nuristan province of Afghanistan, the first time that such a large number of Afghan fighters had entered Kashmir in recent years.

The Pakistani attempt to enter Kashmir through Kargil failed, however, and under pressure from the West, the country's then Prime Minister, Nawaz Sharif, appealed to the militants to withdraw from the heights that they had captured. The militants, on their part, were reluctant to obey, and they saw Sharif's capitulation to the USA as a betrayal of their jihad. Instead of toeing Sharif's line, they announced what they called 'the second stage' of the Kashmir jihad—taking the battle against the Indian army right inside the Kashmir valley itself, in order, as Zaki ur-Rahman Lakhvi, the amir of the Lashkar, put it, 'to avenge' the atrocities of the Indian army. According to the amir of the Markaz, Hafiz Muhammad Sa'eed, in this second phase 'the jihad would spread all across Kashmir. It would spread to every peak, every forest and every path'. As part of this new strategy, the Lashkar came up with a new means of attack—suicide bombers, which it named as Ibn Taimiya Fida'i Missions, in memory of the medieval Arab Islamic scholar who crusaded against what he saw as un-Islamic practices, and to whom the Ahl-i Hadith as well as the Lashkar owe much of their inspiration. So far, the Lashkar has conducted scores of fida'i missions in Kashmir and beyond. In all, the Lashkar claimed that by early 2000, it had killed some 2100 Indian army personnel, including senior officers, and to have lost some 500 of its own men in its Kashmir operations.

In the wake of a Lashkar attack on the Indian army headquarters in Srinagar, the capital of Kashmir, in 1999, the head of the Markaz, Hafiz Muhammad Sa'eed declared before an audience of an estimated three hundred thousand people that his fighters could now 'strike anywhere in India', threatening to target even the Indian prime minister's office if India did not stop its aggression on the Kashmiri Muslims and vacate Kashmir.

The jihad, declared Hafiz, was not limited simply to freeing Kashmir from Indian control. Rather, he stressed, it was aimed at 'liberating' India itself. He revealed that the Lashkar was now planning to extend its activities beyond the borders of Kashmir, deep inside India. 'To set up a mujahidin network across India is our target', said Zaki ur-Rahman Lakhvi, chief of the Lashkar, addressing the same congregation. He claimed that his organization was 'preparing the Muslims of India against India' and that once they were ready, 'it would be the start of the disintegration of India'. Some 50,000 Pakistani youth are said to have responded to this appeal to join the grand anti-India crusade.

THE HISTORY OF KASHMIRI JIHAD

More than half a century after Partition, the vexed Kashmir issue continues to fester, threatening to plunge India and Pakistan into the throes of nuclear war. Meanwhile, an estimated 80,000 Kashmiris have lost their lives in the on-going civil war in the area, leaving thousands more raped, orphaned and permanently maimed for life. Religion plays a central role in defining the very way in which the Kashmir issue is seen, by the Kashmiris themselves, and by both India and Pakistan. As a Muslim majority state, albeit with a significant Hindu minority, Pakistan insists that the very logic of the 'two-nation' theory on which it is founded demands that Kashmir should be a part of it. India, on the other hand, claims that the Kashmiris had thrown in their lot with it in 1947, thus forcefully challenging the legitimacy of the theory of Hindus and Muslims being two separate and antagonistic nations. For many Kashmiri themselves, religion per se is not at the root of the problem, which is seen as essentially political, a quest for self-determination of their own political future. A considerable section of the Kashmiris themselves would seem to support the idea of an independent Kashmir. Indeed, the Kashmiri nationalists who launched the militant struggle in the region in the late 1980s aimed at setting up a sovereign, democratic state, with equal rights for all its citizens, irrespective of religion. From the early 1990s, however, owing particularly to growing Pakistani involvement, Islam emerged as a central issue defining the way in which the Kashmiri struggle came to be framed. For a new breed of Islamist militants, their struggle against India was seen as an Islamic jihad, fired by an irrepressible zeal against the 'enemies' of the faith. This so-called jihad is now being sought to be taken further into India, with attacks by Islamist suicide squads on temples, government buildings and other sensitive locations in various parts of the country.

Muslim militancy in Kashmir and Hindu militancy in India feed on each other, with Hindu chauvinist outfits portraying the conflict in Kashmir as a defence of the indivisible 'Hindu' motherland from marauding Islamic hordes. The events in Kashmir have led to a complete breakdown of inter-faith relations in the state of Jammu and Kashmir, with most of the Hindus of the Kashmir valley having fled their homes, and scores of Hindus and Muslims having lost their lives in internecine violence. Elsewhere in India, the Kashmir imbroglio has contributed to a general heightening of Hindu-Muslim strife and conflict, as well as a rapid deterioration of relations between India and Pakistan, setting off fears of a nuclear catastrophe in the region.

This article looks at how the terms of discourse of the Kashmiri struggle have been transformed over time, and how the secular, nationalist Kashmiri movement has been overtaken by radical Islamists pursuing a very different political project, as represented by the Jama'at-i Islami of Jammu and Kashmir and the Lashkar-i Tayyeba. It focuses, in particular, with the issue of how Islam has been understood by Islamists to legitimize their involvement in the current struggle in the region as a jihad, looking at what this means for relations between Kashmiri Muslims and the Kashmiri Hindus and for the ways in which the former are expected to relate to the Indian state. It seeks to grapple with the crucial question of the shifting identities of the Kashmiri Muslims, faced with the might of the Indian state, increasingly defined by an aggressively militant Hindu agenda, on the one hand, and with the increasing salience of Islamist organizations, on the other.

Roots of Revolt

The early Kashmiri independence movement, whose roots go back to the uprising against the Hindu Dogra regime in the 1930s, saw itself principally as a nationalist struggle. From the 1930s till 1947, the Kashmiri movement, under the charismatic Shaikh Muhammad 'Abdullah, aimed at challenging the autocratic rule of the Dogras, demanding proper representation for the Kashmiri Muslims in the administration of the state. In 1947, most of Kashmir came under Indian rule, and from then onwards, a sizeable section of the Muslims of Kashmir carried on, largely through peaceful agitation, a movement for the establishment of an independent state. As 'Abdullah's charisma's gradually declined, with the failure of his National Conference to meet the aspirations of the people and to preserve the autonomy of Kashmir, a new breed of Kashmiri nationalists emerged, disillusioned with what they saw as 'Abdullah's complicity with the Indian state. The leadership of the movement was provided by young Kashmiri Muslims who had received a modern education in the colleges that began to be set up in the region after 1947. Their principal demand was that India should fulfil its commitments to the United Nations and allow a plebiscite to be held in the territory to enable the people to decide their own political future. Challenging the legitimacy of Indian rule, these Kashmiri nationalists advocated an independent, secular democratic Jammu and Kashmir. The ideology informing their nationalist project was that of Kashmiriyat or 'Kashmiri identity', which they saw as a unique amalgam of traditions drawing upon local Muslim, Hindu and other sources. The Kashmiri nationalist project was spearheaded by several organizations and parties, the foremost being the JKLF, established in 1964. The JKLF demanded that the state of Jammu and Kashmir as it existed prior to 1947 be united as 'one fully independent and truly democratic State'. It advocated 'equal political, economic, religious and social rights' for all citizens in the proposed state, 'irrespective of race, religion, region, culture and sex'.

Parallel to the rise of the Kashmiri nationalists, Kashmir in the late 1930s also witnessed the emergence of an Islamist movement. The roots of the Islamist emergence can be traced to the reformist efforts of the Ahl-i Hadith ('People of the Prophetic Tradition'), established in Kashmir in 1925. The Ahl-i Hadith saw themselves as inheritors of the legacy of the Prophet and his Companions, crusading against popular Sufism, the dominant form of Islamic expression in Kashmir, branding it as un-Islamic. Given the deep-rootedness of the Sufi tradition in Kashmir, the Ahl-i Hadith singularly failed to develop a mass following. Rather, it remained, as it does even today, a largely elitist phenomenon, with its core support base among a limited section of the urban middle classes. Ahl-i Hadith-style reformism did, however, provide fertile ground for the emergence of other Islamist trends from the 1930s onwards. Islamism in Kashmir found its most vocal champion in the Jama'at-i Islami, established in 1941 by Sayyed Abul 'Ala Maududi, and organised as an independent organisation and political party in Kashmir in 1952.

The Jama'at-i Islami of Jammu Kashmir (JIJK) remained, at least at the political level, a marginal force in Kashmir till the 1980s, but with the launching of the armed struggle in 1989 it came to play a central role in Kashmiri politics. It forcefully sought to present the armed struggle as a jihad between Islam and disbelief (kufr), thereby challenging the Kashmiri nationalists' definition of the struggle as one between the Kashmiri nation and the Indian state. The Jama'at sees the struggle as a war between Muslims and the 'enemies' of the faith, and is bitterly critical of the notion of a separate Kashmiri national identity. Rather, it insists that the Kashmiris are simply a part of the worldwide Muslim ummah, not a nation by themselves, for, according to it, Islam and nationalism are incompatible with each other. Hence, it argues, the mission of the Kashmiri struggle is not to set up an independent state, which is what the nationalists' project is all about, but, rather, to make Kashmir a part of Muslim Pakistan.

The JIJK's efforts at restructuring the framework of discourse within which the Kashmiri struggle sought to express itself has, from the early 1990s, been given further impetus by the growing intervention in Kashmir of Islamist groups based in Pakistan. These groups tend to see the Kashmiri struggle not simply as a jihad between the Muslims of Kashmir and the Indian state, but in far wider terms: as a 'holy war' between the Muslims of the world, on the one hand, and the Hindus as an entire community, in league with other 'disbelieving' 'enemies of Islam', on the other.

In this grand battle, all national and geographical barriers are completely demolished—all Muslims, wherever they may be, are seen as being responsible for contributing in some way or the other in this jihad. On the other hand, Hindus are seen as complicit in the oppression of the Kashmiri Muslims, and hence, considered as enemies. Interestingly, the Hindus are regarded as being hand in glove with other 'enemies' of the Muslim ummah—the Jews and the Christian West—against whom, too, a jihad needs to be waged.

The JIJK and the Kashmiri Jihad

The JIJK was established as an independent organization in 1952, although from the late 1930s a growing number of Kashmiri Muslims had come under the influence of the founder of the Jama'at, Maulana Maududi, principally through his powerful writings. The JIJK presented itself as committed to establishing an Islamic state in Kashmir based on the shari'ah, but using democratic means of peaceful persuasion for attaining its goals. This was stressed in its Constitution, adopted in 1953. Article 2 [b] of its Constitution states that

The Jama'at shall not employ ways and means against ethics, truthfulness and honesty or which may contribute to strife on earth.

Article 2 [c] of its Constitution lays down that the Jama'at shall use democratic and constitutional methods, while working for the reform and righteous revolution. Till the late 1960s, the JIJK sought to cultivate a constituency for itself through publishing and distributing literature, establishing reading rooms and discussion groups, setting up a network of schools all over the state, and through public lectures. In 1969, for the first time, the JIJK decided to enter the electoral fray, by sponsoring a number of candidates for the local level (panchayati) elections which were held on a non-party basis. Apparently, it was felt that by remaining outside the sphere of electoral politics it was being rendered increasingly ineffective. It was thought, therefore, that elections were 'the best platform to popularize the message of the movement'. Later, the JIJK went on to participate in successive provincial as well as general elections as an independent political party. It failed, however, to win an impressive number of seats in any election, owing both to widespread rigging engineered by the Indian authorities as well as a definite lack of enthusiasm for the JIJK's agenda on the part of the electorate.

The last time that the JIJK participated in the electoral field was in the 1987 elections, as part of the eleven-party alliance, the Muslim Muttahida Mahaz (Muslim United Front or MUF), a group of several Kashmiri parties championing the right to political self-determination of the Kashmiri people. It was widely expected that the MUF would do well in the elections and might even be able to win a majority. However, these elections, like all the others previously held in Kashmir, were marked by massive rigging by the Indian authorities, as a result of which only four MUF candidates were officially declared elected. The election results met with an upsurge of rage and opposition, with mass demonstrations being held against the Indian state for subverting the democratic process. Then, in 1988, having tired of the democratic path of seeking to win the right to self-determination, an armed struggle for the liberation of Kashmir from Indian rule was launched. On 31 July 1989, two massive bomb blasts in the heart of Srinagar, the capital of the state, heralded the launching of the armed struggle. The JKLF claimed responsibility for the act.

The armed struggle launched by the JKLF for the independence of Kashmir found mass support among the Kashmiri Muslims, disillusioned as they were with Indian rule and with the subversion of democratic institutions in Kashmir. The MUF initially hesitated in joining the armed struggle, directing its four representatives within the state assembly, including Sayyed 'Ali Gilani, chief ideologue of the JIJK, to retain their seats so as to be able to air the grievances of the people. However, the rising tide of the JKLF-led struggle soon proved too much for the MUF high command to ignore, and in 1989, it instructed its members in the state assembly to resign and to join the struggle. The JIJK now decided to fully immerse itself in the militant movement, and in 1990 it set up its own militant wing, the Hizb ul-Mujahidin ('The Army of the Holy Warriors', HM).

Given the JKLF's immense popularity among the Kashmiri Muslims, and the mass support for its goal of an independent, democratic and secular Jammu and Kashmir, the JIJK and the HM had to struggle against great odds in putting forward their own agenda of making Kashmir part of Pakistan and establishing an Islamic state in the region. One of the major hurdles that the JIJK had to face in expanding its base beyond a narrow circle of middle class sympathizers was its perceived attitude towards popular Sufi traditions. The JIJK, rooted as it was in a fierce opposition to popular Sufism, was seen by many Kashmiris as opposed to the Sufi saints as such, whom they held in great respect, and despite its efforts to convince people that this was not the case, the JIJK was unable to dispel the notion. Since Sufism is still a dominant form of Islamic expression in Kashmir, this was seen by many as hostility towards Islam itself. Making the JIJK's project more difficult for itself was the fact that although most Kashmiri Muslims were certainly disillusioned with India, it is unlikely that a majority of them would have preferred to join Pakistan instead or to be ruled under a strict Islamist regime, as the JIJK and the HM advocated. To make matters even more difficult for the Islamists was the widespread abuses of human rights by the Indian armed forces, resulting in the killings of many Kashmiri Muslims, among whom were several known Islamist activists and sympathizers.

Despite the immense odds that the Islamists had to contend with, from both the Kashmiri nationalists as well as the Indian armed forces, they strove, through publications, mass meetings, public rallies and the work of their activists, to convince the Kashmiris that the solution to the crisis lay in the project that they were advocating, a counter to both Indian rule and demands for independent nationhood. In this manner, a shift was sought to be made in the terms within which the liberation struggle was being waged. Islam, not Kashmiriyat, and accession to Pakistan, not an independent Kashmir, were presented as the solutions to the Kashmir problem. Such arguments now began to exercise a broader appeal, especially with the rise of militant anti-Muslim Hindu groups in India, and the subsequent large-scale killings of Muslims in the wake of the destruction of the Babri mosque in 1992. Indeed, the growing popularity of the Islamists in Kashmir and the consequent marginalization of the Kashmiri nationalists has much to do with the rapid spread of the radical Hindu Right in India. The very real dangers that the rise of Hindutva posed to Muslim lives and identity in India, and to the Muslims of Kashmir as well, made the argument more convincing that the struggle being waged in Kashmir was one between kufr and Islam.

The Islamist reworking of the discursive framework in which the Kashmiri struggle has sought to express itself is well illustrated in the case of the writings of Sayyed 'Ali Shah Gilani. Gilani has held many top positions in the JIJK, and was for long the chief political spokesman of the party, besides holding the post of chairman of the All-Parties' Hurriyat Conference, an alliance of thirty-four Kashmiri Muslim parties and organizations fighting for Kashmir's freedom from Indian control. He is one of the most senior present-day Kashmiri political leaders and also has the distinction of being the most prolific writer among them all.

Gilani's major writings all date to the 1990s, a period when the JIJK had already immersed itself in the armed struggle, in which Gilani himself played a key role, and for which he was forced to spend several years in various jails. Not surprisingly, Gilani's writings focus almost solely on the issue of Kashmir's freedom from Indian control. He devotes little attention in his writings to Islamic law, theology and doctrines, for being an ideologue of the JIJK, he takes Maududi's voluminous writings on these subjects as authoritative. Gilani's concern is to place the Kashmiri struggle within the Islamist discursive framework. Thus, the struggle is depicted as a jihad, the goal of which is the merger of Kashmir with Pakistan and the establishing of an Islamic state in the region. As we shall see, however, Gilani's understanding of the struggle differs at some crucial points with the views of the Pakistan-based jihadist outfits, being considerably less radical and uncompromising, at least in some crucial aspects.

Three features are of particular importance in Gilani's description of what he calls the Kashmiri jihad. Firstly, the jihad is seen as directed against the Indian state and its agents, and not against Hindus or Indians as such. Secondly, the jihad has the limited goal of freeing Kashmir from Indian control. Thirdly, the mujihadin have no intention of intervening in Indian internal affairs after the liberation of Kashmir. Once the Kashmir issue is solved by freeing the territory from Indian control and merging it with Pakistan, India and Pakistan, Gilani writes, will be able to establish peaceful and cordial relations with each other, for the root cause of the tensions between the two countries is the dispute over the issue of Kashmir.

Gilani sees the armed struggle being waged in Kashmir not as a war of national liberation, but as a jihad between Islam, on the one hand, and the forces of kufr or disbelief, on the other. He argues that a combination of various developments—India's denial to the Kashmiris of their right to self-determination, its brutal suppression of the Kashmiri struggle which has resulted in the deaths of many thousand Kashmiris, and the rapid rise in India of anti-Muslim Hindu chauvinism—have necessitated the launching of a jihad against India. He writes that the Indian state has, by its actions, 'proved its extreme hostility towards the religious and moral sensibilities [of the Muslims] and the tenets of Islam'. 'Wherever and whenever the laws of Islam are held out for insult and the religious rights [of the Muslims] are trampled upon', he declares, 'jihad becomes a binding obligation (farz) for all Muslims'. Such a situation, he says, prevails in Kashmir, and hence the need for a jihad to be waged there. This jihad, he stresses, calls for the participation of all Muslims, not just Kashmiris alone. In a telephonic interview in 1992 with a Lahore-based journalist soon after his release from a long spell in prison, Gilani declared:

It has now become incumbent, in the light of the teachings of the Holy Qur'an, upon all the people of Pakistan to participate in the [Kashmir] jihad. They should now stand up determinedly and assist their Kashmiri brethren in the practical jihad. This jihad is a religious duty binding not only on the people of Pakistan, but, in fact, on the entire Muslim ummah [...] The extreme oppression that the Kashmiri Muslims are having to face is an open challenge for the entire Muslim ummah. All Muslims must now move ahead, help the oppressed Muslims [of Kashmir] and stop the hands of the oppressors.

While declaring the armed struggle a jihad, Gilani makes it clear, however, that the armed struggle is directed against the Indian state and not against Hindus or Indian citizens per se. He makes a clear distinction between the Indian state, on the one hand, and ordinary Indians and Hindus, on the other. Thus, in an appeal to the Kashmiri militants in April 1992 Gilani asserted that, 'The mujahidin have just two enemies: the Indian state and its agents. To waste the power of our youth on targets other than these two is like pouring salt on the wounds of our oppressed people'. Gilani has, on numerous occasions, appealed for communal harmony between Hindus and Muslims in Kashmir. He stresses that Hindu-Muslim relations in the state have traditionally always been cordial, and that in the past the Valley has never known the wild bloodletting between Hindus and Muslims that has erupted periodically, and now on a menacingly increasing scale, in India. Defending the armed struggle from charges of being anti-Hindu, he asserts that the mass exodus of the Kashmiri Pandits in the early 1990s was actually instigated by the Indian authorities in order to project the Kashmiri struggle as an 'Islamic terrorist' movement, so as to discredit it in the eyes of the West. Gilani has issued several appeals to the Kashmiri Pandits who have fled from their homes to return and join their Muslim brethren in the struggle. He has also warned the mujahidin that they should desist from any actions 'which will give their opponents a chance to brand them as terrorists'.

Gilani's opposition to the Indian state is limited insofar as his prime objective is to liberate Kashmir from Indian control. The jihad against India, in other words, is circumscribed by the limited objective of freeing Kashmir from Indian rule. Thus, he asserts that after Kashmir is freed from Indian occupation, the JIJK would 'like to see India as free, prosperous and peaceful'. Criticizing certain un-named Kashmiri militant groups for spreading anti-India hatred, he says:

Emotional slogans such as 'Crush India!' are neither realistic nor do they reflect the spirit of Islam. At root, Islam is based on invitation to prosperity, witness to the truth, salvation in the Hereafter, protection of the truth, the ending of every form of oppression and creating understanding between all children of Adam. This, indeed, is the message of the life of the Prophet Muhammad (may peace be upon him). Even when the people of Ta'if unleashed a wave of unlimited oppression on the Prophet of Islam (may peace be upon him), he did not pray to God that they should be destroyed but, rather, that He should guide them [to the right path]. This is why I believe our struggle should be geared only to gaining our rights [...] The slogan of Islam is not one of destruction but of invitation [to the Truth], prosperity, peace and truth.

The legitimacy of the category of the 'Kashmiri nation' that forms the subject of Kashmiri nationalist discourse is vehemently denied by Gilani, this being a logical outcome of his own Islamist position that sees Islam and nationalism as being in complete contradiction to each other. Here, of course, Gilani seeks to question the very basis of the political agenda of the major rivals of the JIJK, the various Kashmiri nationalist groups such as the JKLF. Gilani argues that nationalism is a 'poisonous philosophy' which the 'enemies of Islam', foremost being 'various Western philosophies', have deliberately sought to infect Muslims with so as to divide and weaken them so that they can be kept under their control. He insists that the Muslim world-wide ummah is one, monolithic ideological community, cemented together on the basis of 'common belief and faith', which sees no differences of colour, race, language, caste, tribe or family. He asserts that 'whenever Muslims have ignored the principles of Islam, which sees no boundaries of region, they have lost their power and have become like any other community'. Territorial nationalism, he writes, has proved to be the bane of the Muslims, for it has divided them into different states and, thereby, has deflected them from the task of 'changing the conditions of the entire human race'.

Islam, says Gilani, makes a clear distinction between 'love for their country' (watan dosti), which it allows, and territorial nationalism or 'nation worship' (watan parasti), which it clearly forbids. 'Nation worship', based on the principle of 'my nation, right or wrong', Gilani writes, leads to group prejudice, a quality of the period of the pre-Islamic period of jahiliya, an age of utter darkness. He lays much of the blame for strife, war and bloodshed that characterizes the world today on territorial nationalism.

'Nationalism is the slogan of the jahiliya', he argues, because the nation has usurped from Islam the 'right to decide the criterion for what is right and what is wrong'. Because of this, large states, such as India, prey on smaller, weaker states, causing endless suffering and misery, 'with millions of people being sacrificed at the altar of nationalism'—in the Kashmiri case, 'at the hands of the priests of Mother India'. However, he asserts, by denying the narrow boundaries that 'nation worship' has inscribed, Islam has 'destroyed into smithereens the idol of nationalism until the Day of Resurrection'.

All Muslims being considered as one nation, Muslims and Hindus in India, and Kashmir as well, are considered to be members of two different nations despite living in the same territory. This, Gilani says, is 'an undeniable truth' (na qabil-i tardid haqiqat). He writes, conveniently glossing over the remarkable degree to which Muslims in India and Kashmir share a common culture with the Hindus, that not just in matters of faith, beliefs and customs do the two differ, but that they are also distinct and sharply set apart from each other in such matters as food, clothing and lifestyles. For Muslims to stay among Hindus or in an environment which is very different from their own is said to be as difficult as it is 'for a fish to stay alive in a desert'. Muslims, he says, cannot live harmoniously with a Hindu majority without their own religion and traditions coming under a grave threat, one major factor being Hinduism's capacity to absorb other religions and communities into its fold. Hence, for Islam to be preserved and promoted in Kashmir, he insists, it is necessary for Kashmir to be separated from India. Curiously enough, he is silent on the fate of the over 150 million Muslims living in the rest of India.

If all Muslims form one nation and nationalism is antithetical to Islam, then, Gilani implicitly argues, the Kashmiri nationalist project of groups such as the JKLF is itself 'un-Islamic'. From this it follows that the 'Islamic' solution to the Kashmir question is not the establishment of an independent Kashmiri nation-state but, rather, the incorporation of Kashmir into an already-existing existing Muslim state, Pakistan. This is seen as the first step towards the eventual unity of all Muslims. In a pamphlet titled Masla Ka

Hal ('The Solution to the Problem'), issued in 1992, Gilani expressed this view thus:

To advocate that one Muslim group (qaum) be kept apart from the rest would be against the very definition of a people (millat), whose communal identity is based only on one pure creed (kalima tayyiba), especially so when that group shares common ideological, cultural and communal relations with a neighbouring [Muslim] group as well as a common border [...] For such a group to maintain a separate political identity of its own is against the broader interests of the entire Muslim millat.

The JIJK has, in fact, been among the most vocal champions of the merger of Jammu and Kashmir with Pakistan. In a letter to Nawaz Sharif, the then Prime Minister of Pakistan, in June 1993, Gilani commented that in Kashmir the JIJK and the HM 'were the most reliable groups supporting the ideology of Pakistan', and declared that the final goal of the JIJK was Kashmir's accession to that country. In the Kashmir jihad, therefore, the Pakistanis state is seen as having a central role to play, in addition, of course, to the Pakistani people, who are asked to assist the jihad. Thus, in his letter Gilani appealed to the Pakistani Prime Minister for further assistance, but bitterly criticized Pakistan's alleged policy of 'taking everyone together', by which he meant Pakistani support for Kashmiri nationalist groups, in addition to the Islamists. Gilani complained that such a policy was not only 'un-Islamic'; it also is against the very interests of Pakistan itself. He labeled the nationalists as 'enemies of the jihad', and foes of Pakistan, and cautioned that assistance to such groups as advocate secular nationalism posed a grave threat 'to Pakistan's stability and existence'.

THE PROLIFERATION OF JIHADIST ORGANIZATIONS IN PAKISTAN

The proliferation of jihadist organizations in Pakistan over the previous two decades had been the result of a militant culture espoused by radical madrasas like Darul Uloom Haqqania. Thousands of madrasas across the country became hubs for militancy and religious extremism, having a spill-over effect and presenting a serious threat to Pakistan's internal security. Pakistani madrasas were once considered centres for basic religious learning, mostly attached to local mosques.

The more formal ones were used for educating clergy. The development of simple, sparse religious schools into training centres for Kalashnikov-toting religious warriors was directly linked with the rise of militant Islam. Many of the religious parties operating the madrasas turned to militancy courtesy of the US-sponsored Jihad in Afghanistan. From waging Jihad against infidels in that foreign land, taking on perceived enemies of Islam at home was just a small step away. The influx of huge sums of money and a growing sense of power transformed the mullah's image from that of a docile and humble man to a mafia thug with a four-wheel-drive Jeep and armed bodyguards.

The influence of mullahs with local Pakistani leaders had also become formidable. Successive governments ignored their activities out of political expediency and also because most of the foreigners supporting them were 'brotherly Muslim' countries. The Islamic revolution in Iran in 1979 opened up the first wave of foreign funding for madrasas in Pakistan. Fearful of growing Iranian influence and the spread of revolution, Kuwait, Saudi Arabia, Iraq and some other oil-rich Muslim countries started pumping money into hardline Pakistani Sunni religious organizations willing to counter the supposed Shia threat. Millions of dollars were poured into setting up madrasas across the country, particularly in Balochistan province, bordering Iran. The Islamization process started by General Zia ul-Haq's regime in 1979 also contributed to the mushrooming of madrasas. For the first time in Pakistani history, the state started providing financial support for the expansion of religious education from Zakat and Ushr funds. The Islamization of education and levying of Islamic taxes had a profound long-term effect.

Zakat, one of the five pillars of Islam, had been treated as a private matter in most Muslim states. General Zia's regime broke with that tradition by deducting it from bank accounts each year during the Islamic holy month of Ramadan. The substantial amount raised by Zakat was used to finance the traditional religious schools, most of them belonging to the Deobandi movement, which is akin to Saudi Wahabism. Zakat did little to improve the lot of millions of Pakistanis living in abject poverty. The only visible consequence was the transformation of the religious landscape of the nation. The foreign and government-funded madrasas also became the main centres for spreading sectarian hatred. Saudi Arabian patronage, especially of more radical Ahle Hadith madrasas, played a major role in worsening the situation.

Madrasas also had a key place in Pakistani religious and social life. Most of the seminary students came from the poorest sections of Pakistani society and were provided with free religious education, lodging and meals. The influx of the impoverished rural population to the madrasas was a major reason for their growth, with Punjab and the North West Frontier Province having the highest number of religious seminaries. Divided along sectarian and political lines, religious seminaries were largely controlled by the two main branches of Sunni Islam in South Asia – the Deobandi and the Barelvi. Ahle Hadith or Wahabi Muslims had their own schools, as did the Shias. The religious doctrinal differences among these sects were irreconcilable. Most of the madrasas were centuries apart from the outside world. Generally the students were poor, from broken homes, or were orphans. Conditions in schools were regularly condemned by human rights groups as crowded and inhumane. The students were often subjected to a regimen as harsh as any jail, and physical abuses were commonplace. In many schools, students were put in chains and iron fetters for the slightest violation of the rules. There were almost no extracurricular activities and television and radio were banned. Teaching was rudimentary and students were taught religion within a highly rigorous and traditional perspective, giving them a deeply retrograde world-view.

At the primary stage, madrasa pupils learnt to read, memorize and recite the Qur'an. Exegeses of the holy script and other branches of Islamic studies were introduced at the higher stages of learning. Though the focus was on religious learning, some institutions also taught elementary mathematics, science and English. The most dangerous consequence of the content and style of teaching in religious schools was that the people that emerged could do nothing apart from guide the faithful in rituals that demand no experts. Job opportunities for madrasa graduates were few and narrow. They could only work in mosques, madrasas, the parent religious sectarian party, or its affiliate businesses or organizations.

The education imparted by traditional madrasas often spawned factional, religious and cultural conflict. It created barriers to modern knowledge, stifled creativity and bred bigotry, thus laying the foundation on which fundamentalism – militant or otherwise – was based. Divided by sectarian identities, these institutions were, by their very nature, driven by their zeal to outnumber and dominate rival sects. Students were educated and trained to counter the arguments of opposing sects on matters of theology, jurisprudence and doctrines. Promoting a particular sect inevitably implied the rejection of other sects, sowing the seeds of extremism in the minds of the students. The literature produced by their parent religious organizations promoted sectarian hatred and was aimed at proving the rival sects as infidels and apostates. The efforts by the successive government to modernize madrasa curricula and introduce secular subjects failed because of stiff resistance from the religious organizations controlling the religious schools.

The rise of Jihad culture since the 1980s gave madrasas a new sense of purpose. As a result, their numbers multiplied and the clergy emerged as a powerful political and social force. At independence in 1947, there were only 137 madrasas in Pakistan; in the next ten years their number rose to 244. After that, they doubled every ten years. A significant number remained unregistered and therefore it was hard to know precisely how many there were. Government sources put the figure at 13,000, with total enrolment close to 1.7 million. The vast majority of students were between five and 18 years old. Only those advancing into higher religious studies were older. According to the government's own estimates, ten to 15 per cent of the madrasas had links with sectarian militancy or international terrorism. The trail of international terror often led to the madrasas and mosques. Madrasas were basically conservative institutions before they were radicalized during the 1980s Afghan Jihad. The growing army of extremists fought the anti-Soviet Afghan Jihad alongside Arabs and Afghans. They later served the cause of Jihad from Kashmir to Chechnya to Bosnia, Egypt and Yemen. At the height of the Afghan Jihad – 1982–1988 – more than 1,000 new madrasas were opened in Pakistan, mostly along the borders with Afghanistan in the North West Frontier Province and Balochistan. Almost all belonged to hardline Sunni religious parties like Jamiat-e-Ulema Islam (JUI) and Jamaat-i-Islami (JI), which were Zia's political allies as well as partners in the Afghan Jihad.

Their location in the two border provinces, which had close cultural, linguistic and sectarian affinities with Afghan Pashtuns, made it easier to motivate the pupils to fight for their brethren in distress.

These madrasas did not conduct military training or provide arms to students, but encouraged them to join the 'holy war'. The purpose was to ensure a continued supply of recruits for the Afghan resistance. The message was simple: all Muslims must perform the duty of Jihad in whatever capacity they could. It was the responsibility of the Pakistani military, particularly the ISI, to provide training to the recruits in camps inside Afghanistan and Pakistan's tribal region. As the Afghan Jihad progressed, so did the influence of the jihadists coming out of these madrasas. The USA indirectly – and sometimes directly – promoted militancy, the culture of Jihad and supported the clergy in its war against communism.

Special textbooks were published in Dari and Pashto by the University of Nebraska-Omaha and funded by USAID with an aim to promote jihadist values and militant training. Millions of such books were distributed at Afghan refugee camps and Pakistani madrasas, where students learnt basic maths by counting dead Russians and Kalashnikov rifles. The same textbooks were later used by the Taliban in their madrasas.

As General Zia attempted to consolidate his authority through Islamization at home and Jihad in Afghanistan, the madrasa system was profoundly transformed. The Islamization process nurtured many, often mutually hostile, varieties of fundamentalism. In a society where many sects coexisted, the measures representing the belief of the dominant sect acted as an identity marker, heightening sectarian divisions and promoting sectarian conflicts. As a result, sectarian divisions were militarized. The zealots began to look inwards and fight a new Jihad against sectarian rivals, particularly Shias. The madrasa phenomenon drew international attention, particularly following the rise of the conservative Taliban regime in Afghanistan. The movement was largely the product of hundreds of seminaries in the Pashtun belt on the border with Afghanistan.

The link between madrasas and the Afghan Jihad is exemplified by the Darul Uloom Haqqania madrasa. Founded in 1947 by Haq's father, Maulana Abdul Haq, a well-respected Islamic scholar belonging to the Deobandi order, Darul Uloom Haqqania developed into a centre for pan-Islamism with the beginning of the Afghan war. It saw a huge expansion with the support of the government and funds from abroad. Like other Deobandi institutions, Darul Uloom was controlled by a faction of JUI, a mainstream religio-political party that was part of a six-party conservative alliance known as Muttehida Majlis Amal (MMA). The party became an important part of the Afghan Jihad. The seminary traditionally had a large number of students from Afghanistan, but they increased considerably with the influx of Afghan refugees.

By 1985, about 60 per cent of the students in the seminary were Afghans. It also attracted students from Tajikistan, Uzbekistan and Turkmenistan. From the beginning of the Afghan Jihad, the school had relaxed the rules concerning attendance, allowing the students to take time off to participate in the 'holy war'. The seminary, however, drew immense international attention in the 1990s with the emergence of the conservative Taliban movement. Thousands of Afghan, as well as Pakistani students crossed the border into Afghanistan to join the Islamic militia. In 1997 the school was closed for several months to allow the students to participate in the Taliban's war to capture Afghanistan's northern province of Mazar-i-Sharif. Such a large-scale cross-border movement would not have been possible without the collusion of Pakistani intelligence agencies.

Just months before the 11 September terrorist attacks in New York and Washington, the school hosted a conference of Islamic parties and militant groups to express solidarity with bin Laden and the Taliban regime. Masked gunmen in camouflage guerrilla outfits stood guard as Islamic leaders from Pakistan and Afghanistan congregated at the sprawling auditorium on 9 January 2001, vowing to defend bin Laden and to launch a holy war against the West. Besides the 300 leaders representing various radical Islamic groups, the meeting was also attended by a former army chief, General Aslam Beg, and a former ISI chief, General Hamid Gul. They declared it a religious duty of Muslims all over the world to protect the Saudi dissident whom they described as a 'great Muslim warrior'. One of the objectives of the assembly was to press Islamabad not to comply with UN sanctions against the Taliban. Interestingly, the military government, which had banned political parties holding public rallies, did not try to stop the conference. No action was taken against the militants for the public display of weapons. They obviously had the backing of the intelligence agencies. Islamic seminaries and clerics had never been as numerous and so powerful in Pakistan.

Islamic seminaries also became a transit point for foreign militants aspiring to join al-Qaeda and the Taliban forces in Afghanistan. Very few people had heard about the primitive fundamentalist Madrasa-i-Arabia outside the remote corner of north-west Pakistan until its name sprung on the international scene in connection with the American Taliban, John Walker Lindh. The young American was wounded in battle and captured by US-supported Northern Alliance forces in the Afghan northern province of Kunduz in December 2001.

It was in this isolated and spartan school where there were no amenities that the 19-year-old American learnt his lesson in Islamic sharia and Jihad. A new convert to Islam, he spent some six months in this austere madrasa housed in a one-storey building before leaving for Afghanistan in May 2001 to join the Taliban. Lindh, who had grown up in upper-middle-class surroundings in California, chose the school to properly understand Islam. Mufti Mohammed Iltimas, the white-bearded head of the school, remembered him as a hard-working student who was determined to memorize every word of the Qur'an. He slept on a rope bed in a place where there was no hot water and no electricity after 10 pm. Lindh's introduction to the madrasa came through a Pakistani missionary he met in California in 1998. A Pashtun, Khizar Hayat, who had travelled to America on a preaching mission, was closely linked with the local militant organizations. Even though he was much older than the other boys, Lindh was granted admission to the school. Lindh, who went by the name Suleyman al-Faris, was not in Pakistan to engage solely in scholarly pursuits. During his stay in the madrasa, he frequently met visiting Taliban activists. In May 2001, Hayat took him to the office of a pro-Taliban Islamic militant group, HuM, where he enrolled for guerrilla training.

Lindh was sent to a HuM camp near Islamabad. After learning the use of firearms, he was dispatched to Afghanistan to work with the Taliban. He was not the only American and not the only westerner to have joined al-Qaeda and the Taliban. Many western men, a lot of them Afro-American, were recruited by the Tablighi Jamaat and its front organizations and sent to Afghanistan after receiving basic religious training in Pakistani madrasas and guerrilla training at the camps run by militant groups, closely affiliated with the religious institutions. Some of the madrasas had links with international Islamist organizations like Egypt's Akhwan-ul Muslimeen (Muslim Brotherhood), Indonesia's Jemmah Islamiyah, Algeria's Islamic Salvation Front (FIS) and the Philippines' Abu Sayyaf group, all of whom extended support to alQaeda.

Radical madrasas were not restricted to the remote border region in northern Pakistan. In fact, the country's largest city and its main financial centre Karachi, became the hub of militant seminaries. According to one estimate, more than 200,000 students were enrolled in around one thousand madrasas in the city. Not all, but many of them, had links with sectarian or Islamic militant groups. The largest among them was the Jamia Ulumia Islami or Jamia Binoria. The sprawling red-brick campus, with tall minarets right in the heart of the city, served as the backbone of militant

Islam and was the breeding ground for 'Islamic warriors'. The country's premier institution for Islamic learning had also become the citadel of Sunni extremist groups. The main campus and eight other affiliated madrasas enrolled more than ten thousand students from Pakistan as well as 30 other countries including China, Central Asia, Chechnya, Malaysia, the Philippines and Britain. Students were taught the concept of Jihad as a special subject to prepare them to fight for the cause of Islam. Many of the Taliban leaders were graduates and took guidance from their former teachers for running the fundamentalist Islamic state. The students were sent regularly to Afghanistan for training and orientation during Taliban rule. At the main gate stood a huge banner exhorting Muslims to join Taliban forces in Afghanistan. Over the last two decades, thousands of its students fought in Afghanistan and Kashmir.

Dozens of other smaller and relatively low-profile madrasas spread across Karachi became the base for al-Qaeda 'sleeper' cells in Pakistan. A lean and shy Ahmed Hadi was an ordinary student at Jamia Abu Bakr and the last person one would suspect of being an important cog in the international terrorist network. It was only after Pakistani security forces raided the seminary in Karachi's middle-class neighbourhood of Gulshan-e-Iqbal in September 2003 that his real identity was revealed. Gun Gun Rusman Gunawan was a leading member of Indonesia's Jemmah Islamiyah and the brother of Hambali, the mastermind of the 2002 bombing in the Indonesian holiday resort of Bali in which more than 200 people died. The Indonesian, who was captured along with 11 other Southeast Asian students, had spent four years at the seminary under a fake identity.

Hambali, who was arrested in Thailand in 2003, had contacts with alQaeda's top leaders Ramzi bin al-Shibh and Khalid Sheikh Mohammed, both of whom were apprehended in Pakistan. It was the first indicator of a terrorist sleeper cell operating in Pakistan's main commercial hub. Gunawan was granted admission to the Jamia Abu Bakr Islamia in 1999. He was among 15,000 students from Muslim countries who came to Pakistan to study in Pakistani madrasas during the 1990s. Founded in 1978, the seminary had a large number of foreign students mainly from Thailand,

Indonesia, Malaysia and African countries. The arrest of Gunawan provided some indication of the strong links between Islamic seminaries and the international terrorist network. His arrest was followed by a series of raids less than a kilometre away from the Abu Bakr seminary.

Another eight Southeast Asian students were arrested from the Jamia Darasitul Islamia, a seminary run by Jamaatud Da'awa, the political wing of Lashkar-e-Taiba. This connection compelled investigators to explore Jemmah Islamiyah's links with Pakistan's militant groups. Pakistani intelligence agencies suspected that Gunawan was instrumental in channelling funds provided by al-Qaeda to the Jemmah Islamiyah. Despite the government's crackdown, many madrasas continued to provide safe haven to al-Qaeda sleeper cells.

Over the past several years, there had been a visible rise in the number of madrasa students belonging to families of the expatriate Pakistani community, particularly those living in the USA and Britain. Fired by the desire to become 'true Muslims', hundreds of second-generation expatriates joined Pakistani seminaries each year. Most of them from prosperous middle-class families, they took time off from their schools to learn about their faith. While the majority of the boys confined themselves to Islamic learning, dozens of them got involved in jihadist activities under the influence of militant groups that operated inside some of the madrasas.

It was one such radical madrasa where Shehzad Tanweer, one of the suicide bombers involved in the 7 July 2005 terror attacks in London, spent time during his last visit to Pakistan. Twenty-two-yearold Shehzad, who blew himself up on a subway train near Aldgate station in East London, was the eldest son of Mohammed Mumtaz Tanweer, who had migrated to England in the 1960s. He grew up in the Beeston area of Leeds, but remained connected with Pakistan through his extended family members who lived in a farming village in Faisalabad district. In December 2004, Shehzad went to Manzoor ul Islamia madrasa in Lahore, which was linked with JeM. He intended to stay there for nine months of religious education, but left just a week later.

There are strong suspicions that Shehzad might have met the mastermind of the London bombings during his brief stay there. The suspected Pakistani connection to the 7/7 attacks brought Musharraf under a renewed pressure to act against militant madrasas. As in the past, he responded this time by ordering a nationwide crackdown on Islamic extremist groups. The police again stormed a number of madrasas and arrested hundreds of suspected extremists. But the entire operation appeared merely superficial; most of them were released after a few weeks. In his new role as a key ally in the US-led war on terror, Musharraf toned down many policies that had previously fostered militancy and religious extremism. But most of the measures, particularly against the home-grown jihadists, were taken under external pressure and lacked conviction. Very little was done to rein in the militant madrasas, despite their continuing involvement in jihadist politics. While talk about reform went on, fresh batches of volunteers ready to confront what they perceived as enemies of their faith continued to graduate from madrasas.

Even after the ousting of the Taliban regime, many madrasas in parts of Balochistan continued to preach Jihad to Afghan students. A major part of Musharraf's anti-extremism drive was to regulate and transform those madrasas whose role in promoting Jihad had come under increasing international scrutiny. The move was stalled because of the administration's failure to stop their funding from Pakistanis working abroad, as well as from foreign Muslim charities.

The biggest source of financing for madrasas was external – from Muslim countries as well as private donors and Pakistani expatriates. A report by the Brussels-based International Crisis Group (ICG) revealed that Pakistani madrasas and religious centres had received more than 90 billion rupees ($1.5 billion) every year through charitable donations. The amount was almost equal to the government's annual direct income tax revenue. Most of the madrasas, which had in the past received government funding, now relied solely on private charity. Ninety-four per cent of charitable donations made by Pakistani individuals and business corporations went to the religious institutions. Though most donors did not support the politics of religious parties, they felt that Islamic education and the preservation of Islam were the most worthy choice for their donations. Many religious leaders who ran the Islamic seminaries had strong links in Arab countries that went back to the Afghan Jihad. For many it had become a 'status symbol' to receive funding from foreign sources.

Muslims in Britain had been one of the largest donors to the Pakistani Islamic institutions and Muslim militant groups, some of whom had been declared terrorists and outlawed by Pakistan's military government. UK-based charities were the main financiers for Islamic groups. Diversion of funds for educational and humanitarian projects to the Islamic militant groups had become a normal practice. 'It is difficult to separate finances for terror from those for charity,' said the ICG report. LeT and JeM, reportedly collected more than £5 million each year in mosques in Britain. Although both the groups were banned in Britain, the Kashmiri diaspora continued to make donations to them. While Islamabad had repeatedly downplayed the link between extremism and the madrasas, most religious schools continued to preach Jihad. After the failed attempts on Musharraf's life in December 2003, the administration launched raids on some extremist madrasas, but such half-hearted and piecemeal measures could hardly help improve the situation.

Pakistan's failure to curb extremism owed less to the difficulty of implementing reforms than to the administration's own unwillingness. Musharraf had promised to ban the use of mosques and madrasas for spreading religious and sectarian hatred. However, all those pledges remained largely rhetorical and seemed to have been made under international pressure. The sectarian groups continued to challenge the authority of the state in different ways. Pakistan's failure to strictly enforce laws against the preaching of religious hatred and reining in of the extremist madrasas had largely been responsible for the rise in sectarian-based violence.

The failure to deliver to any substantial degree on pledges to reform madrasas and contain the growth of jihadist networks had not only given rise to religious extremism in Pakistan, but also continued to present a threat to domestic, regional and international security. Several madrasas continued to provide recruits for Taliban insurgents in Afghanistan. Run by JUI, part of the coalition government in the western Balochistan province, the seminaries not only provided the Taliban with ideological training, but also extended material help. Pashtunabad, a congested slum district in the provincial capital, Quetta, had a large concentration of former Taliban activists. A stronghold of radical Islamic groups, it looked more like a Kandahar neighbourhood under the former Taliban regime, and several former Taliban leaders were believed to have taken refuge there. The main madrasa in the neighbourhood was run by Maulana Noor Mohammed, a MMA member of the National Assembly. He appeared convinced that the Taliban would re-establish their control over Afghanistan. 'They will ultimately triumph,' declared the 75-year-old cleric.

KASHMIR—EXPANDING THE CONFLICT THEATER

Faced with India's conventional superiority, Pakistan believed that its interests were favored by a military equation that saw the largest number of Indian troops diverted and towards internal security operations and away from a possible Indian strike force aimed at Pakistan. Islamabad also believed that it could calibrate and control this policy, an assessment that generally held until the Afghan Jihad ended with the fall of Najibullah's communist regime in Kabul in April 1992.

Although Islamabad's policy remained constant, several other external factors made IHK an increasingly volatile flashpoint. First, the victory over the Union of Soviet Socialist Republics (USSR) inspired Kashmiri militants to believe that New Delhi could also be beaten. Second, a moderate number of Pakistani and Indian Kashmiris received training and combat experience in Afghanistan during the war against the Soviets and believed that they were ready to fight Indian forces.

Third, Islamist NGOs from the Arabian Peninsula looked for post-Afghan causes to support and Kashmiri separatists figured prominently. Lastly, after al-Qaeda's formation in 1988, it took a strong interest in the Kashmiri militants and began to assist them after the Soviet withdrawal. Each of these factors lessened

Islamabad's ability to effectively regulate the violence in Kashmir and thereby limit chances of a military confrontation with India. Even if Islamabad tightened the spigot, assistance came from other sources.

Pakistan's covert operations alone would not have posed a threat to Indian security and stability, but rising anti-Hindu sentiments among India's 150 million-strong Muslim community have complemented Pakistani operations and enhanced the threat posed to India's communal harmony and economy, something that increases the likelihood of an unintended India-Pakistan war. Nonetheless, this situation was still manageable, but with the rise of Hindu nationalism and cultural chauvinism, or Hindutva, the situation has become more severe. The rapid growth of the Bharatiya Janafa Party (BJP—a Hindu nationalist political party) and the simultaneous expansion of the Mumbai-based Shiv Sena (Army of Shiva) began to challenge the secular credentials of the Indian state in a manner that was openly anti-Muslim. By the late 1990s Hindu nationalist leaders were pushing for the imposition of domestic policies, namely in the area of counterterrorism, that widened the Hindu-Muslim communal divide and created a permissive environment for the development of anti-Hindu Islamist militancy in India. Further, since the U.S.led invasion of Afghanistan in 2001, Pakistan has continued its covert operations in Kashmir, and as a response to Indian moves in Afghanistan, aims to create an insurgent/terrorist capability across India to attack the booming economy.

After lying low for a few months following the November 2008 Mumbai carnage, and the subsequent crackdown on its Pakistan-based camps and leadership, LeT began scaling its operations back up in IHK. LeT fighters engaged Indian regulars of 1 Para and 6 Battalion Rashtriya Rifles (a counterterrorism paramilitary unit created in 1990 for use in Kashmir) in a 5-day firefight beginning on March 20, 2009, in the Shamasbari forest range of Kupwara district near the LoC. LeT claimed responsibility for the ambush on an army patrol and the following encounter in which 17 militants and eight soldiers (including a major) were killed.

The Indian Army attributed its losses to the technical sophistication of the insurgents and their use of global positioning systems (GPS) in the densely forested region. India claims that it has also recovered snow gear, advanced maps, satellite phones, rations, and medical supplies. This equipment points to continued involvement by elements within Pakistan's security forces. Following the admission of involvement in LeT by the sole surviving Mumbai terrorist, the group's image suffered tremendously throughout Pakistan as well as Kashmir, as it risked pulling the decades-old dispute into the greater war on terror framework, something that would allow India to become even more inflexible regarding negotiations on the issue.

LeT appears keenly aware that its core source of legitimacy stems from its fight against Indian security forces in Kashmir, and that this cannot be compromised. Wisely, LeT waited for the regional security environment to settle somewhat before reengaging the Kashmir theater. These actions sought to clearly communicate to New Delhi and the Kashmiris that LeT remains resolutely focused on Kashmir while also attempting to signal to ordinary Pakistanis and their allies in the security forces that LeT is still a reliable partner that seeks to forward Pakistani objectives vis-à-vis India. By continuing to fight in Kashmir, LeT makes it more difficult and politically unpopular to crack down on its activities in Pakistan despite the fact that its other actions in India and elsewhere clearly undermine Pakistani security.

After recently overhauling its infrastructure in IHK, LeT has vowed to continue its operations against security forces and vital installations in the state. Further, unconfirmed reports state that LeT has opened up more camps in Muzzafarabad, Mirpur, and Kotli for the fresh recruitment and training of new fighters and has replaced the commanders that were taken into Pakistani custody. As such, many have raised questions regarding how LeT was able to bounce back so quickly even after Pakistan's so-called crackdown following the Mumbai attacks.

Reports about training camps are often exaggerated and nearly impossible to verify. However, until Pakistan's border dispute with India as well as Afghanistan is resolved, Islamabad is not likely to drop its support for irregulars, as Pakistan has come to view many of them as an insurance policy against what Islamabad assesses to be hostile neighbors. Unless these fundamental issues are addressed, Pakistan is likely to continue on this ultimately self-destructive path much to the detriment of regional and international security.

Veteran Kashmiri guerrilla commander Ilyas Kashmir is overseeing the development of the new "neo-Taliban" strategy in Afghanistan which seeks to complement the traditional guerrilla war of the Kandahari clan in southwestern Afghanistan and suicide operations in and around Kabul and in southeastern Afghanistan. These neo-Taliban also intend to spread chaos throughout Pakistan and India through kidnappings, high profile attacks, and other asymmetric tactics. After this, they intend to go a step further by actively engaging security forces once military operations are diverted by the chaos that has been caused. The Arab and former Kashmiri fighters that form the bulk of the neo-Taliban have been fighting under the command and strategy of the Taliban in Afghanistan but have now formed into a separate entity. Given the background of this group and the nature of terrorism and insurgency in the region, this organization likely has links to Kashmir and can shift back to that theater if they become disenchanted in Afghanistan or if the conflict ends. In the event that this group returns to Kashmir and greater India, it will be even more capable after spending years engaging American and NATO forces in Afghanistan.

The Mehsud tribe is believed to provide base camps for these fighters and also raises money. It is estimated that between November 2008 and April 2009 alone, Tehrik-i-Taliban Pakistan's (TTP) network in Karachi generated at least 250 million rupees (US $3.1 million) through various operations, including extorting fuel contractors for coalition troops in Afghanistan and ransom money from kidnappings and threats. These proceeds have been used to open up new guerrilla training camps in both Pakistan and Afghanistan. TTP has links with mainstream LeT, so these fighters in Afghanistan can hardly be viewed as insulated from the Kashmir insurgency. TTP also uses LeT and other infrastructure of the

Punjabi-dominated groups to attack in settled areas of Pakistan such as Lahore and Islamabad as well as rural southern Punjab. This will inevitably have an impact on India, and with additional safe havens to plan and train, another spectacular attack by LeT or a related group on Indian territory cannot be ruled out. Pakistan's Punjabi militants are highly trained and have become battled hardened after years of fighting in India and IHK. In such an event, there is no guarantee that American diplomacy could prevent a major conventional war.

It is believed that the March 2009 attacks on a police academy in Lahore were carried out by militants who have been associated with LeT and Harakat-ul-Jihadi-Islami Pakistan (HUJI-P). Security sources claim that the group travelled to Lahore from a militant camp in the North Waziristan town of Razmak. After killing a number of cadets and taking many others hostage, the lead militants are reported to have slipped away, leaving behind a few men to keep the shootout with security forces going for 8 hours. The fugitives most likely then travelled to cities in southern Punjab, namely Multan.

Intelligence agencies maintain that some of the militants came from Punjab and spoke Urdu, Punjabi, and Seraiki, even though FATA-based TTP claimed responsibility for the attack. These attacks and the attack on the Sri Lankan cricket team in Lahore represent some dangerous muscle-flexing by Pakistan's original jihadis, mostly Punjabis trained by the military in the 1990s as the first line of defense for the country, especially in Kashmir.

These militants remained neutral after the U.S. invasion of Afghanistan in 2001 and only joined the Taliban's fight against foreign forces in Afghanistan in 2004 through the provision of training and logistics. However, they did not involve themselves in the hostilities in the tribal areas. This has now clearly changed, thus rendering any distinctions between militants even more indisputably obsolete and demonstrates that Pakistan's outfits, including its supposed allies like LeT, have made a strategic decision to escalate their campaigns in the country even if it pushes Pakistan to the brink. LeT's parent outfit, Jamaat-ud-Dawa (JuD), is considered to be the best organized Islamic charity in South Asia with a social network unmatched by other Islamic groups or militant outfits. By responding to social and economic ills under the platform of Islamic social justice, groups like JuD have done extremely well in meeting the population's expectations in times of crises or natural disasters and winning their loyalty as a result. Through these provisions of social services, JuD is able to connect in a way that the Pakistani state cannot.

This puts pressure on the state and also prevents external actors from exploiting the local population to steer them away from the Islamists' camp. In doing so, JuD, and by extension LeT, are able to expand their organization through social networking. This allows them to maintain a level of independence and qualify as legitimate authorities to a population that increasingly perceives the civilian government as corrupt and weak in the face of Western demands. This is a major impediment to shutting down LeT infrastructure as it could create a massive vacuum that would likely be filled by another nonstate actor. By thinking strategically, LeT and JuD have taken steps to ensure that any effort to uproot them will be most painful for society and the government.

LeT seems to have a heightened awareness of the power of emotions and a need to continue to engage in surprising moves to maintain their elevated status. LeT/JuD also seeks to appeal to a global audience despite being a local group, something that has prompted comparisons with al-Qaeda. It also attracts members from outside of Pakistan and has infrastructure in Central Asia and the Arab World. This likely has much to do with LeT's inflated ambitions, but it still cannot afford to shift its primary focus from Kashmir and India. For this, LeT has to maintain its infrastructure in IHK, carry out innovative spectaculars in India, and continue to nurture IM.

Assam: The Next Front?

The October 30, 2008, Assam blasts claimed 85 lives and injured nearly 500 people. Sophisticated weaponry and unknown smuggling networks were used to carry out these attacks as opposed to the relatively crude locally assembled explosives used elsewhere in India such as New Delhi, Mumbai, Hyderabad, and Varanasi.

The bombs used in Assam have raised concerns over the region's porous borders as well as links between local separatist militant groups, especially from Bangladesh and Myanmar. Security experts say that the car and motorcycle bombs used were often laden with over 80 kilograms of RDX, well beyond the capability of domestic separatist outfits such as the United Liberation Front of Assam (ULFA) or the National Democratic Front of Bodoland (NDFB). Prior to the bombings, there had been brutal anti-Bengali/Muslim riots and communal tensions were high.

India's Home Ministry believes that HUJI-B was involved in the Assam bombings and that the group maintains close ties with IM. In Assam, HUJI-B is believed to utilize its close connections with illegal immigrants from Bangladesh for new recruits, safe houses, and logistical support, and reports suggest that the Indian government has identified 46 points along the border with Bangladesh that are being used as exit and entry points by HUJI-B. Bangladesh is facing a major yet little-publicized national security challenge from terrorist groups. Unfortunately, a common perception exists amongst the greater counterterrorism community that Bangladeshi terrorist groups do not have significant linkages with groups outside the country and therefore do not pose a challenge to international security. Put simply, the common viewpoint is that these groups are waging an internal struggle and are not linked to global terrorism.

Potential Radicalization of Security Personnel in Bangladesh?

While investigations are still underway into the Bangladesh Rifles (BDR—a paramilitary border security force) mutiny that took place in February 2009, there have been allegations made in several quarters, including by the minister responsible for coordinating the investigations, about a possible involvement by Bangladesh-based Jamaat-ul Mujahideen Bangladesh and other terrorist organizations. If the suspicion proves to be true, this would have serious implications for Bangladesh's national security. Many of the bodies of the Bangladeshi Army officers that were killed in the mutiny were mutilated in a barbaric, brutal fashion. Does this point towards a possible radicalization of certain members of the security forces? If that is the case, then that would raise serious concerns and would require Bangladeshi authorities to have a hard look at the internal oversight procedures of the security apparatus. It is also of note that over 1,800 BDR personnel still have not returned for duty and are dispersed throughout the country. Despite Operation REBEL HUNT, some of these deserters are not likely to be located. Potentially radicalized paramilitary and regular soldiers are especially dangerous for a number of reasons. First, they tend to be well trained in combat techniques and the use of weaponry. Second, as they have previously served in the armed forces or paramilitaries, they have knowledge of the layout of various facilities and the strengths and weaknesses of the security forces. Third, their actions can serve as a powerful motivator for many fence-sitters, who are also disillusioned with their positions, as well as with society at large. Finally, extremist ex-soldiers may have a line of communication open with still-serving personnel. These soldiers not only constitute a large group of well-trained men, but they also may have a significant portion of the weapons and ammunition that were looted from BDR during the mutiny.

With extremist groups now equipped with the necessary resources, Bangladesh and India have to contend with the possibility of the ranks of existing groups mushrooming or witnessing a dangerous proliferation of self-starter groups, either of which will have knock-on effects in India, especially in nearby areas where there is communal tension and a conducive environment like Assam. Further, IM is not likely to have remained idle while massive amounts of weapons flowed out of BDR headquarters, and Bangladesh's border defenses were also down. As such, IM's biggest operational upgrade may come from Bangladesh instead of Pakistan.

Bangladesh-Afghanistan Connection

A fact that is often ignored is that the senior leadership of Bangladeshi terrorist groups such as JMB and HUJI-B took an active part in the armed resistance against the Soviet Union. The leaders of HUJI-B saw action in several provinces in Afghanistan, and it was during this time that they came into close contact with individuals who later went on to assume important leadership positions in militant groups across the South Asian region and beyond. For around a decade, these individuals participated side by side against the USSR, and these relationships did not likely fade following the Soviet withdrawal. In addition to JMB and HUJI-B, the senior leadership of the vast majority of Islamist terrorist groups in South Asia still includes individuals who fought in the Afghan anti-Soviet resistance. Therefore, there is a very real possibility that Bangladeshi terrorist leaders are able to leverage the long-term relationships they forged with their counterparts in South Asia and possibly the Middle East, and can translate this into a strong collaborative operational relationship between their groups. The bonds that were initially formed in Afghanistan are more than likely to have been further cemented over the years as they continue to engage in activities that are driven by the same ideological reasoning. As such, it is vital that this phenomenon be examined, and that the transnational linkages of Bangladeshi terror groups are adequately understood if counterterrorism policies, strategies, and tactics are to be effective.

Different Enemies, Common Justifications

A concept that frequently appears in the strategic communications put forward by South Asian terrorist groups is the comparison of everything that they stand against with *Taghoot* or the force of evil. Referring to some verses in the Quran and interpreting it to suit their requirements, these groups try to portray their enemies as alongside the forces of evil. The same reasoning is used by JMB, Pakistan-based LeT and Jaish-e-Mohammad, and a number of other Islamist terrorist organizations across South Asia.

The forces that these groups claim to fight against are diverse. For example, while JMB is fighting Dhaka to establish a puritanical Islamic state in Bangladesh, LeT and JeM are fighting against the Indian state using Kashmir as their main justification. However, while the targets are different, the ideological justifications are usually the same. They also share an almost pathological disdain for the West, and the United States in particular. When JMB sends a message, while the Bangladeshi state and society remains the main enemy, the West and the United States are also targeted. Further, HUJI-B espouses the same extremist Deobandi ideology which inspires JeM and other groups in the region.

Understanding the Threat from Bangladeshi Groups

While distinct organizations, both JMB and HUJI-B share some striking similarities. In Pakistan, even groups such as Tehrik-i-Taliban Pakistan and others which are actively engaged in hostilities with Pakistan's security forces still espouse nationalist rhetoric and offered to stand and fight with the Pakistan Army in the event of an Indian attack following the carnage in Mumbai in November 2008. They are also in lockstep with the position of many Pakistanis regarding the Kashmir dispute. However, HUJI-B and JMB are fundamentally against all tenets of the Bangladeshi state and society and seek to overthrow the secular government, replace the Western-style court system, and establish a Taliban-style state in Bangladesh. It should be remembered that several of HUJI-B's most senior leaders are veterans of the Afghan conflict against the Soviet Union, and that Osama bin Laden provided critical financial backing during the group's infant stages. Despite being a much younger organization that is believed to have been formed around 1998, JMB's ideology and vision for Bangladesh's future does not differ dramatically from HUJI-B's. JMB is an extremely formidable outfit as was demonstrated by its ability to carry out over 400 coordinated bomb blasts within one hour in all but one district in Bangladesh. Further, the threat posed by JMB as well as HUJI-B recently forced Sheikh Hasina to curtail her travel plans following her recent election.

Among the counterterrorism community, while Indian and Pakistan terror groups get a lot of attention, the groups operating in Bangladesh are often believed to be substantially weaker and operating mainly with local motivations. However, certain events over the past few years point towards a different direction. For example, in 2003 several JMB members were apprehended by the Bangladeshi police with uranium. Police and sources at Bangladesh's Atomic Energy Commission later remarked that they possessed enough uranium to manufacture a dirty bomb. To this day, it is not clearly established why those JMB terrorists were carrying such fissile material and it is still unknown whether they were planning an operation in Bangladesh or acting as couriers for one of their regional partners. Whatever the mission may have been, the consequences of its success would have been cataclysmic.

Second, as briefly mentioned earlier, JMB carried out a near simultaneous terrorist attack on August 17, 2005, when it detonated a total of 463 bombs over a span of 50 minutes in 63 out of 64 district towns in Bangladesh. This was by no means a simple feat as an operation of that nature required superb organization, planning, and coordination to achieve the desired results. Furthermore, each attack site was also left with a leaflet carrying the key messages of the group. The motivations may have been local, but it is unlikely that without support of either a tactical or logistical nature from an international partner, such an operation could have been mounted.

Third, there is now an elaborate structure of financing that is used by Bangladeshi terror groups. A recent study undertaken by the Centre for Strategic and International Studies (CSIS) has shown that both HUJI-B and JMB extensively use the large Bangladeshi expatriate population for fund raising and are known to have received funds from Europe and the Middle East. They have also received funds from NGOs in the Middle East. In addition, a HUJI-B terrorist apprehended in 2008 admitted during interrogation that he had undertaken several visits to countries in Southeast Asia. It is also important to note that Maulana Tajuddin, one of the key masterminds of the deadly bomb attack on the Awami League political rally (where the incumbent Bangladeshi Prime Minister was seriously wounded) on August 21, 2004, is currently in South Africa according to various reports. It is believed that South African organizations have been used for raising funds, and, as such, it is clear that the organization has spread far and wide, and its linkages transcend well beyond Bangladesh's immediate vicinity.

The international community must note with caution the potential fissures and divisions that exist within Bangladeshi society. Bangladesh has evolved into a secular society where culture and religion cohabit in the same space without having any contradiction or collision. The terrorist and extremist groups operating in Bangladesh find this to be disdainful, and these groups will continually try to resist the forces in favor of preserving the secular liberal nature of the state. Further, in the aftermath of the mutiny of the BDR in February 2009, it is critically important to examine the kind of fissures that terror groups can create within the security forces of Bangladesh while bearing in mind that HUJI-B also tried to stage a coup in 1995. The attempt was meant to topple the elected government and install an Islamist regime, but the coup was averted due to early intelligence reports. Given the historical, operational, and administrative links that exist between HUJI-P and HUJI-B, this is something that needs to be taken into account. Therefore, there is a requirement to study this dimension of the problem very closely, and it is critical to understand if there has been any Islamist penetration of the security apparatus since it can have catastrophic consequences for the security of Bangladesh and the region.

Links to Groups in India

Many analysts as well as Indian security officials believe that HUJI-B actively works with the banned SIMI, is a component of the Indian Mujahideen as part of its design to expand its support base and to destabilize India, and was possibly involved in the November 2008 Mumbai attacks. HUJI-B poses a very serious threat to Indian security not only because of its links to other transnational terrorist groups that are antagonistic towards New Delhi and have a proven ability to carry out large-scale attacks, but also because many of its cadre do not arouse suspicion as they speak a language (Bangla) and are of an ethnic background (Bengali) that is also prominent in India. This is compounded by the porous nature of the poorly-policed Indo-Bangladesh border and the lack of an extradition treaty between the two countries. As such, future efforts to prevent infiltration will prove most difficult even if sufficient political will is available, something that is debatable.

Like most of India's smaller South Asian neighbors, there is considerable apprehension in Bangladesh regarding New Delhi's ambitions in the subcontinent as well as its perceived interference in Bangladesh's internal affairs. However, at the same time it is not in Bangladesh's interest to have a hostile relationship with its giant neighbor and, as such, any leadership in Dhaka must toe a fine line by maintaining at least a stable relationship with India while not appearing to be too close to New Delhi. Failure to do so risks jeopardizing their domestic as well as international legitimacy and regime security.

Following the most recent election late last year, Sheikh Hasina returned to power. Largely perceived to be pro-India, it has been widely anticipated that her administration will seek to crack down on groups that threaten regional stability, such as JMB and HUJI-B, but also several insurgent groups in India's Northeast that New Delhi believes have taken refuge in Bangladesh. Much of Hasina's credibility in India will rest upon the extent to which she can effectively reign in these groups, and, given her previous failures, her half-life with the Indians is not incredibly generous. This fact is not lost on her Islamist adversaries who recognize that carrying out attacks in India has a multiplier effect in that it increases the group's profile, enhances its credentials as an international terrorist outfit, and also actively undercuts any potential for improvement in Indo-Bangladesh ties, something that could put a major dent in their activities. It can also provoke irrational responses by India and strengthen hardliners in New Delhi thus creating an environment that is even more conducive to militant activity in both countries. Any attack that HUJI-B or JMB carries out in India has multiple objectives and sophisticated political aims.

Links to groups in Pakistan

HUJI-B was initially an offshoot of HUJI-P, a Pakistan-based Kashmir-centered group that had strong links with the Pakistani security apparatus and, until recently, was the stronger half. Traditionally, HUJI-B has taken much of its training and arms supply from Muzaffarabad in Pakistan-administered Kashmir (PAK) as part of its partnership with HUJI-P, but this has now changed and it has become the role of HUJI-B to maintain relevance by continuing to carry out attacks in Bangladesh and India. Nonetheless, HUJI-B still maintains some of its most critical

Pakistani links and interrogations of captured militants have revealed that the group has recently employed trainers from Pakistan-based LeT and JeM. However, as the international spotlight shines brightly on Pakistan, HUJI-B has shifted many of its training and logistical operations into Bangladesh itself, though information sharing still likely continues.

Jalaluddin Haqqani's network has existed in Pakistan since the Soviet era and also extends throughout the Pashtun areas of Afghanistan and into Kabul. Haqqani is arguably the most credible mujahideen, given his personal history and lack of involvement in Afghanistan's brutal civil war. Further, unlike the Tehrik-i-Taliban Pakistan, the Haqqani network is friendly towards Pakistan, urges other groups to avoid engaging the Pakistani security forces, and focuses all of its resources on Afghanistan. As such, while still being on the receiving end of many American drone strikes, his network has not been the focal point of military operations by the Pakistani Army. Any cooperation between the Haqqani network and HUJI-B could greatly enhance the latter's operational capabilities through training, while also providing HUJI-B with an established infrastructure to raise funds and to hide wanted members. It is of note that over 20 Bangladeshis were arrested while trying to cross the Afghan-Pakistan border in 2008.

Haqqani runs an extensive unregulated network of madrassas near the border with Afghanistan. These schools are often blamed for helping to spawn the Taliban movement in Afghanistan in the 1990s and were known to provide thousands of frontline troops during their advances. Most of the madrassas are still operational and have also been the target of American drone attacks, thus suggesting that they still support insurgents in Afghanistan, domestic and foreign. Bangladesh also has an unregulated network of thousands of private "Qaumi" madrassas that develop their own curriculum and are not required to make their sources of funding known to Dhaka. Any further transfer of radical ideology from overseas into Bangladesh's Qaumi madrassas is extremely dangerous, as this has been a major driver behind groups such as JMB beginning to look beyond Bangladesh in their strategic planning. Further, while Pakistani groups like the TTP and the

Tehreek-e-Nafaz-e-Shariat-e-Mohammadi (TNSM) are still somewhat nationalist in nature and locally focused, this is not the case with HUJI-B, a group that is increasingly identifying itself with global terrorism and making less of a distinction between the "far" and "near" enemy. Increased contacts with other radical madrassa networks in South Asia could accelerate this trend. However, it should be noted that, by and large, unregulated Bangladeshi madrassas produce lower-ranking members for HUJI-B and JMB as they do not equip graduates with many practical skills. Nonetheless, these individuals still form the bulk of the membership of these groups and are the ones who are charged with executing attacks and implementing various strategies and directives.

HUJI-B and JMB have undoubtedly been watching developments in Pakistan's Malakand Division (which houses Swat) with much interest since, like Sufi Mohammed and the TNSM, one of their main complaints with the Bangladeshi state is over the lack of Sharia law and the slow, inefficient, and corrupt practices that are commonplace in the British-style judiciary. A careful analysis of strategies and tactics used by the TNSM is likely underway, and information exchange cannot be ruled out. HUJI-B and JMB also have latecomer's advantage in that they have been able to witness the successes and failures of previous groups and can avoid many potential pitfalls. As such, expect a deliberate and precise strategy by HUJI-B and JMB that seeks to incorporate many of the lessons learned from other terrorist/insurgent theaters. Already we are seeing them attempting to employ their own ink blot strategy by building their support base and cadre strength district by district. Further, these groups seek active participation in the legitimate political process: HUJI-B attempted to run in the elections in late 2008 under the Islamic Democratic Party but was denied permission by the Election Commission. Also, JMB has now split and established a mainstream ideological wing that claims to operate separately from the militant outfit and has reconstituted its Shura. All of these developments point to long-term strategic thinking and the intent to systematically intensify their campaigns in the country.

Implications

Just like financial markets, terrorist or insurgent markets influence each other. Successes by terrorist or insurgent organizations in other South Asian theaters will embolden the Bangladeshi groups as well as IM, something that can lead to an increase in recruiting as well as more audacious tactics. Also, as HUJI-B, JMB, and IM are considerably younger and less well-known than most of their regional counterparts, they will likely attempt to springboard into the limelight through more violent yet innovative methods of attack and subversion. However, this will require guidance from external sources.

Like the rest of the world's most prolific terrorist groups, Bangladesh's organizations have recognized the power of ideas and increasingly sophisticated propaganda videos have begun to appear that are available in multiple forms in order to reach as many potential recruits as possible. In addition, JMB's information operations (IO) are very effective and place great emphasis on leaflets and on immediately explaining the rationale for their actions in a clear and concise manner. For example, JMB explained the lack of massive casualties during their coordinated bomb blasts in 2005 as being the result of an intentional decision to not cause harm to innocents. Instead, they claimed that the bombs were designed to serve as a demonstration of power and a warning to Dhaka. If IM is to become a long-term factor in India, it will also have to develop a more advanced IO capacity.

As JMB is operating in an environment that shares many similarities with India (official secularism, constitutional governance, democratic institutions, etc.), its rationale and justifications for its attacks could provide a useful framework for IM. In addition, the influence of the pan-Islamic Hizbut Tahrir has mushroomed in Bangladesh, while the country still faces a critical shortage of iconic moderate Muslim clerics to counter this development and the increased propagation of radical Islamic ideology. Without an effective counterweight, breaking the recruitment cycle of groups such as HUJI-B and JMB will prove most difficult, if not impossible.

Like the Afghan Taliban in the 1990s, TTP, al-Qaeda, and others, JMB and HUJI-B have creatively blended select Islamic themes and socio-economic issues in a simple, easy-to-digest manner that does not require much critical thinking. This ensures that their ideology is not solely dependent on Islamic arguments, messages that can be countered by qualified religious leaders, thus enhancing its survivability and long-term viability. These groups have also successfully identified their target audience (semi-educated 18-25-yearold Bangladeshis with limited employment prospects) and are carrying out an aggressive marketing campaign. HUJI-B and JMB have also seen how causing high civilian casualties and not adhering to local traditions can quickly drain the oxygen out of a movement, something that al-Qaeda in Iraq (AQI) learned the hard way.

Given the close ties between LeT and the HUJI chapters in both Pakistan and Bangladesh that have been forged over the years in Kashmir and elsewhere, coordination of efforts to enhance IM's capabilities is likely. While the world closely analyses Pakistan's every move regarding counterterrorism, Bangladesh is still considered a nonfactor by many. As such, HUJI-B, JMB, and LeT may be able to use Bangladeshi territory to aid IM's efforts to carry out consistent low-tech attacks throughout India, while leaving spectaculars to LeT for the time being. This is not to play down the threat to India originating from Pakistani soil, but several South Asian terrorist groups likely view Bangladesh in the same manner that an investor views an emerging market. Efforts to increase terrorist capacity in India and nearby Bangladesh will be spearheaded by LeT as a component of its strategy to become the most prolific terrorist group in the region.

Concluding Thoughts

Although LeT was a key component of Islamabad's regional strategy in the past, the organization is growing beyond Pakistan's control and is undertaking its own independent operations. LeT still views Kashmir as a vital issue, but now feels it is a part of a larger Pan-Islamic strategy. Pursuant to this objective, LeT has forged selective partnerships with fellow Pakistani and other regional militant groups, as well as criminal syndicates, whose activities undermine Pakistan's own security, escalate terrorism campaigns throughout South Asia, and increase the risk of an inadvertent war between India and Pakistan. One such group is al-Qaeda, an organization whose presence on Pakistani soil Islamabad has promised to eradicate. LeT is also believed to have been involved in attempts on the lives of several Pakistani leaders, including General Musharraf, and the recent attacks in Mumbai. As such, it appears that LeT leaders no longer feel that they are accountable to their former patron as a whole, but rather to themselves and a select few officers in ISI and the Pakistani military (current and/or retired). However, if support for LeT from the Pakistani intelligence and military establishment continues unabated, LeT will become a multinational organization that determines its own agenda as it will have a wide range of sponsors and sources of funding, and will have fighters and other vital resources spread throughout several regions. This clearly defies the logic, used by several state sponsors of terrorism, that irregulars can be sustainably used in an asymmetric fashion to achieve limited objectives against a conventionally superior adversary, and that such groups will not eventually deviate from the process of not escalating tensions past a certain point. This throws into doubt claims that ties between groups like Hizballah and Tehran/ Damascus are a permanent reality and are not vulnerable to fractionalization.

LeT has not had problems in recruitment, as many madrassas in Pakistan remain unsupervised and do not equip graduates with practical skills. Further, communal tension within India has allowed LeT to develop a working relationship with SIMI and to establish IM, assist its operations, and guide its development and strategic planning. In addition, these tensions have made it possible for LeT to recruit within India, thus providing it with ideal operatives that speak without foreign accents, are highly familiar with their surroundings, and have an extensive network of local contacts. Equally troubling is the fact that LeT has upgraded its activities and has begun to operate throughout India and will likely target transportation and economic infrastructure and the political establishment as opposed to Indian security forces exclusively. It has also adopted new methods of destabilization such as recruiting from India's troubled Northeast and smuggling militants into India by sea, a serious infringement on India's sovereignty.

Despite being a proscribed outfit, LeT still enjoys funding from ISI and through donations from a wide range of domestic and overseas sympathizers, including Indian Muslims. Further, after capitalizing on the 2005 earthquake, LeT has been able to reestablish some of its fund-raising activities within Pakistan. On top of this, LeT now raises funds on the internet and has become market-savvy while making legitimate investments in a range of sectors. LeT is also very likely involved in trafficking Afghan heroin, an extremely high-yielding venture given the low overhead costs and high domestic and overseas demand. All of this has resulted in a diversification of LeT's financial pipeline, thus reducing the possibility of it being held hostage to a particular party, decreasing its vulnerability to a decapitating strike, and ensuring its continued existence even if it is abandoned by Islamabad entirely.

India will continue to face a serious threat from Pakistan-based terrorist groups for the foreseeable future. However, India lacks military options that have strategic-level effects without a significant risk of a military response by Pakistan, and neither Indian nor U.S. policy is likely to be able to reduce the terrorist threat substantially in the short to medium term. Due to this, other Indian extremists will inevitably find inspiration and instruction from the November 2008 Mumbai attacks.

Local radicalization is a major goal of the terrorists, and this will remain a major social and political challenge for India. Although LeT spectaculars grab international attention, and inspire others, their impacts on India and Mumbai in particular are not usually long-lasting, thus rendering LeT unable to translate short-term tactical victories into long-term strategic gains while operating on its own from Pakistan.

Due to this, LeT and others will rely more heavily on IM to increase its membership and to engage in low-tech terrorism campaigns throughout India if it expects to succeed in undermining the Indian economy, disturbing communal relations, and dashing any hopes of improving ties between India and Pakistan.

Although LeT and groups like HUJI-B have high hopes for IM, the group remains relatively primitive in terms of operational capacity and information operations. LeT's rise to prominence has largely followed a more sophisticated understanding of politics and strategic thought, thus causing the group to come to view violence as a tool rather than an end in itself. IM's urban terrorism currently appears to be reactive and driven by anger rather than by more complex strategic objectives, something that LeT undoubtedly seeks to change. At present, IM's attacks do not require a safe haven or training in Pakistan as they are relatively simple, but if the group intends to evolve, then the role of both Pakistan and Bangladesh will become more prominent. However, although LeT would like to see a much more advanced IM, it will still seek to claim the title of South Asia's most effective terrorist group. If this is to occur, LeT will continue to plan major Mumbai-style operations in India while also scaling up attacks in IHK so as to maintain legitimacy.

Since many of LeT's cadre are Pakistani and IM is still a somewhat disjointed organization, D-Company's logistical network will be critical, especially in major urban centers such as Mumbai. This network can be utilized for recruiting, smuggling weapons and militants in and out of India, and providing pre-and post-operation services like surveillance, reconnaissance, and assisting terrorists in moving through India undetected. Without D-Company's vast cross-border network, LeT is unlikely to be able to achieve its objectives in India and the growth of IM will be inhibited, thus limiting it to inconsistent low-tech terrorism which has few lasting effects despite the loss of human life and damage to property. Though investigations are still ongoing and the full story may never be available, as is the case with the 1993 Mumbai (Bombay) blasts, any revelation of D-Company involvement in the 2008 Mumbai attacks should not surprise analysts.

India faces a considerable security challenge from Bangladesh with two major terrorist groups that have ties to LeT and other groups in Pakistan and are increasing their capabilities alongside their ambitions and political awareness while the country has been neglected by international counterterrorism efforts. The bomb blasts in Assam and the BDR mutiny serve as a startling preview of what is to come if current trends are not reversed. Given the porous nature of the Indo-Bangladeshi border and the shared ethnicity between the two countries, knock-on effects in India and on IM's capabilities would be nearly unavoidable. Further, in the event that Pakistan actually engages in a meaningful crackdown on terrorist groups operating from its territory, Bangladesh would become IM's most viable option for strategic guidance and material support.

No group from Pakistan, Bangladesh, or elsewhere could make headway in India unless conditions in select areas were conducive to such activity. Without the Indian component, these groups would remain confined to carrying out occasional large-scale attacks that do not result in political gains, and the IM project could not be successful. This fact is something that New Delhi must continuously emphasize to its civilian population as opposed to focusing a disproportionate amount of attention on foreign groups. As long as the Indian media and political leadership continue to point the finger exclusively towards external forces, many in the security bodies and the general public will look overseas along with them. If a new counterterrorism body is formed under these misconceptions, there is little to suggest that it will be any more effective than its predecessors. In addition, New Delhi's approach could alienate its regional neighbors, thus unnecessarily undermining any potential for stronger inter-state cooperation. Until New Delhi faces up to this, it is unlikely that it will be able to implement a functioning counterterrorism strategy and these attacks will tragically continue. This will prove most detrimental to India's internal stability, business climate, and the faith of its people in the nation's political leadership and security forces, and could drag South Asia's nuclear-armed rivals into a war.

4

Jihad Against the 'Enemies of Islam'

The subject of armed jihad runs right through the writings and pronouncements of Markaz spokesmen and is, in fact, the most prominent theme in the Markaz's discourse. Indeed, its understanding of Islam maybe seen as determined almost wholly by this preoccupation, so much so that its reading of Islam seems to be a product of its own political project. The contours of its ideological framework are constructed in such a way that the theme of armed jihad appears as its central, over-riding concern. Not surprisingly, therefore, it constructs a discursive framework that, like Gilani's and the JIJK's, completely denies the legitimacy of the Kashmiri nationalist project, but at the same time goes considerably beyond the limited aims of the JIJK's jihad as Gilani conceives them in his writings.

There has been much discussion on the nature and forms of jihad in writings about Islam. Liberals have tended to explain it in terms of self-defence, while others have taken recourse to certain Sufi positions, where the foremost jihad (jihad-i akbar) is said to the struggle against the nafs or one's 'baser self' or ego. Yet others have suggested that jihad in the path of God (jihad fi sabil illah) can take many forms, and that armed struggle is just one of these. However, in the writings and speeches of Markaz spokesmen jihad appears unabashedly as qital or violent conflict waged against unbelievers. Indeed, it is projected as the one of the most central tenets of Islam, although it has traditionally not been included as one of the 'five pillars' of the faith. Thus, it is claimed that 'There is so much emphasis on this subject that some commentators and scholars of the Qur'an have remarked that the topic of the Qur'an is jihad', and that 'There is consensus of opinion among researchers of the Qur'an that no other action has been explained in such great detail as jihad'.

In order to properly understand the role of jihad for the Markaz's political project, it is necessary to situate it within the broader context of the Markaz's own understanding of Islam. Like other Islamist groups, the Markaz sees Islam as a perfect, all-embracing system and way of life. Islam is said to govern all aspects of personal as well as social life, in the form of the shari'ah. For the establishing of an Islamic system, an Islamic state is necessary, which would impose the shar'iah as the law of the land. This is seen as 'the solution to all our problems'. If such a state were to be set up and all Muslims were to live strictly according to 'the laws that Allah has laid down', then, it is believed, 'they would be able to control the whole world and exercise their supremacy'. Since Islam is seen as the very antithesis of nationalism, it demands the establishment of one universal Islamic state, ruled by a single khalifa. Thus, the present division of the Muslims into many nation-states must be overcome. Since 'the ummah is one', it follows from this that 'the system of khilafah does not recognize the physical borders or the independence of one Muslim country from another'. Hence, 'the state is one, the army is one, the flag is one, the budget is one, etc.'.

Islam is seen as a universal ideology meant for all humankind, and hence its message, and, in other words, the boundaries of the Islamic state, must be extended till the entire world comes under its domination. In order for the Islamic call to reach all peoples, it is the duty of the Islamic state to 'carry it to new lands'. This, it is acknowledged, 'will lead to a conflict with other states and ideologies', which can be resolved either peacefully, through diplomatic means, or by force. The Islamic state must first try the former option, but if that fails it is incumbent on it to take recourse to force and wage a jihad. No one can be forced to accept Islam, however, and jihad is to be waged only to bring 'recalcitrant' states under Islamic control by incorporating them within the ever-expanding boundaries of the Islamic state so that the new territories can be 'provided with the security that comes from the application of Islam', in other words, to be ruled by the shari'ah. The people of the conquered lands, if they choose not to convert to Islam, may continue to practise their own religion. In this way, jihad is seen as 'the method adopted by Islam to protect its lands and save humanity from slavery to man-made regimes'. It is, in short, 'the foreign policy of the Islamic State'.

The global jihadist programme of the Markaz presents itself in a liberationist garb, basing itself on widespread feelings of discontent and suffering of sections of Muslims who see themselves as being persecuted by Western-oriented elites in their own countries, as well as by the West more generally. The greatest problem of the Muslims, says Hafeez Muhammad Sa'eed, head of the Markaz, is their 'subjugation to the West'. Thus, the Markaz is reported to have gone so far as to call for a jihad against the USA. Jihad is contrasted with other forms of war that are pursued for purely worldly concerns, and is described as 'the act of supreme sacrifice to preserve human rights bestowed by Allah'. It is portrayed as a struggle 'to help the oppressed against the atrocities committed by the aggressors', and is compared with 'a surgeon using a blade during an operation'. Jihad is thus a means for challenging oppression and of establishing the rule of Islam.

Eight specific objectives are laid out for this grand jihadist enterprise. These objectives, in the words of an official Markaz statement, are:

- To end persecution and tumult.
- To enforce the Islamic world order.
- To force the disbelievers to pay jizya.
- To protect and shield the weak and the oppressed from oppression.
- To avenge the millions of Muslims who were and are being mercilessly slaughtered in various parts of the world.
- To punish those who have broken covenants made with the Muslims.

- To restore Muslims' possession of territories now occupied by disbelievers, such as Spain, India, Ba'it ul-Muqaddas (Jerusalem), Turkistan (Xinjiang).
- To defend and protect the Muslims continuously facing offensives from the disbelievers all over the world

Jihad is seen as the secret of Muslim power in the past when much of the known world was under Muslim rule, and it is argued that when Muslims 'abandoned jihad and other injunctions they began to degenerate'. In Markaz discourse, jihad is seen as a religious duty binding on all Muslims today. Thus, it is claimed that the prevailing global situation warrants all Muslims to be involved in some way of the other in jihad against non-Muslims. As an official Markaz publication puts its, 'Struggle and fighting against the disbelievers is a comprehensive process, very vast in its nature and scope, and it cannot be carried out successfully and duly unless all the classes of the Muslim community [...] participate in it'. In this grand war there are different roles for different people to play. Those who are ordered by the khalifa to fight must do so, while others may be required to assist the mujahidin by supplying them food, arms and other supplies, providing medical assistance, looking after their families in their absence or even by exhorting others to participate in the war. Thus, every Muslim, man or woman, must be mobilized to assist in the struggle in some form or the other, and if any Muslim has 'never intended to fight against the disbelievers', his or her faith 'is not without traces of hypocrisy'. Those believers who have the capacity to participate or assist in the jihad but do not do so are said to 'be living a sinful life'.

DEFINITION OF ISLAMISM

Having all these interrogations in mind, we propose a definition as follows: 'Islamism' is a religious ideology with a holistic interpretation of Islam whose final aim is the conquest of the world by all means. This definition is composed of four interrelated elements. The first is a *religious ideology*, the second a *holistic interpretation of Islam*, the third *conquest of the world*, and finally the fourth and the last element is the use of *all means* in the search for the final objective. Each of these four elements will be briefly examined in the following.

Islamism is a religious ideology

Among western thinkers and scholars, there has been a tendency to attribute a kind of religious aureole to non-religious ideologies. Jean-Jacques Rousseau calls what he regarded as the moral and spiritual foundation essential for any modern society 'civil religion'. To some authors, contemporary political ideologies such as communism, fascism and Nazism are considered as 'political religion'.

Compared with the above-mentioned, Islamism has a particularity: it is already a *religious* phenomenon, and labels like 'civil', 'secular' or 'political' religions do not apply to it. 'Clerical fascism' is perhaps the nearest concept which comes closest to Islamism.

The concept of 'Islamism' is composed of two elements: 'Islam' and 'ism'. The former stands for a religion and a civilisation with its specific history, and the latter indicates a non-Islamic suffix. The composition of these two elements refers to a bi-pillar construction, composed by religion and ideology. Islam is a religion with a long history and with different theological and juridical schools. The Qur'an is not really a coherent book able to provide Muslims with clear and unambiguous guidelines. Roughly speaking, it is divided into two very different and somewhat contradictory sets of statements, principles and commandments.

The *surats* [chapters] are divided into the Mecca period of 12 years' length (from 610 to 622), and the Medina period of ten years' length (from 622 to 632). The first and initial period is characterised by relative moderation, toleration and pluralism. You find this aspect of Islam in some verses in the Qur'an. For example the Qur'an states: 'You shall have your religion and I shall have my religion' (surat 109, verse 6).

We may call the Mecca period the moderate phase of Islam. In contrast, the Medina period is essentially characterised by politics, power and war. The moderate and open-minded language and behaviour give place to a power language. The following verse shows the change in the Qur'an's language when it states: And slay them wherever ye find them, and drive them out of the places whence they drove you out, for persecution is worse than slaughter. And fight not with them at the Inviolable Place of Worship until they first attack you there, but if they attack you (there) then slay them. Such is the reward of disbelievers (s. 2, v. 191).

This example is an illustration of the Qur'an's ambiguous discourse and its ambivalence in recommended behaviour. The Medina period can be termed as the radical phase of Islam. The Qur'an also reflects this part of Islam. The fact is that some Muslims (known as 'cultural Muslims') refer to the Mecca period alone, and others (Islamists in particular) consider the Medina period as the achievement of Islam in its final shape. Then there is a third group (the overwhelming majority of Muslims) which refers to both periods. This consideration among many others demonstrates that it is practically impossible to identify the 'real message' of Islam. Therefore, the world is facing various manifestations of Islam at a time when no consensus exists among Muslims on fundamental aspects of their faith, except for two cardinal, and thus very general points: the acceptance of the unity of God (Allah), and the reliability of the prophecy of Muhammad as the last Prophet.

This means that if we take only the Qur'an, which is the main source of Islam and which should be the point of convergence between Muslims, it leads us to further confusion about Islam. If we add to the Qur'an other sources of Islamic creed as for example Sunna, Hadith, Rivaya, Fatwas and so on, we get more than one billion disoriented and confused persons, all Muslims of divergent articles of faith, all convinced that their own version and their own understanding of Islam represent the only truth. Yet, while 'Islam' is a general, elusive and ambiguous phenomenon, 'Islamism' as an ideology represents a coherent, specific and identifiable construction.

Ideology may be defined as: 'sets of ideas by which men explain and justify the ends and means of organised social action, with the aim of preserving or reconstructing a given reality'. In totalitarian systems ideologies are a powerful instrument for the mobilisation of the masses as well as sources of legitimacy, sources of the sense of mission of a leader or a ruling group. In this sense, Islamism is more than merely a 'religion' in the narrow sense of theological belief, private prayer and ritual worship, but also serves as a total way of life with guidance for political, economic and social behaviour. Selectively, Islamists pick up some elements in Islam and turn them into an ideological precept. Islamism indeed fulfils all requirements of an ideology, but it goes beyond the purely ideological dimension and sacralises the very essence of ideology. Therefore, Islamism differs on this point from other totalitarian ideologies as it takes its legitimacy from a *double* source: *ideology* and *religion*. Owing to its double character, actions undertaken by Islamists are seen by them as religious duties. Where a Nazi feels responsible to his Führer, an Islamist is responsible to his Leader *and* before Allah.

Islamism is also a regressive ideology which is oriented towards the past (*salaf*). Its ideal is the Medina model under Prophet Muhammad as well as the caliphate of the first four caliphs (*Khulafâ al-Râshidûn*). In this respect, Sayyid Qutb is explicit when he declares: 'If Islam is again to play the role of the leader of mankind, then it is necessary that the Muslim community be restored to its original form'.

The Holistic Interpretation of Islam

In the above discussion, we said that Islamists are selective when choosing religious principles from the original sources of Islam. How can a set of selective elements be holistic? There is no contradiction here. In the first place, Islamists argue that their set of selected elements is, in reality, the 'true' Islam and, in the second place, they are convinced that this 'true' Islam' is holistic and embraces all aspects of Muslims' life in eternity.

The holism is based on the absolute indivisibility of the trinity *Dîn* [Religion], *Dunya* [Way of life] and *Dawla* [Government]. This indivisibility is supposed to be permanent and eternal. Its ultimate goal boils down to the fulfillment of this mentioned triad on a global scale. The triad's totalitarian character is confirmed by the writings of the main contemporary Islamist thinkers and leaders:

Hasan al-Banna and Sayyid Qutb of Egypt, Ayatollah Khomeini of Iran and Abu Alâ Mawdudi of Pakistan.

Conquest of the World

To Islamists, the existing world is both wrong and repressive. It is wrong because the existing world does not correspond to Islamic principles. Islam as a political power is no longer as predominant as it used to be in the past. The world is also considered repressive because non-Muslims occupy what the Islamists consider to be Muslim territory (e.g. Palestine, Kashmir, Chechnya) or because Muslims live under severe repression from their own (anti-Islamic) governments.

In order to get rid of these conditions of repression and wrong-doing, the Islamists mainly propose two other 'ideal reference points'. The first is the 'Medina model', e.g. society as it was shaped by Muhammad himself. The second is the classical era of the Caliphate. The Caliphate is one of the longest political institutions in history. Its lifespan extended from the year 632, right after the death of Muhammad the Prophet, until its abolition by Mustafa Kemal in the year 1924. During this very long period of time, the Caliphate experiences were of course not all of the same nature, and not all the experiences were triumphant. The Caliphate was sometimes unified, strong and glorious, whereas at other times it was divided, in conflict, in crisis and weak. The first type of experiences was of incomparably shorter duration than the second. The second reservation concerns the non-Sunni Muslims, especially the Shi'a communities. According to the general position of Shi'a, the Imamate, not the Caliphate, is the rightful and legitimate institution. However, Shi'a Islamists like Ayatollah Khomeini, without hiding their preference for the Imamate, have moved slowly but consistently towards a more consensual attitude. Together with the Sunni Islamists, they share pride in, but also nostalgia for the disappeared past. Therefore, it is fair to say that the restoration of the Caliphate today represents a general claim of all Islamists, independently of their sectarian membership.

To the Islamists, the restoration of the Caliphate is the first step towards the 'Islamisation' of the world. From their perspective,

Islam constitutes a universal religion whose aim is to rule over the entire world. After all, Allah promised the regency on the earth to His 'virtuous servants', as claimed in the Qur'an:

the earth is Allah's, to give as a heritage to such of His servants as He please; and the end is (best) for the righteous. He said: 'It may be that your Lord will destroy your enemy and make you inheritors in the earth; that so He may try you by your deeds' (s.VII, v. 128–9).

Utopia? Perhaps. But a powerful one, capable of inspiring action and motivating people to sacrifice their lives.

By all means The Islamist

The Islamists' spectrum of means to reach the above mentioned goal is quite wide, expanding from propagation, peaceful indoctrination and political struggle to violent methods such as assassination, hostage taking, terrorist and suicide actions, and even massacre of civil populations. However, the use of violence is not systematic. All Islamists do not use violence all the time, but some have recourse to it sometimes and, since there are various Islamist groups of different obedience and with different affiliations and histories, the use of violence by Islamists remains non-concomitant.

It is possible that, simultaneously, some Islamists use extremely violent methods in one part of the world while other Islamists use non-violent methods in another part. This variation in patterns of action is determined by different factors. It can be the consequence of a strategic and deliberate choice by the leadership, as is the case for al-Qaeda.

It can also be the result of prudential considerations when a group of Islamists living in a particular situation prefer to follow a relatively quietist and hence pacifistic line for a while. This line of action was for example adopted by the Muslim Brotherhood in Jordan, and for certain periods of time in Egypt. In Europe, *Hizb al-Tahrir al-Islami* [the Islamic Liberation Party] is a good example of an Islamist movement which for the time being claims to be non-violent. The quietist attitude of some Islamists is an exception. In general, the use of violence is integral to their strategy for achieving their ends. Among the various violent methods, terror is proven to be the preferred one, and is indeed frequently used by Islamist groups. The use of terrorism by Islamists confirms a general rule that Hannah Arendt formulated in her study of totalitarianism: 'Total terrorism (is) the essence of totalitarian government ... guiding principles and criteria of action are, according to Montesquieu, *honor* in monarchy, *virtue* in a republic and *fear* in a tyranny'.Terrorism, and diffusion of fear in the civil population, is therefore the instrument of choice in the hands of Islamist groups.

MODERATE ISLAM-IN OTHER WORDS, TRUE ISLAM

For half a century after the first verse was revealed to the Prophet Muhammad (may God bless him and grant him peace), Islam underwent such an expansion as has seldom been seen. It spread from the Arabian Peninsula to the whole of the Middle East, North Africa and even Spain, drawing the attention of many in the West. In the words of the famous Islamic expert John L. Esposito, "What is most striking about the early expansion of Islam is its rapidity and success.

Western scholars have marveled at it."12 Over the next centuries, Islam reached all corners of the world, from Indonesia to Latin America. Today, Islam is accepted as the fastest growing religion, and its roughly one billion followers represent about one-fifth of the world's population. Interest in Islam particularly increased after the terrorist attacks of September 11, 2001.

Looking at today's Islamic world today, we see a wide range of religious practices, depending on societies' different customs and traditions, their cultural heritage, and world views. This has led some individuals researching or trying to understand Islam to form mistaken impressions.

Those differences may symbolize only the traditional values of the society under examination, but Islam itself. The only way of arriving at an accurate opinion of Islam is to put aside these differences and turn to the Qur'an, where the essence of Islamic morality is set out, and to the actions of our Prophet (may God bless him and grant him peace).

Even if Muslims comprise the majority in a community, that does not mean that community's behavior, views and judgments will necessarily be Islamic, nor that they need be defended in the name of Islam. When evaluating an individual's—or community's—view of Islam, that must always be borne in mind. Differences may stem from prevailing conditions. The only way to ascertain whether those views are correct is by turning to the Qur'an, the most accurate source of truth about Islam, and to the actions of our Prophet (may God bless him and grant him peace). It is most unfair to pass judgment on Islam and Muslims without studying the Qur'an to learn whether a particular practice appears in it. Examining the lifestyle of a single community only can seriously mislead anyone who tries to understand Islam and form opinions about it. First, what needs to be done is to learn about Islam from its true source. Then, once the various models in different parts of the world are considered in the light of those criteria, many who only imagined they knew about Islam will actually come to do so for the first time; and can free themselves from the errors they have been laboring under so far.

Morality of Islam

Every Muslim has the duty to call others to the morality of Islam, to inform them of the existence of God and the proofs of His creation. God Himself has revealed that responsibility in Verse 3: 104: "Let there be a community among you who call to the good, and enjoin the right, and forbid the wrong. They are the ones who have success." He also reveals how that invitation is to be made:

> *Call [them] to the way of your Lord with wisdom and fair admonition, and argue with them in the kindest way. Your Lord knows best who is misguided from His way, and He knows best who are guided. (16:125)*
>
> *Correct and courteous words accompanied by forgiveness are better than charity followed by insulting words. God is Rich Beyond Need, All-Forbearing. (2:263)*

True believers know the importance of this responsibility, described in Verse 3:114: "They believe in God and the Last Day, and enjoin the right and forbid the wrong, and compete in doing good. They are among the righteous." Therefore, they call on all those around them—friends, relatives, everyone they can reach—to believe in God, fear Him, and display a proper morality. This pleasing characteristic of Muslims is described in Verse 9:71:

> *The men and women of the believers are friends of one another. They command what is right and forbid what is wrong, and perform prayer and pay charity tax, and obey God and His Messenger. They are the people on whom God will have mercy. God is Almighty, All-Wise.*

From this verse, it's clear that all believers, throughout the course of their lives, are charged with explaining that proper morality, living by it themselves, recommending good deeds to others and advising them to avoid evil. God commands believers to use soft words, "Say to My servants that they should only say the best..." (17:53)

God describes good words and bad in this analogy in the Qur'an (14:24-27):

> *Do you do not see how God makes a metaphor of a good word: a good tree whose roots are firm and whose branches are in heaven? It bears fruit regularly by its Lord's permission. God makes metaphors for people so that hopefully they will be reminded. The metaphor of a corrupt word is that of a rotten tree, uprooted on the surface of the earth. It has no staying-power. God makes those who believe firm with the Firm Word in the life of this world and the hereafter. But God misguides the wrongdoers. God does whatever He wills.*

Anyone who wishes to lead a virtuous life should encourage others toward virtue.

Anyone who wants to see good should make an effort to help spread it. Anyone who wants to see others behave according to their conscience should encourage them to do so, and anyone who opposes cruelty should warn those who engage in it. In short, anyone who wants right to prevail should call on all others to abide by it.

When issuing that call, however, it's most important to keep in mind that only God can inspire people to become Muslims, and cause words pleasing to them to have any effect. God has revealed that our Prophet (may God bless him and grant him peace), as a result of his noble character and superior morality, always treated people well—and has recommended him as a role model for all mankind.

Islam Commands

In the Qur'an (5:2), God has issued this command:

... help each other to goodness and godliness. Do not help each other to wrongdoing and enmity. Have fear of God. God is severe in retribution.

As that verse makes clear, the faithful struggle only for what is good. They consider the words of God in Verse 4:127 of the Qur'an: "Whatever good you do, God knows it."

They never forget that they will be recompensed for all they do in the sight of our Lord, but God reveals that pleasing mutual aid needs to be in a framework of "good and godliness." The meaning of goodness is also explained in Verse 2:177:

It is not devoutness to turn your faces to the East or to the West. Rather, those with true devoutness are those who believe in God and the Last Day, the Angels, the Book and the Prophets, and who, despite their love for it, give away their wealth to their relatives and to orphans and the very poor, and to travelers and beggars, and to set slaves free, and who perform prayer and pay charity tax; those who honor their contracts when they make them, and are steadfast in poverty and illness and in battle. Those are the people who act loyal. They are the people who guard against evil.

True goodness, therefore, is rather different from the way society in general perceives it. Those who do not live by the morality of the Qur'an view good deeds as favors they confer, whenever they happen to feel like it. Usually they restrict such good deeds to giving money to a beggar, or giving up their seat on the bus to an elderly person.

Yet as we have seen from the above verse, the Qur'an describes goodness as a concept encompassing the whole of a believer's life, as an obligation that must be fulfilled throughout the course of his life, not only when he feels like it or happens to remember it.

As a servant, any Muslim possesses true sincerity and helps the poor and needy, even if he himself is in need, even giving up the things he loves (Qur'an, 76:8).

In Verse 51:19, which reads, "And beggars and the destitute received a due share of their wealth," God has revealed that rendering assistance, helping others, and doing good are all incumbent upon Muslims. They give help unconditionally; and believers are ready to make any sacrifice to encourage others towards what is good. They expect nothing in return, apart from winning the pleasure of God. In Verse 76:9-10, God describes such behavior by believers:

We feed you only out of desire for the Face of God. We do not want any repayment from you nor any thanks. Truly We fear from our Lord a glowering, calamitous Day. Muslims know that God is the Lord of infinite justice, and never forget that their good behavior will be suitably rewarded in the hereafter. Nor do they forget that life in this world is only temporary, and that their true home lies in the sight of God. In the Qur'an, He warns people of their inevitable end, and calls on them all to behave in a manner pleasing to Him:

> *We did not create the heavens and earth and everything between them, except with truth. The Hour is certainly coming, so turn away graciously. (15:85)*
>
> *Worship God and do not associate anything with Him. Be good to your parents and relatives and to orphans and the very poor, and to neighbours who are related to you and neighbours who are not related to you,. and to companions and travelers and your slaves. God does not love anyone vain or boastful. (4:36)*

The recompense for those who exhibit pleasing behavior is of great good news for all of mankind, and is revealed in these verses, in these terms:

> *But as for those who believe and do right actions, We will not let the wage of good-doers go to waste. (50:30)*

When those who have done their duty are asked, "What has your Lord sent down?" their reply is, "Good!" There is good in this world for those who do good, and the abode of the hereafter is even better. How wonderful is the abode of those who guard against evil: Gardens of Eden which they enter, with rivers flowing under them, where they have whatever they desire. That is how God repays those who guard against evil. (16:30-31)

Islam Commands Us to Do Good and Avoid Evil

Believers learn the true meaning of good and evil from the Qur'an, a book revealed by God as the Standard by which to discern the true from the false." Concepts such as good and bad, right and wrong, are elucidated in the Qur'an with examples that everyone can understand. The faithful's fear of God gives them light and understanding to help them distinguish between good and bad. (8:29)

Muslims spend their whole lives implementing their awareness of the good and evil, as described in the Qur'an. Yet they take another important responsibility onto their shoulders: inviting others to see the truth, to avoid evil, and live by the morality of the Qur'an. Believers spend their lives telling people about the difference between good and evil, because to the faithful, God has given the following command (3:104):

Let there be a community among you who call to the good, and enjoin the right, and forbid the wrong. They are the ones who have success.

In Verse 3:110, God stresses how those who abide by this commandment are much more auspicious than others:

You are the best nation ever to be produced before mankind. You enjoin the right, forbid the wrong and believe in God. If the People of the Book were to believe, it would be better for them. Some of them are believers, but most of them are deviators.

The faithful perform that Qur'anic duty not only in respect for those ignorant of the difference between right and wrong and with no knowledge of religion, but also in respect for the faithful themselves. People fall into error not only out of ignorance, but sometimes out of forgetfulness, by mistake, or when driven by earthly desires. That being so, the faithful encourage good and prevent evil by reminding one another of the Qur'an's commandments. They warn each other that in this world, those who fail to avoid evil will suffer the torments of hell; that only those who do good and devoutly carry out their religious obligations will be rewarded with Paradise. That delightful responsibility means that they never need feel wearied or discouraged while continuing to warn others compassionately and affectionately, no matter what mistakes they might have made. In many verses, God reveals that He loves those who have patience, and calls on the faithful to be patient when practicing the morality of the Qur'an:

> *You who believe! Seek help in steadfastness and prayer. God is with the steadfast. (2:153)*
>
> *... Those who are steadfast and do right actions. They will receive forgiveness and a large reward. (11:11)*

Islam Commands us to Repay Evil with Good

A good action and a bad action are not the same. Repel the bad with something better and, if there is enmity between you and someone else, he will be like a bosom friend. (41:34)

Ward off evil with what is better. We know very well what they express. (23:96)

In these verses, God promises the faithful that they can secure positive results, so long as they adopt a pleasant attitude in the face of wrongdoing. The Qur'an emphasizes that even when a believer is dealing with an enemy, still he can establish a warm friendship. Responding to evil with good is also an essential part of compassion. When any believer sees others adopting an attitude that will not be pleasing to God, he considers first of all how that will affect them in the hereafter. Then he approaches them with toleration and humility, refusing to let himself become puffed up with pride.

Over the course of their lives, believers may come across people of very different characters. Yet they will not change their view of morality according to the people they meet. Others may speak mockingly, use ugly words, become angry, or even behave in a hostile manner. Yet the true believer never ceases to be polite, modest, and compassionate. He will not respond to ugly words with more of the same. He will not laugh at those who mock him, nor answer anger with anger, but remains patient and tolerant. In the face of insulting behavior, he will respond with proper morality, and with such compassion that the other will feel ashamed.

That is the morality our Prophet (may God bless him and grant him peace) recommends to us. In one of the hadiths, he says, *"You do not return evil for evil, but excuse and forgive."*— 18 In another hadith, he calls on the faithful in these terms: *"None of you must be the kind of weak person who says, 'He who has no compassion will receive none."*

In the Qur'an (5:13), our Prophet (may God bless him and grant him peace) was told to be forgiving when betrayed by some of the children of Israel:

> ... *They have forgotten a good portion of what they were reminded of. You will never cease to come upon some act of treachery on their part, except for a few of them. Yet pardon them, and overlook. God loves good-doers.*

As this verse shows, poor morality displayed by someone else is no justification for displaying the same thing. Each individual is solely responsible to God for his actions. According to the Qur'an, acting with compassion, affection and proper morality in the face of someone else's bad behavior is a sign of superior morality that reveals the extent of a believer's devotion to God. One verse (10:26) reveals the reward that such a pleasing attitude will bring:

> *Those who do good will have the best, and more! Neither dust nor debasement will darken their faces. They are the Companions of the Garden, remaining in it timelessly, forever.*

Islam Forbids the Killing of Innocents

According to the Qur'an (5:32), it is a great sin to kill an innocent person, and anyone who does so will suffer great torment in the hereafter:

> ... *If someone kills another person—unless it is in retaliation for someone else or for causing corruption in the earth—it is as if he had murdered all mankind. And if anyone gives life to another person, it is as if he had given life to all mankind. Our Messengers came to them with Clear Signs, but even after that, many of them committed outrages in the earth."*

This verse equals the killing of one innocent to slaughtering all of humanity! Another verse (25:68) expresses the importance that the faithful attach to life:

> *Those who do not appeal to any other deity besides God [alone]; nor kill any soul whom God has forbidden [them to] except with the right to do so; nor fornicate. Anyone who does so will incur a penalty.*

In yet another verse (6:151), God issues the following commandment:

Say: "Come, and I will recite to you what your Lord has forbidden for you": that you do not associate anything with Him; that you are good to your parents; that you do not kill your children because of poverty—We will provide for you and them; that you do not approach indecency - outward or inward; that you do not kill any person God has made inviolate – except with the right to do so. That is what He instructs you to do, so that hopefully, you will use your intellect.

Any Muslim who believes in God with a sincere heart, who scrupulously abides by His holy verses and fears suffering in the hereafter, will avoid harming even one other person. He knows that the Lord of Infinite Justice will suitably reward him for all his deeds. In one of the hadiths, our Prophet (may God bless him and grant him peace) listed the kinds of people who are not pleasing to God:

> *"Those who act cruelly and justly in the sacred lands, those who yearn for the ways of the ignorant, and those who wrongly shed human blood."*

Islam Commands People to Behave Justly

Islamic morality commands believers to behave justly and morally in making a decision, speaking, or working—in short, in every area of their lives. God's commandments in the Qur'an and the sunnah of our Prophet (may God bless him and grant him peace) describe that understanding of justice in great detail. With their warnings, all the Messengers revealed to us in the Qur'an brought peace and justice to all the communities where they were sent. The prophets helped lift cruelty and despotism from the shoulders of the community of the faithful. As God has revealed in one verse (10:47):

> *Every nation has a Messenger, and when their Messenger comes, everything is decided between them justly. They are not wronged.*

A most important feature of Islamic understanding of justice is that it commands justice at all times, even if one is dealing with a person who is near and dear. As God commands in another verse (4:135):

> *You who believe! Be upholders of justice, bearing witness for God alone, even against yourselves or your parents and relatives. Whether they are rich or poor, God is well able to look after them. Do not follow your own desires and deviate from the truth. If you twist or turn away, God is aware of what you do.*

That verse clearly states that to a believer, the wealth or social status of whomever one deals with is of no importance. What is important is fairness—no one should be treated unjustly—and to scrupulously implement the holy verses of God. In another verse (5:8), it is commanded:

You who believe! Show integrity for the sake of God, bearing witness with justice. Do not let hatred for a people incite you into not being just. Be just. That is closer to heedfulness. Heed God. God is aware of what you do.

In that verse, God orders the faithful to act justly always, even with their own enemies. No Muslim can make a spontaneous decision, based on the fact that the person he's dealing with has once harmed him or left him in a difficult situation. Even when he is a personal enemy, if the other side is genuinely in the wrong, any Muslim has the duty to respond with good will and to display the morality God has commanded. To believers, God has issued the following commandment (60:8): "God does not forbid you from being good to those who have not fought you in the religion or driven you from your homes, or from being just towards them. God loves those who are just." Here, He informs Muslims how their relationships with other people should be. These verses are the very foundation of a believer's attitude towards others, formed not by the nature of the people he is dealing with, but by God's revelations in the Qur'an. That is why Muslims with pure hearts always support what is right. Their determination on this matter is revealed in these terms (Qur'an, 7:181): "Among those We have created, there is a community who guide by the Truth and act justly according to it."

Other verses in the Qur'an on the subject of justice read:

God commands you to return to their owners the things you hold on trust and, when you judge between people, to judge with justice. How excellent is what God exhorts you to do! God is All-Hearing, All-Seeing. (4:58)

Say: "My Lord has commanded justice. Stand and face Him in every mosque and call on Him, making your religion sincerely His. As He originated you, so you will return." (7:29)

God commands justice and doing good and giving to relatives. And He forbids indecency and doing wrong and tyranny. He warns you so that hopefully, you will pay heed. (16:90)

All over the world, people are subjected to cruel treatment because of their race, language or skin color. Yet according to the view of justice as set out in the Qur'an, a person's ethnicity, race or gender are of no importance, because Islam maintains that all people are equal. Our Prophet's (may God bless him and grant him peace) words, *"All of you belong to one ancestry of Adam, and Adam was created out of clay,"*14 stress that there is no difference between people. Skin color, social status and wealth confer no superiority on anyone.

According to the Qur'an, one reason why different tribes, peoples, and nations were created is so that they "might come to know one another." All are servants of God and must come to learn one another's different cultures, languages, customs and abilities. One intent behind the existence of different nations and races is cultural wealth, not war and conflict. All true believers know that only godliness —in other words, the fear of God and faith in Him—can impart superiority. As God has revealed in the Qur'an (49:13):

Mankind! We created you from a male and female, and made you into peoples and tribes so that you might come to know each other. The noblest among you in God's sight is that one of you who best performs his duty. God is All-Knowing, All-Aware.

Elsewhere (30:22), He has revealed that:

Among His Signs is the creation of the heavens and earth and the variety of your languages and colours. There are certainly Signs in that for every being.

History offers many examples of the faithful behaving with complete justice towards other peoples, helping Islam grow with unbelievable speed over a wide area, taking in North Africa, the whole Middle East and even the Iberian Peninsula. By means of these conquests, the civility and tolerance of Islamic morality was spread to many races, nations, communities and individuals, bringing together millions in a bond of mutual tolerance, the likes of which had never been seen before. The renowned researcher Joel Augustus Rogers has examined the various races and the relationship between the black race and other countries. In his book *Sex and Race,* he describes Islam's influence on the world in these terms: One reason why Islam was able to survive so brightly for centuries is the almost complete absence in this religion of value-judgements based on race and class, the disregarding of the colour of an individual's skin or his social class and the fact that promotion to the highest levels of a community is based on ability alone... Islam established the greatest and at the same time the freest racial melting-pot in history, and the mixing of these races took place within the body of the most extensive empire the world has ever seen. At the height of its power the Islamic Empire stretched from Spain and central France in the West to India, China and the Pacific Ocean in the East, including Central Asia. The rulers of these extensive territories were of various colours. The colour of peoples' skins was even less important for Muslims than the colours of the flowers in a garden is to the flowers themselves.

Professor Hamilton Alexander Rossken Gibb is one of the world's foremost experts on Islam. In his book *Whither Islam?*, he describes the Islamic view of other races:

No other society has such a record of success uniting in an equality of status, of opportunity, and of endeavors so many and so various races of mankind... Islam has still the power to reconcile apparently irreconcilable elements of race and tradition. If ever the opposition of the great societies of East and West is to be replaced by cooperation, the mediation of Islam is an indispensable condition. Islamic morality aims at a society built on brotherhood and peace, freedom and security.

That is why all communities that come into contact with Islam have given up their oppressive, cruel and aggressive ways and have, instead, built peaceful and civilized societies. In their works, many Western historians have documented Islam's deep and positive affects on communities that came into contact with it. In *The Making of Humanity*, Professor Robert Briffault discusses the relationship between Western society and Islam:

> *The ideas that inspired the French Revolution and the Declaration of Rights, that guided the framing of the American Constitution and inflamed that struggle for independence in the Latin American countries [and elsewhere] were not inventions of the West. They find their ultimate inspiration and source in the Holy Quran.*

These extracts indicate how, down through the centuries, Islamic morality has taught people about peace, tolerance and justice. Nowadays, nearly everyone is seeking just such a model, and there is no reason why such a culture should not come about once again. All that is needed is people's desire to live by the morality of the Qur'an, starting with themselves and later, making efforts to convey it to others. When everyone, from the highest ranks to the very lowest, begins to implement the morality commanded in the Qur'an, they will become just, compassionate, tolerant, full of love, respectful and forgiving. That, in turn, will bring peace to all of society.

Islam Commands The Faithful to be Forgiving, Always

One important sign of compassion is a person's ability to forgive. In Verse 7:199, God calls upon His servants to "make allowances for people, command what is right, and turn away from the ignorant."

Some may find this attitude difficult, but in the sight of God, it will be well rewarded. Those caught up in anger may well refuse to forgive mistakes. But to the faithful, God has revealed that it is better to forgive and, in Verse 26:40, has recommended this morality:

The repayment of a bad action is one equivalent to it. But if someone pardons and puts things right, his reward is with God...

In another verse (26:43), God reveals, "But if someone is steadfast and forgives, that is the most resolute course to follow." Verse 24:22 emphasizes that this is a very superior form of morality:

Those of you possessing affluence and ample wealth should not make oaths that they will not give to their relatives and the very poor and those who have emigrated in the way of God. They should rather pardon and overlook. Would you not love God to forgive you? God is Ever-Forgiving, Most Merciful."

In these words, He encourages the faithful to consider their own positions when it comes to forgiveness. Because everyone wants God to forgive him, to protect and show him mercy, so do we hope that all others will excuse and forgive our mistakes. Therefore, God has commanded the faithful to treat others in the same way they would like to be treated themselves. That important responsibility encourages the faithful to be forgiving towards one another. Our Prophet (may God bless him and grant him peace) encouraged them in these words: *"That person is nearest to God, who pardons, when he has someone in his power, one who would have injured him."*

Believers, knowing that at any moment they may make a mistake, behave tolerantly towards others. Those verses in the Qur'an dealing with repentance make it clear that never making mistakes isn't as important as the determination never to repeat them. One of these verses (4:17) reads:

God accepts only the repentance of those who do evil in ignorance and then quickly repent after doing it. God turns towards such people. God is All-Knowing, All-Wise. Under conditions that reveal an individual's sincerity, the faithful behave forgivingly and compassionately towards one another. If he who has committed error sincerely repents having done so, they cannot judge him for his past deeds. Even when the faithful are totally in the right and the other completely in the wrong, still they have no compunction about forgiveness, because God recommends such behavior as an example of proper morality (3:134):

> *Those who give in times of both ease and hardship, those who control their rage and pardon other people—God loves the good-doers.*

When it comes to forgiving, the faithful don't distinguish between great and small errors, nor do they tailor their view of forgiveness accordingly. Someone may have committed an error inflicting severe harm on others, great financial loss, even loss of life. Yet the faithful know everything happens by the permission of God, as part of His destiny. When it comes to such things, they therefore place themselves in the hands of God and feel no personal anger.

Alternatively, if someone transgresses this Qur'anic rule and exceeds the bounds set by God, only God can judge that person's behavior. It is never up to the faithful to judge—or refuse to forgive—anyone on any matter.

The truly sorry and repentant person will have his reward only in the sight of God. In many verses, God has revealed that apart from "associating partners to Him," He will forgive the errors of the faithful who repent sincerely. Since one man cannot know another's repentance, the faithful simply forgive in the manner God revealed to them. If the Qur'an has anything to say on a particular subject, they treat the person who has committed error in that light.

Islam Commands People To Behave Gently

God has infinite compassion, and is forgiving, protective and gentle toward believers. The Compassionate and Merciful has placed all the blessings in the universe at Man's disposal, supporting him with messengers to reveal the true path. He directs all men to be His sincere servants by means of His revelations, each of which is a guidepost to that path.

Our Lord is the *Halim* (the Clement), *Adl* (Lord of Infinite Justice), *'Afuw* (the Pardoner), *Asim* (the Protector), *Barr* (the Source of All Goodness), *Ghafir* (the Forgiver), *Hafiz* (the Protector), *Karim* (the Generous One), *Latif* (the Subtle One), *Muhsin* (Lord of Infinite

Kindness), *Ra'uf* (the Compassionate), *Salam* (the Author of Safety), *Tawwab* (the Accepter of Repentance) and *Wahhab* (the Bestower).

Believers know that they are under our Lord's protection and are aware of His infinite goodness and kindness. For that reason, they are eager to become the kind of servants that are pleasing to Him, who merit His mercy, and Paradise. As we have seen, one characteristic distinguishing believers is they are full of love and compassion. A Muslim behaves very gently, always treating others kindly. God has offered our Prophet's (may God bless him and grant him peace) gentle nature as an example to all believers (3:159):

It is a mercy from God that you were gentle with them. If you had been rough or hard of heart, they would have scattered from around you. So pardon them and ask forgiveness for them, and consult with them about the matter. Then when you have reached a firm decision, put your trust in God. God loves those who put their trust in Him. That verse describes how our Prophet's (may God bless him and grant him peace) gentle, moral nature exerted a positive influence on people, whereby they grew even more devoted to him.

The Qur'an gives the gentle natures of other loving prophets as role models. One verse (11:87) recounts how, when the Prophet Shuayb (peace be upon him) was sent to the people of Midian, they told him, "... You are clearly the forbearing, the rightly-guided!" The superior morality of the Prophet Abraham (peace be upon him) is another example for everyone. The Qur'an tells us that he was sensitive, gentle and full of love. The verses in question read:

> *Abraham would not have asked forgiveness for his father, but for a promise he made to him, and when it became clear to him that he was an enemy of God, he renounced him. Abraham was tenderhearted and forbearing. (9:114)*
>
> *Abraham was forbearing, compassionate, penitent. (11:75)*
>
> *God has commanded his believers always to behave in a pleasant manner, to speak kindly, and to treat others well. His prophets behaved accordingly. For example, when the Prophet Musa (Moses) (peace be upon him) was about to go to Pharaoh, one*

of the most repressive and cruel rulers of all times, God called on Moses in these terms (20:42-44):

Go, you and your brother, with My Signs, and do not slacken in remembering Me. Go to Pharaoh; he has overstepped the bounds. But speak to him with gentle words so that hopefully, he will be reminded or show some fear.

These verses are an important reminder that everyone has a duty to live by the morality that the Qur'an reveals, and to adopt the morality of the prophets. The Qur'an proposes the following ideals for mankind: Love to all creatures God created; being kind and gentle in the best possible ways; always favoring compromise and tolerance; never speaking harshly, even under the most trying circumstances; making sacrifices happily and willingly; always desiring and seeking the best for others; pushing one's own personal desires to the background; wishing for others exactly what one wishes for oneself; being always quick to offer assistance in cases of need; and rejecting all forms of cruelty. That, no doubt, is exactly the ethical model that mankind is searching for.

Islam Supports Freedom of Belief

In matters of belief, Islam offers people complete freedom, and in the very clearest language. That has been so ever since Islam was first revealed, and forms the basis of today's Islamic morality. The verses on the subject (2:256) are perfectly clear:

There is no compulsion where religion is concerned. Right guidance has become clearly distinct from error. Anyone who rejects false gods and believes in God has grasped the Firmest Handhold, which will never give way. God is All-Hearing, All-Knowing.

According to Islam, people are free to choose whatever beliefs they wish, and nobody can oblige anyone else.

Yes, a Muslim has a duty to communicate Islam and explain the existence of God, to state that the Qur'an is the book of His revelation, that the Prophet Muhammad (may God bless him and grant him peace) was His messenger, to speak of the hereafter and the Day of Judgment and of the beauty of Islamic morality. Yet that duty is restricted to explaining the religion only.

In one verse (16:125), God informs our Prophet (may God bless him and grant him peace) that he is only a messenger:

> *Call to the way of your Lord with wisdom and fair admonition, and argue with them in the kindest way. Your Lord knows best who is misguided from His way. And He knows best who are guided.*

Another verse (18:29) states, "... It is the truth from your Lord; so let whoever wishes believe and whoever wishes disbelieve..." In Verse 26:3, our Lord warns the Prophet (may God bless him and grant him peace), "Perhaps you will destroy yourself with grief because they will not become believers." He also issues His Prophet (may God bless him and grant him peace) this reminder (50:45):

> *We know best what they say. You are not a dictator over them. So remind, with the Qur'an, whoever fears My Threat.*

People are free to choose correctly or wrongly. When Islam—the true path that God has revealed—is explained, they come to believe of their own free will, reaching this decision with no pressure being put on them.

If they make wrong choices, they will face its consequences in the hereafter. On this subject, Verse 10: 99 of the Qur'an contains the clearest command and reminder: "If your Lord had willed, all the people on the earth would have believed. Do you think you can force people to be believers?"

When one of the faithful explains matters, one person might come to believe straightaway, whereas another might adopt a mocking and aggressive attitude. One who follows his conscience might decide to devote his life to pleasing God, even while another, doing as the deniers did, might respond to those same kind words with wickedness. Yet his denial won't lead whoever issued the invitation to suffer or despair. In Verses 12: 103-104, God has stated, "But most people, for all your eagerness, are not believers. You do not ask them for any wage for it. It is only a reminder to all beings."

What's important is that no matter what reaction he meets with, the person who abides by the Qur'an keeps on displaying the kind of morality that is pleasing to God, refuses to make any concessions on it, and leaves matters in God's hands. God has told us that His religion is to be explained in the most pleasing manner. In the words of the Qur'an (29:46):

> *Argue with the People of the Book only in the kindest way—except in the case of those of them who do wrong–saying, "We believe in what has been sent down to us and what was sent down to you. Our God and your God are one and we submit to Him."*

We must not forget that every event, large or small, takes place according to a destiny created by God. He reveals the true path to anyone invited to believe in Him. For that reason, the faithful feel no distress at the behavior of those who reject Him. The Qur'an gives several examples. In Verse 18:6, God tells our Prophet (may God bless him and grant him peace) not to be distressed when those whom he calls on to believe refuse to do so: "Perhaps you may destroy yourself with grief, chasing after them, if they do not believe in these words." Another verse (28:56) reads, "You cannot guide those you would like to, but God guides those He wills. He has best knowledge of the guided."

That means that whatever invitations an individual issues, all his pleasant words, and every detail he goes into can make an effect only by the will of God. A believer's only responsibility is to call people to the Qur'an. He cannot be blamed for atheists' refusal to amend their ways, nor with how they will earn the torments of hell for themselves. In Verse 2:119, our Lord told our Prophet (may God bless him and grant him peace), "We have sent you with the Truth, bringing good news and giving warning. Do not ask about the inhabitants of the Blazing Fire."

God has given mankind both reason and a conscience. His messengers and the divine books revealed to them have shown the true path, and people are responsible for their own choices. Islamic morality can be lived only by a sincere decision to do so—by surrendering oneself to God and listening to one's conscience, which always commands one to do what is right. It is a total violation of Islamic morality to force anyone to believe, because what matters is an individual's surrendering himself to God with all his heart and believing sincerely. If any system obliges people to have faith, then those "converts" will become religious only out of fear. The only acceptable way to live a religion is within an environment that leaves one's conscience completely free. This is what God revealed to our Prophet (may God bless him and grant him peace) (88:21-26):

So remind them! You are only a reminder. You are not in control of them. But as for anyone who turns away and disbelieves, God will punish him with the Greatest Punishment. Certainly it is to Us they will return Then their Reckoning is Our concern.

It's worth emphasizing that Islam leaves people free to make their own choices regarding religion and commands them to respect other religions. Even if someone believes in what the Qur'an describes as superstition, still he can live in peace and security in Muslim lands and freely perform his own religious obligations. In Verses 109:2-6, God commanded our Prophet (may God bless him and grant him peace) to tell those who denied Him:

"I do not worship what you worship, and you do not worship what I worship. Nor will I worship what you worship, nor will you worship what I worship. You have your religion, and I have my religion." Under the morality of Islam, everyone is free to carry out the obligations in accord with his own particular belief. Nobody can prevent any others from performing their particular religious duties, nor can he oblige them to worship in the manner he desires. That violates the morality of Islam, and is unacceptable to God. In the Islamic model of society emerges in which everyone is free to worship and perform the obligations attendant upon his particular chosen beliefs. The Qur'an (22:40) describes monasteries, churches, synagogues, and the places of worship of the Peoples of the Book as all under God's protection:

> *... If God had not driven some people back by means of others, [then] monasteries, churches, synagogues and mosques, where God's name is mentioned much, would have been pulled down and destroyed. God will certainly help those who help Him — God is All-Strong, Almighty.*

Our Prophet's (may God bless him and grant him peace) life is full of such examples. When Christians came to see him pray in his own mosque, he left it for them to use. That kind of tolerance was maintained during the times of the caliphs who succeeded the Prophet (may God bless him and grant him peace). After Damascus was captured, a church that had been turned into a mosque was divided into two, so that Christians might worship in one half and Muslims in the other.

THE ISLAMIC DOCTRINE OF JIHAD

Islam is not a religion of peace. It provides a recipe for perpetual war. It is the only major religion in the world of today that institutionalizes violence against non-Muslims, which it calls jihad (normally translated "holy war," as it is usually used in that context. The literal translation is "struggle" or "strive"). Many verses in the Qur'an exhort Muslims to wage jihad against those who reject Islam, and against Muslims who do not practice Islam to its fullest. An entire sura 8 is called al-Anfal which means "spoils of war." There is no sura called "peace." Only 56 verses in the entire Qur'an mention peace, and most of them occur in the context of the Islamic greeting of "peace be upon you." Others deal with the peace that occurs after a military battle. The most vivid and repeated themes in the Qur'an are on jihad and the punishment of hell.

The Arabic word "jihad" appears in its various forms about thirty-five times in the Qur'an: nine times in the Meccan chapters (suras), and twenty-six times in the Medinan ones. The Arabic word "qatal," means "kill" (it does not mean inner struggle against vices). It appears in its various forms, meaning "kill" or "fight," about one hundred and twenty-three times in the Qur'an: thirty-four times in the Meccan chapters (suras), and eighty-nine times in the Medinan suras. The increase of these words in the Medinan Qur'an reflects the rise of the military power of the prophet of Islam after he immigrated to Medina, though a few uses of these words are not in a military context. In sura 9, al-Tawbah of the Qur'an, thought to be one of last suras given, each of these two words appear ten times in the context of war. In fact, verses al-Tawbah 9: 111 and an-Nisa' 4: 74 each contains three words rooted in the Arabic word "qatal" (meaning to kill): "God has bought of the believers their lives and their possessions, promising them paradise in return, so they fight (from "qatal") in God's cause, and kill (from "qatal"), and are killed (from "qatal")..." (al-Tawbah 9: 111).

In contrast with that, the Holy Bible (KJV) provides 420 verses on the subject of peace. Man strove for peace since ancient times (Isaiah 52: 7). Deep inner peace is the gift of the living God. Man cannot create his own peace. "The peace of God, which surpasses all understanding, will guard your hearts and minds through Christ Jesus" (Philippians 4: 7); "Now may the Lord of peace Himself give you peace always in every way" (2 Thessalonians 3: 16; James 3: 17-18); "There is no peace," says the LORD, "for the wicked" (Isaiah 48: 22; 57: 20-21; 59: 1-4, 7-11; etc).

In fact, the whole of the Qur'an and Islam support jihad in its various forms: jihad with money, with the written and spoken word and with the sword. The verses that do not refer to jihad directly or indirectly marshal the Muslims into a militant fraternity (ummah) on the basis of a common belief system, a common set of rituals, and a common code of conduct. Jihad in any form can be practiced only when there is an organized and disciplined community to practice it. The Qur'an marshals and motivates the ummah to impose Islam on the rest of mankind by every possible means, including the sword.

The purpose of jihad is the islamization of the conquered populations either by pressuring them to convert to Islam, or by forcing them to submit to Islamic rule. The main purpose of jihad is political, not religious. It is an instrument for both the universalization of the Islamic religion, and the establishment of an imperial world state. Islamic jihad must continue until the whole world is under the rule of Islamic law. All the Sunni and Shia Islamic schools of jurisprudence command waging war against unbelievers in order to establish the rule of Islamic law over them. War is the main vehicle of Islamic religious expansion. Without the sword of Muhammad and his followers after him, Islam will not exist today. Over a thousand years of unprecedented military expansion, the Islamic armies invaded vast territories in the Middle East, North Africa and even Europe. Muslim Arabs and Moors had controlled Spanish territory for eight hundred years, Portugal for six hundred years, Greece and Bulgaria for five hundred years,

Romania and Serbia for four hundred years, Sicily for three hundred years, and Hungary for one hundred fifty years.

Authoritative Muslim historians, such as Ahmad ibn Yahya al-Baladhuri (d. 892) and al-Tabari (838-923), attest the fact that Islam was spread by the sword.

Jihad in the Qur'an, Hadith and Sharia

Violent jihad is a central Islamic doctrine. The prophet of Islam repeatedly stressed that there is nothing better and nobler for a Muslim to do than to engage in jihad warfare (Bukhari 1.2.26; Muslim 20.4642). He claimed that engaging in jihad warfare is more meritorious than prayers, fasting, pilgrimage, etc. He warned Muslims who did not participate in jihad warfare of punishment (Abu Dawud 14.2497). He taught that Muslims who fight in jihad would be rewarded with a higher level in the Islamic paradise (an-Nisa' 4: 95; Muslim 20.4645).

Muslims are called upon to proclaim Islam by subduing and conquering non-Muslims, murdering them, destroying their temples, and looting their possessions.

In general, the obligation to participate in violent jihad is a collective one. It becomes a personal imperative one for every Muslim when Muslim lands are invaded by uninvited non-Muslim forces (Reliance of the Traveler, o9.3).

The violent activities of the Muslim zealots are fully supported and encouraged by the Islamic teachings. Muhammad said: "I have been ordered to fight with the people till they say, 'None has the right to be worshipped but Allah ..." (Bukhari 4.52.196; 1.2.25; etc). Jihad is a Muslim religious duty and obligation, like pilgrimage (al-Baqarah 2: 216). Rejecting jihad amounts to rejecting a fundamental Qur'anic dogma. The Qur'an condemns Muslims who refuse to fight in jihad (al-Anfal 8: 20, 47, 49; al-Tawbah 9: 24, 39, 81-82). Some Islamist groups consider Muslims that do not participate in jihad infidels. Those who wage jihad rank highest in Islam.

References to jihad, and killing of infidels who reject Islam and of apostates who leave Islam abound in the Qur'an. It contains about 164 verses that refer to jihad warfare against non-Muslims and distributing the spoils of war. 24% of Medinan Qur'an is devoted to jihad.

"Fight against such of those to whom the Scriptures were given (Christians and Jews) as believe in neither god (the god of Islam) nor the last day, who do not forbid what god and his apostle (Muhammad) have forbidden, and do not embrace the true faith (Islam), until they pay tribute out of hand and are utterly subdued" (al-Tawbah 9: 29)

"When the forbidden months are past, then fight and slay the Pagans wherever you find them, and seize them, beleaguer them, and lie in wait for them in every stratagem; but if they repent, and establish regular prayers and practice regular charity, then open the way for them: for Allah is Oft-Forgiving, Most Merciful" (al-Tawbah 9: 5, 12, 14, 19, 20, 29, 36, 38, 39, 41, 73, 81, 86, 88, 111, 123; al-Baqarah 2: 190, 193, 216, 244; Al-Imran 3: 169; an-Nisa' 4: 47, 74, 76, 77, 84, 89, 95; al-Ma'idah 5: 33, 51; al-Anfal 8: 12-17, 39, 59-60, 65, 67, 74; al-Anbiya' 21: 44; Muhammad 47: 4-6, 35; al-Fath 48: 16; al-Hujurat 49: 15; al-Mumtahanah 60: 1, 11; as-Saff 61: 4; at-Tahrim 66: 9; etc).

The Qur'an urges Muslims to kill, even those willing to surrender (al-Anfal 8: 67). The Qur'an claims that Islam is superior to all other religions (Al-Imran 3: 85; al-Tawbah 9: 33; al-Fath 48: 28; as-Saff 61: 9; etc). The jihad warfare commands for waging offensive, aggressive and unjust wars to Islamize all the non-Muslim populations are open-ended, perpetual, global, and generic in nature. That is what motivates Islamists to terrorize and kill non-Muslims following the example of Muhammad, the architect of Islam.

To read such blood thirsty injunctions in the Qur'an, the holiest book of Islam, is shocking. It grants Muslim jihadis a license to kill in the name of the Islamic god in the Islamic jihad. Extreme hatred and bloody violence against the non-believers are built into the religion of Islam. It is a historical fact that, with the exception of some Indonesian islands, no nation has ever willingly converted to Islam. On the other hand, no nation has ever unwillingly been converted to Christianity in the first three centuries of the Christian era.

In addition, the Hadith collections of Sahih al-Bukhari and Sahih Muslim include hundreds of references to jihad warfare. A sampling of the Islamic teaching on violence is provided herein from the Hadith of Sahih al-Bukhari which is second in authority only to the Qur'an in Sunni Islam. It contains about 199 references to jihad in the sense of armed warfare against non-Muslims. Muhammad, the prophet of Islam, said:

"The example of a Mujahid in Allah's Cause— and Allah knows better who really strives in His Cause——is like a person who fasts and prays continuously. Allah guarantees that He will admit the Mujahid in His Cause into Paradise if he is killed, otherwise He will return him to his home safely with rewards and war booty" (Bukhari 4.52.46; 1.2.35);

"Nobody who dies and finds good from Allah (in the Hereafter) would wish to come back to this world even if he were given the whole world and whatever is in it, except the martyr who, on seeing the superiority of martyrdom, would like to come back to the world and get killed again (in Allah's Cause)" (Bukhari 4.52.53);

"There is no migration (after the Conquest of Mecca), but Jihad and good intentions, and when you are called for Jihad, you should immediately respond to the call" (Bukhari 4.52.42; etc).

All the four principal Sunni schools of jurisprudence, the Maliki, Hanbali, Hanafi, and Shafi'i, agree on the importance of jihad. Prominent Islamic scholars of antiquity from each of the four major schools of jurisprudence in historical Islam clearly understood the Qur'anic injunctions of jihad to command holy war. This includes al-Tabari (838-923), al-Biadawi (d. 1286), Ibn Khaldun (1332-1406), Ibn Kathir (1301-1373), Ibn Taymiyya (1263-1328), al-Ghazzali (1058-1111) who was a peaceful Sufi, etc.

Reliance of the Traveler (Undat al-Salik), the Shafi'i manual of Islamic law, devotes three sections o9, o10, o11 (eleven pages) to jihad. Making war on unbelievers is one of the responsibilities of the Muslim nation. The Islamic umma (nation) must exist in a state of perpetual war, interrupted only by temporary truces, with the non-Muslim world in order to compel either conversion to Islam, or subjugation to its rulers. When the Islamist regime is militarily weak, it reaches out for truce and peace simply in order to buy time to build up its strength (Muhammad 47: 35). Those that reject the invitation to convert to Islam are required to pay the poll tax (jizya) in humiliation and subjugation in their homelands. Should they refuse, war is to be declared against them (Muslim 19.4294; etc). In addition, Shia Islam calls for the necessity of jihad. Islam lacks any doctrine of equal coexistence. Islam lacks any doctrine of coexistence with non-Muslims in equality. In fact, peaceful coexistence as equals in a pluralistic society is not an option in Islam.

Islam divides humanity into two classes: a superior class of Muslims (Al-'Imran 3: 110; at-Tawbah 9: 33), and an inferior class of non-Muslims (infidels). There are more than four hundred verses in the Qur'an that describe the torment of hell that the god of Islam has prepared for the infidel. There are approximately seven hundred verses in more than fifty Qur'anic suras that have explicit negative references to the Jews (an-Nisa' 4: 47; al-Ma'idah 5: 13; etc.). The Qur'an dehumanizes and demonizes the non-Muslim infidels and calls them "... the vilest of animals ..." (al-Anfal 8: 55; al-A'raf 7: 179), and the vilest of all creatures (al-Bayyinah 98: 6; al-Mujadilah 58: 20). It claims that Jews were transformed into apes (al-Baqarah 2: 65 and al-A'raf 7: 166), and Jews and Christians into swine (al-Ma'idah 5: 59-60)? It likens Jews to asses (al-Jum'ah 62: 5). It tells Muslims that Jews are cursed because of their unbelief (al-Ma'idah 5: 78). Muhammad claimed that Muslims will eventually exterminate the Jews in a global holocaust. "Allah's Apostle said, The Hour will not be established until you fight with the Jews, and the stone behind which a Jew will be hiding will say, O Muslim! There is a Jew hiding behind me, so kill him" (Bukhari 4.52.177; Muslim 41.6981-5).

The Qur'an goes as far as commanding Muslims to eschew friendships with infidels, including Christians and Jews (Al-'Imran 3: 28, 118; an-Nisa' 4: 89, 101, 144; al-Ma'idah 5: 51, 82), even if they be their fathers, sons, brothers, or kin (al-Tawbah 9: 23; al-Mujadalah 58: 22). Abu Obaida, son of Garah, who was praised by the prophet of Islam, killed his own father who refused Islam. Musaab, son of Omair, never listened for his mother's cries for help and left her to die because she rejected Islam. Abu Bakr, the first guided caliph, told his father he would kill him if he refused Islam.

Traditional orthodox Islam promises the jihadist that if he dies fighting for the god of Muhammad in Islamic jihad, he is guaranteed to be rewarded with the sinful Islamic paradise of sexual promiscuity and gluttony (as-Saff 61: 10-13; ad-Dukhan 44: 51-56; at-Tur 52: 17-29; ar-Rahman 55: 46-78; al-Tawbah 9: 111; Al-Imran 3: 157-8, 169; an-Nisa' 4: 74; al-Fatir 35: 50; Muhammad 47: 6; etc). Muhammad said: "Know that Paradise is under the shades of swords" (Bukhari 4.52.73, 72, 46, 48, 53; 4.53.386). Muhammad promised these fictitious rewards, which are merely a desert mirage, in order to motivate his fighters. Unable to give them a reason to live, he gave them a reason to die.

On the other hand, should the jihadist survive and live, he gets a share from the spoils of war, which enriches him (al-Anfal 8: 41, 60). In addition, he obtains forgiveness of his sins (as-Saff 61: 11-12), and the love of the Islamic god (an-Nisa' 4: 95; al-Anfal 8: 16). According to orthodox Islamic belief, martyrdom in Islamic jihad is the only sure way a Muslim could take to avoid the horrifying torments of the grave and hell, and to get into the Islamic paradise. In fact, when a Muslim dies in jihad, his corpse is not washed or dressed in clean clothes. It goes in his coffin just as he died. The stains of blood on it are a witness for him before the Islamic god. It is a sign of honor that would prompt the angels to treat him in a special distinguished way.

The Example of the Prophet of Islam

The history of Islam to-date has been one long jihad (holy war) against non-Muslims. Muslims are exhorted to emulate Muhammad's pattern of behavior (al-Ahzab 33: 21). In the ten years that he lived in Medina (622-632 AD), Muhammad, the prophet of Islam, was the aggressor in seventy-three of seventy-five raids and conflicts he got involved in. He initiated seventy-three raids, military expeditions, full-scale military campaigns, and small assassination hit bands to kill his opponents. This adds up to more than seven slayings, raids or battles for each of the ten years he ruled in Medina in the beginning of the Islamic era. There is a lot of blood on his hands. He did not personally participate in forty-eight of those raids. He personally accompanied his Muslim fighters in twenty-seven raids. In eight of them, he was in the battlefield fighting alongside with them. Muhammad used to order his followers and commanders to kill those who disbelieved in his god, not making any distinction between combatants, and civilians.

The prophet of Islam financed his military expeditions through a variety of avenues. His economic lifeblood was the plunder usurped from defeated enemies, and the jizya tax levied on unbelievers.

The majority of the Arabs who adopted Islam and fought in the military battles of jihad did so in order to acquire booty usurped from the conquered tribes and peoples who did not submit to Islam.

The Muslim fighters have been motivated mainly by their greed for the booty of wealth and women (al-Fath 48: 19-20). Four-fifths of the booty went to them, and one-fifth to Muhammad, or to the caliph after him (al-Anfal 8: 41). That was how the god of Islam made Muhammad and his followers wealthy (ad-Duha 93: 8; al-Tawbah 9: 74; Bukhari 3.37.495). Muhammad distributed his share of the booty as he wished to close relatives, orphans, the needy, travelers, and new converts to Islam to coax them to stay in Islam (al-Tawbah 9: 60; Bukhari 4.53.373; 4.55.558; Muslim 5.2313).

Sura 8 is titled "al-Anfal," which means "the spoils of war." The entire book no. 53 of Bukhari is called "One-fifth of Booty to the Cause of Allah (Khumus)." The battle plunder included captive women and children who were sold as slaves for profit. Slave trading flourished in Arabia in the early Islamic era. The Qur'an describes the loot as "...lawful and good...," and supports pillaging and plundering infidels, enslaving their children, and placing their women in concubinage (al-Anfal 8: 69; an-Nisa' 4: 24; etc). In fact, the first Islamic raid on the peaceful Meccan merchant caravan at Nakhlah was to loot and rob the caravan. This is what motivates bandits and pirates.

The Rules of Jihad

Based on Islamic jurisprudence derived from the Qur'an, the Hadith, and classical Islamic legal opinions, the principal rules of Jihad are summarized herein. These rules are immoral and exploitative:

1. Muslims may enslave women and children of the conquered non-Muslim populations (Reliance of the Traveler, #o9.13). Islam codifies slavery in its religious law (Sharia). Selling humans into slavery produced a lot of wealth for Muhammad and his followers. Slaying women and children is prohibited, not for mercy, but for profit. However, if a Muslim slays them, he is not censured.
2. The marriages of those women are annulled upon their capture. They may be forced to marry their Muslim masters and added to their harim (an-Nisa' 4: 24).
3. Worse off, Muslim jihadists are allowed to rape the captured female prisoners of war. Ali, Muhammad's cousin and son-in-law, did this abomination, and Muhammad defended him (Bukhari 5.59.637). Islam codifies and legalizes rape for conquering jihadist Muslim men (Muslim 8.3371, 3373-7, 3432). Islam is the only religion in the world that condones and encourages the crime of raping female captives of war as a reward to victorious Muslim soldiers for conquering the infidels.
4. Muslim jihadists are allowed to kill old men and Christian monks (Reliance of the Traveler, #o9.10), and women and children in night raids (Bukhari 4.52.256; Muslim 19.4321-4323).
5. The non-Muslim prisoners of war may be killed, enslaved, ransomed (exchanged for money or a Muslim captive), or released (al-Ahzab 33: 26; Muhammad 47: 4; Reliance of the Traveler, #o9.14).
6. Pagan Arabs were pressured to convert to Islam on pain of death. Enemy men who converted to Islam were allowed to keep their property and children (al-Tawbah 9: 5, 11, 14, 33; Bukhari 4.52.263).

7. The Muslim jihadist invaders may confiscate or destroy non-Muslim civilian property, including homes and groves (al-Ahzab 33: 27; al-Hashr 59: 5, 2; Bukhari 4.52.262, 263; Muslim 19.4324).
8. A Muslim jihadist who kills a non-Muslim in jihad gets his belongings. This is called personal booty. In addition, he gets his share from the four-fifths of the collective spoils of the battle.
9. The Muslim jihadist invaders give the people of the Book (Jews and Christians) three options (al-Tawbah 9: 29) either to convert to Islam, to keep their faith and pay the submission tax of jizya (poll tax) while living under Islamic rule, or to get killed fighting if they refused the first two options. However, Muslims can mount surprise attacks on the infidels, slay them and usurp their property. This is not censured because the victims are not Muslims, and they are not protected in the Islamic state.

Although Islam permits Jews and Christians to remain in their faiths as dhimmis under Islamic rule (second class citizens in their homelands), from the dawn of Islamic history till the present, forced conversions are widely practiced in the Islamic world. This is because Islamic teachings scorn non-Muslim infidels who are, according to Islamic culture, bound to the Islamic hell. Battle, animosity and hatred directed towards the non-Muslim infidels are part of Islamic mindset.

The Dhimma

The concept of the dhimma was first introduced by the prophet of Islam. After conquering the Jews of the oasis of Khaybar in 628, he agreed to let them continue to cultivate their oasis only if they gave him half their produce. He reserved the right to cancel out this treaty and expel the Jews whenever he liked (Bukhari 4.53.380). This type of treaty is called a "dhimma."

Peoples that came under Islamic rule and agreed to pay tribute (jizya) in return for Muslim protection are referred to as "dhimmis." They were ultimately reduced to the status of a tiny culturally derivative marginalized minority in their homelands. The only peoples that escaped Islamic dhimmitude were those who were successful in resisting and eventually, after centuries of armed struggle, defeating Islamic imperialistic jihad: the Christians of Europe and the Hindus of India.

The dhimmis (Jews, Christians, etc. under Islamic rule) were not equal to Muslims in dignity and rights. They lived in subjugation to Islamic rule. The terms of the dhimma were first articulated by the second guided caliph, Umar ibn al-Khattab (634-644). The dhimma was an agreement imposed on conquered populations.

It required them not to build churches, monasteries, and synagogues, nor restore them. It also required them to wear clothes different from those worn by Muslims, not to acquire weapons, not to ride horses, to refrain from using church bells and from erecting crosses on top of the churches, not to proselytize Muslims, to pay the poll tax (jizya), etc.

The jizya indicated the dhimmis submission and inferiority to Islamic rule (at-Tawbah 9: 29). It led to the overall humiliation and abasement of non-Muslims. Payment of the jizya often took place in a demeaning ceremony to ensure the belittlement and humiliation of the dhimmi.

The Muslim tax-collector slapped the Christian man on the back of his neck or on his head telling him: 'O unbeliever, pay al-jizya.' This was followed by the Christian man handing him the tax money with his head bowed down and his back bent while the tax-collector held him by the beard.

The dhimmi was not allowed to marry a Muslim woman. The penalty for such marriage was death. The dhimmi was barred from public office. The history of Muslim dealings with the dhimmis is one of oppression, random massacres, avaricious greed and plunder, extortion under the threat of persecution, rape, systematic degradation and slavery.

According the Shafi'i school of Islamic Sharia, the dhimma pact is broken if the dhimmi fights the Muslims, refuses to pay the jizya, or disobeys Muslim laws. It is also broken if the dhimmi violates the dhimma's additional stipulations, if any, by having relation with a Muslim woman, leading a Muslim away from Islam, killing a Muslim, or slandering Muhammad and his god. When the dhimma is broken, the rules of the prisoners of war will apply on the dhimmi subjecting him to either death, slavery, ransoming, or release.

By denying basic human rights to non-Muslims in Islamic controlled lands, Islam has sanctioned slavery on an unprecedented scale. Jihad slavery in its various forms (slave soldiers, harem slavery, child slavery, etc.) became a powerful tool to both expansive islamization and the support of Muslim society.

The dhimma terms and requirements are codified in Islamic Sharia (Reliance of the Traveler, #o11). Under Western pressure on the weakened Ottoman Empire, the dhimmis were emancipated in the mid-nineteenth century.

Although Islamic Sharia is enforced at this time only in a few countries, such as Saudi Arabia, Iran, and the Sudan, many of its elements are practiced in Islamic countries.

It is surprising indeed that the dhimmi communities have survived at all despite the Islamic pressures on them throughout centuries of Islamic rule.

ISLAMIC MILITANT MOVEMENTS BETWEEN TRADITION AND MODERNITY

The Arab world is in turmoil. In most parts of the transcontinental land that extends from Casablanca to Baghdad, internal conflict has become the norm and uneasy stability is the exception. The growing cult of Islamic militancy in the Arab world owes much more to socio-political than to religious factors. The major causes of Islam being articulated as answer to the prevailing ills of the Arab polities are basically two:

1) The failure of the Arab political elites to evolve responsive political systems to take the place of traditional ones which no longer exist; and
2) The humiliating defeat of the Arabs in the Arab-Israeli Six-Day War of June 1967 causing reverberations not only in the Middle East but the wider Muslim world.

Islamic Theory

In traditional Islamic political theory the state rested on three pillars: the *Ummah* (the community of Muslim believers), the Caliphate, and the *Shariah* (Islamic Law). Except perhaps in the early decades of Islam, this theory, however, did not always conform to what happened in real life.

The *Ummah* embodied an ideal which could not be realised in full even in the early period of Islam. As long as Islam was confined to the Arabian Peninsula, the *Ummah* was a homogeneous community held together by the bonds of Islam. But once Islam spread into the non-Arab territories to the north, the dichotomy between the Arab and non-Arab Muslims arose.

The Arabs found it difficult to accept the non-Arabs as full members of the *Ummah* and gave them the unflattering title of *mawla* (client). The Persians accepted Islam but refused to be reconciled to Arab supremacy and led the revolt against the first Arab-Islamic dynasty headed by the Umayyads. The Abbasids, who succeeded the Umayyads, were accommodative to non-Arab Muslims.

From the tenth century onward, regional pressures reinforced by ethnic self-assertion splintered the Islamic empire and it was progressively displaced by feuding kingdoms across the massive arc stretching from the plains of central Asia to the Atlantic coast of Africa.

In the 16th century, the Ottomans did succeed in bringing large chunks of the Arab world under the umbrella of the Turkish empire but remained at loggerheads with the Shiite rulers of Iran, called the Safavids. Towards the end of the 19th century, the Arabs were stirred by sentiments of modern nationalism and took full advantage of the opportunities offered by the First World War to break loose from the Ottoman hegemony. The 20th century has witnessed Iran and Turkey emerge as independent states, and a fragmented Arab world into 20 odd nation-states. The *Ummah* had thus ceased to be a fact of political life long before the advent of the present day nation-states. The institution of Caliphate emerged out of a practical necessity in the aftermath of Prophet Muhammad's death. His closest companion Abu Bakr al-Siddiq was chosen to head the *Ummah*, and he assumed the modest title of *Khalifah* ("caliph" being its Western corruption) or deputy. But within the span of a few decades the caliphate degenerated into an absolute hereditary monarchy.

Islamic political theorists supplied the necessary religious underpinnings for the institution to suit its changing requirements. It was generally held that the caliph must be from Quraish (the Prophet's clan); he was the defender of the faith and the political leader of the *Ummah*. All Muslims were obliged to proclaim allegiance to him.

The principle of hereditary succession also found general acceptance. In later centuries, power slipped from the hands of the caliph but the caliphate lingered on as a notional institution. Kings and sultans of the Muslim world found it expedient to seek the caliph's formal recognition in return for offerings of salutations and gifts.

The *Shi'ah*, of course, did not recognise the caliphs and looked to their own *imams* for political leadership and spiritual guidance. The late Ottomans staked their claim to caliphate, if only to beef up their bargaining power *vis-à-vis* the European states. But when the empire disintegrated after the First World War, the new Turkish leaders, aspiring to build a modern republican state, abolished the caliphate in 1924.

Since then, there has been no serious proposal from any quarter to revive this supra-national politico-religious institution. Even the Islamic Conference Organisation (ICO), which pays lip-service to Islamic solidarity, takes ground realities into consideration to exclude political unification of the Muslim world from its proclaimed agenda.

In the field of *Shariah*, too, the Arab societies have traversed a long way from the early beginnings when the divine law, derived mainly from the *Qur'an* and the *Sunnah* (sayings of the Prophet), governed all aspects of life. In classical argument, the institution of caliphate itself was justified in terms of the need for a central authority to enforce the *Shariah*. Ironically enough, it was under the late Ottoman caliphate that the application of *Shariah* was progressively circumscribed. Beginning in the mid-19th century, the Ottoman sultans launched legal reforms, supplanting the *Shariah* from the penal and commercial fields, under the grand project of "*tanzimat*", or "putting things in order." The project also stipulated creation of "*nizamiyah*" (secular) courts to adjudicate the man-made penal and commercial laws.

The 1917 Ottoman Law of Family Rights made inroads into the hitherto forbidden territory of Muslim personal law by introducing administrative regulations governing divorce and relief to deserted wives. Violation of these regulations was punishable under the secular criminal law.

Most of the Arab countries, stretching from Iraq to Morocco, effected further reforms in the Muslim personal law besides endorsing the general principle of sovereignty of legislatures to enact laws for all aspects of life.

It can thus be said that in most of the Arab countries today the *Shariah* applies only to limited segments of life involving marriage, divorce and inheritance. There are, however, two sets of exceptions to this rule. At one end of the spectrum stand Saudi Arabia and the smaller states of the Arabian Peninsula which enforce, with varying intensity, the Islamic penal codes. Iran, too, falls into this category.

At the other extreme is Turkey which, in the wake of the Kemalist revolution of the early 1920s, adopted a militant secularist stance. It proclaimed modern secular laws for all areas of life including marriage and divorce. It is seldom realised that outside the "communist" fold Turkey is the only Asian nation to opt for full-scale secularisation of social and political life in a strictly modern sense of the term. And it has stayed that way since the days of Mustapha Kemal Atatürk, notwithstanding recurrent clamour by the Islamists for a return to the good old days of the *Shariah*.

It follows from the above that the concept of *ummah* and the institution of caliphate had either become dysfunctional or changed beyond recognition long before the advent of western influence in the region. It was only in the field of *Shariah* that increasing contacts with Europe and modernisation of social and economic life contributed to its shrinking influence.

ALTERNATIVE ORDER

While Arab modernising political elites can justly claim credit for managing the transition to certain areas with reasonable efficacy, they cannot escape blame for their failure to provide a credible alternative to the traditional system of government. This does not mean that no effort was made in this direction.

On the intellectual level, a whole generation of thinkers from Abdel-Rahman al-Kawakibi to Ahmad Lutfi as-Sayyid, Ali Abdel-Raziq and Taha Hussein, joined the quest, in the late 19th and the early part of this century, for an alternative order based on reason and rule of law.

The Syrian-born Abdel-Rahman al-Kawakibi argued that despotism had been the bane of Muslim polities through the ages; that the just state, in which men could find fulfilment, was one in which the individual was free and freely served the community; and that the government should be controlled by the people and act as a watchdog to ensure that freedom. Ahmad Lutfi as-Sayyid, for his part, made the case that good government is one that springs from the will of the people. All other forms end up in tyranny.

The case for an out and out secular order was, however, made by Sheikh Ali Abdel-Raziq in his book *al-Islam wa Usul al-Hukm* (*Islam and the Basis of Political Authority*, 1925). A product of al-Azhar and Oxford, Abdel-Raziq used his theological scholarship and analytical skill to advance the thesis that the entire theory of caliphate (the kingpin of Islamic political thought) had no basis in the *Qur'an* and the *Sunnah* and that the practice of the caliphate was often at variance with its theory. Abdel-Raziq's book aroused a storm of protest. But the works of Dr Taha Hussein (also an alumnus of al-Azhar) were greeted with much less hostility. For Taha Hussein approached his subject from a pragmatic rather than theological angle. In his *Future of Culture in Egypt*, he argued that the dichotomy between religious dogma and everyday secular practice is an inescapable part of life.

Early Arabs, he reasoned, had no inhibitions about borrowing extensively from Greek and Persian civilisations and they gained a great deal in the bargain. Hence, contemporary Arabs need not be averse to borrowing from the Western civilisation.

On a practical footing, the quest for alternative basis of polity found expression in eclectic approach.

It favoured liberal borrowings from Western constitutional forms and adapting them to local needs and circumstances. In quick succession, Iran, Iraq, Syria, Lebanon and Egypt adopted constitutions patterned after the British, French or Belgian models. This stupendous experiment in constitutionalism, however, did not carry much credibility as it was generally devoid of democratic content.

In the 1950s, most of these edifices collapsed like houses of cards. A succession of *coups d'etat* and civil disorders made the whole region reverberate with the sound of crashing thrones. Egypt and Iraq turned into republics and the soaring spirit of republicanism rattled the remaining monarchies in the region.

Then came the era of charismatic leaders espousing heady ideologies of pan-Arabism, socialism and redressal of the unequal relationship with the West. Even the Shah of Iran donned the mantle of a modernising monarch heralding his "white revolution". In most cases, where some form of constitutional structures existed, the single party system of political mobilisation was introduced. But this was mostly used as a facade behind which dictatorial rule thrived. The press and other media were firmly controlled.

The system allowed no possibility of free debate on public priorities or policies. Even the Shah of Iran felt tempted to emulate the undemocratic devices designed by the radical republics in the region which he otherwise abhorred. As for the paternalistic kingdoms and emirates of the Arabian Peninsula, the rate of their social and economic transformation in the wake of the oil boom of the 1970s has been mind-boggling. Literacy advanced in rapid strides and the benefits of housing, health and general economic welfare were extended to all sections of these sparsely populated oil-exporting countries. But there was no corresponding change in the political arena. Political power still vests in kings and sheikhs amidst growing popular clamour for accountability and rule of law.

Divisions and Disjunctions

If the absence of credible political systems responsive to popular expectations has driven the people to protest under the banner of Islam, the failure of the ruling elites to hold their own against an expansionist Israel or to contain super-power pressures on the region gave a militant edge to the call of *Jihad* against the internal and external foes of Islam.

The Islamic militants, commonly called "fundamentalists" because of their strident call for a return to the fundamental tenets of Islam, view the defeat of Arab armies at the hands of the Zionist state in a series of wars, beginning in 1947, and the loss of entire Palestine to Israel in the process, as a catastrophe for the Arab and Islamic peoples.

The fundamentalists no doubt blame the Zionist and their Western backers, in particular the United States, for this calamity; but they blame their own rulers even more.

They ascribe the Arab-Islamic defeat to the alienation of the ruling classes from Islam, their worship of the false idols of nationalism (local as well as pan-Arab) and their addiction to foreign ideologies such as socialism, communism or capitalism. The same malaise, they argue, accounts for the apathy and inaction of the present rulers in face of the ongoing tragedy in Bosnia and Herzegovina.

Exacerbating the grievous injury to the Arab sense of dignity and honour caused by defeat is the relentless pressures on and manipulations of the region by the industrialised West which not only accounts for close to two-thirds of the world's proven oil reserves but also serves as a lucrative market, thanks to the oil boom of the 1970s, for their consumer products and weapons. The Islamists see in this a replay of the medieval crusades.

It is, however, necessary to point out that the fundamentalists in the Arab world are not a monolithic entity nor is their upsurge irreversible.

The fundamentalist camp, although clamouring for Islamic solidarity, suffers from inner divisions and disjunctions. Saudi Arabia, for example, has long been the home of what might be called *controlled fundamentalism*. The Saudi royalty took shelter behind Islam to deny its own people a constitution. And to gain respectability for their archaic domestic set-up, the Saudi rulers created the *Rabitat al-Alam al-Islami* (World Islamic League) to mobilise goodwill of Muslim *'ulama'* from all over the world through an elaborate system of patronage.

With a substantial spurt in oil royalties in the 1970s, Saudi Arabia sponsored the Islamic Conference Organisation as a handy platform to demonstrate its Islamic credentials. It is hardly surprising that the United States found Saudi Arabia's championship of Islam as a convenient weapon to beat the Arab radicals with, and look benignly on it.

In the wake of the Suez War, which spelled disaster for Britain as a custodian of Western interests in the Middle East, US president Dwight Eisenhower seriously toyed with the idea of promoting king Saud as the "pope" of Islam. But the project failed to take off.

For some time now, Saudi Arabia is having second thoughts about the efficacy of its own brand of Islam as an instrument of its foreign policy. It all started with the Iranian clergy mounting a rebellion against the Shah and eventually seizing political power. In 1979, the Pahlavi monarchy of Iran was replaced by an Islamic republic with Ayatollah Khomeini as its "Supreme Guide". The cause of Saudi Arabia's discomfiture lay in the fact that whereas Riyadh had always invoked Islam to uphold political *status quo,* Iran's new rulers presented Islam in a revolutionary attire seeking to topple despotic kings, ushering in an egalitarian social and economic order, and fighting foreign dominance in the region.

The Saudis were indeed scared when, in 1979, a bunch of home-grown fundamentalists occupied the Holy Mosque of Mecca in an undisguised attempt to overthrow the monarchy, ironically, in the name of Islam.

In Iran, too, in the past 16 years since Ayatollah Khomeini returned to Iran from his long exile, public zeal for the Islamic revolution has steadily diminished. Khomeini strongly believed in the unquestioned power and efficacy of Islam to establish and sustain a just social and political order. He encouraged export of the Iranian revolution to other parts of the Islamic world and envisaged eventual triumph of Islam the world over. He came to be identified with what may be called *messianic fundamentalism.*

Khomeini, however, glossed over one basic fact about the Islamic revolution: it was made possible by the active support and sacrifices of a good section of the educated youth and the merchant class who would loathe to see Iran converted into an obscurantist theocracy. As it happened, the clergy squeezed their non-clerical partners out of the newly created governing institutions and eventually suppressed them.

The eight-year-long Iran-Iraq war, which was patently senseless for both sides, scotched all hopes of a just and humane order taking shape in Iran. In the end, Khomeini was compelled by his closest advisers to swallow his pride and call for a cease-fire. The post-Khomeini Iran is surely, though haltingly, moving towards a rational and pragmatic approach to the moulding of Iran's domestic and foreign policies. Dr Qassem Ihsanzadeh, an outspoken member of the Iranian parliament recently observed: "We must decide whether we want a parliamentary system or an Islamic government-the two are incompatible." Predictably, he was shouted down by the Islamists but not before he made it quite clear that there were many more who shared his views but would not utter them publicly.

President Ali Hashimi Rafsanjani, for his part, knows that he cannot bring the fruits of revolution to the restive people of Iran without the inputs of science and technology and modern managerial skills. He is, therefore, keen to loosen the stranglehold of clergy on the system so that Iranian technocrats who fled the country in the wake of the revolution can return and a new generation of technocrats could be trained at home. Rafsanjani admittedly sees no contradiction between modernity and Islam and he speaks of the need for close co-operation between Iran, India and China so that they can have a say in post-cold war world politics. All this is a far cry from the heady days of February 1979 when Ayatollah Khomeini had unfurled the flag of Islamic revolution.

Hence the real breeding grounds of militant Islam and Islamic fundamentalism today are not in Iran or Saudi Arabia or the mini-states of the Gulf. On the contrary, these states are either apprehensive of Islamic militancy or, as in the case of Iran, having second thoughts about its efficacy as an instrument of public policy. Islamic militancy is, however, rampant in the more populous Arab countries of Egypt, Algeria and the Sudan.

All three have certain features in common: population explosion, soaring unemployment and varying degrees of repression of political dissent. And this has given rise to Islamic protest movements which can be generally designated as *retributive fundamentalism*.

The political stalemate in Egypt during the 1940s, resulting from the triangular conflict between the British, the king and the mass-based *Wafd* Party, and public disenchantment with the politicians in the wake of Egyptian defeat in the first Arab-Israeli War of 1947-48, swelled the ranks of *al-Ikhwan al-Muslimun* (Muslim Brothers), founded by Hassan al-Banna in 1929. The *Ikhwan* preached that the redemption of Egypt (and of the Islamic world) lay neither in reform nor in reinterpretation of the Islamic doctrine but in its full-scale resurrection.

They declared that the real issue was not Islam's inadequacy to meet the challenges of modern times but that Islam was never given a chance to prove its efficacy, and that the *Qur'an* and the *Sunnah* provide essentials of a just political order and a universal brotherhood of men. Above all, the *Ikhwan* claimed that the fault lay not in Islam but in its internal and external enemies: the West strangled it politically and economically from the outside and the westernised Muslims undermined it from within.

On the eve of the revolution of July 1952, which toppled the monarchy and put General Muhammad Naguib and Colonel Jamal Abdel-Nasser into power, the *Ikhwan* claimed a million followers in Egypt alone. Two years later the *Ikhwan* faced a showdown with the military regime and lost. For a while, Nasser's Egypt offered a future of hope to its teeming millions. Pursuit of the ideals of socialism, unification of the Arab world into a single polity, and an independent role in world affairs enthused the whole Arab world. But the defeat of Egypt in the June 1967 war turned that dream into a nightmare. Nasser's image as saviour of the Arabs was shattered and he died soon after. That was the time when the Islamists regrouped and mounted a frontal assault taking advantage of Egypt's mounting economic problems, the occupation of Sinai by Israel and the vacillations and waywardness of Anwar al-Sadat who succeeded Nasser.

Al-Sadat's compromise agreement with Israel over Sinai was seen by the Islamists as a betrayal of Egypt and Islam and as a justification to take up arms against the regime.

The turmoil gave birth to several militant groups, collectively know as *al-Jama'at al-Islamiyyah* (Islamic Groups). Currently the intensity of their violence and the virulence of their propaganda make the old *Ikhwan* look like a moderate outfit.

One such group, called *al-Jihad al-Islami*, plotted the assassination of president Anwar al-Sadat in October 1981. Amongst their principal targets are top members of the Coptic Christians, who make up over 15 per cent of Egypt's population, and foreign tourists. The most visible protagonist of the movement is a 55-year-old sightless Dr Omar Abdel-Rahman, now under detention in the United States for his alleged involvement in the car-bomb attack on the World Trade Centre at New York, in February 1993, that killed six people and injured many more.

In Algeria, the monopoly on power enjoyed by the National Liberation Front (FLN) and its failure to find credible solutions to the nation's economic problems, notwithstanding its substantial oil and gas reserves, have thrown up an Islamic backlash. Opponents of the FLN rallied under the banner of Islam not because Islam had ready-made answers to Algeria's political and economic woes but because the ruling group permitted no secular platform to exist outside its own regimented ranks.

In the early 1980s, the Algerian government launched an austerity programme to grapple with rising unemployment. But the crisis aggravated and in October 1988 widespread anti-government riots occurred.

The government then belatedly revised the constitution to permit a multi-party system. Restrictions on the press were relaxed. Among the various political parties that emerged, the most articulate was the Islamic Salvation Front (FIS), headed by Abbas Madani. It benefited greatly from Madani's previous record of opposing the FLN and gained further popularity through impressive relief operations organised in the wake of the 1989 earthquake.

Not surprisingly, therefore, the Islamic Salvation Front won 67 per cent of the provinces and 55 per cent of the municipalities in the regional and local elections held in June 1990.

And in the postponed parliamentary elections, eventually held in December 1991, when the FIS won 188 of the 231 seats in the first round of elections, president al-Shazli Ben-Jedid stepped down to make way for Muhammad Bou-Diaf.

The new president cancelled the elections. In March 1992, the FIS was outlawed. Bou-Diaf was assassinated on June 29th, 1992. Algeria's cautious advance towards democracy came to a grinding halt. In the Sudan General Ga'afar Muhammad al-Numeiri seized power in a bloodless *coup d'état* in 1969, and followed in the footsteps of Egypt's Nasser, adopting a set of socialist policies and mobilising mass support under the banner of the Sudanese Socialist Union, within the framework of a single-party system.

5

The Jihad in Kashmir and India

The Markaz sees the conflict in Kashmir not as a territorial dispute between India and Pakistan, nor even as a clash between cultures, but as nothing less than a war between two different and mutually opposed ideologies: Islam, on the one hand, and disbelief or kufr, on the other. This is portrayed as only one chapter in a long a struggle between the two that is seen as having characterized the history of the last 1400 years ever since the advent of the Prophet Muhammad. The roots of the Kashmir problem are seen in its Muslim rulers having been replaced, first by the Sikhs and then by the Hindu Dogras through British assistance. With India (the 'Hindus') having taken over Kashmir in 1947, a long and protracted reign of bloody terror is said to have been unleashed on the Kashmiri Muslims.

This is seen as a direct and logical consequence of the teachings of Hinduism itself, because, it is alleged, 'the Hindus have no compassion in their religion'. Hence, it is the duty of Muslims to wage jihad against the 'Hindu oppressors'. All Hindus are tarred with the same brush. Thus, Hafiz Muhammad Sa'eed declares: 'In fact, the Hindu is a mean enemy and the proper way to deal with him is the one adopted by our forefathers [...] who crushed them by force. We need to do the same'. This sort of hard-hitting anti-Hindu rhetoric is not a prominent feature in Gilani's writings, and thus represents a further radicalization of the Kashmiri jihadist discourse.

The armed struggle in Kashmir is depicted as only one stage of a wider, indeed global, jihad against the forces of 'disbelief'. Here, the Markaz goes far beyond Gilani's limited jihadist project, which aims at simply freeing Kashmir from Indian control and merging it with Pakistan. The Markaz's jihad is far more ambitious: it aims, at least rhetorically, at nothing less than the conquest of the entire world.

As Qari 'Abdul Wahid, former amir of the Lashkar in Indian-controlled Kashmir put it, 'We will uphold the flag of freedom and Islam through jihad not only in Kashmir but in the whole world'. Likewise, Colonel Nazir Ahmed, in-charge of the public relations department of the Markaz, declares that through the jihad that the mujahidin have launched, 'Islam will be dominant all over the world, Inshallah (God willing)'.

This war is seen as a solution to all the ills and oppression afflicting all Muslims, and it is claimed that 'if we want to live with honour and dignity, then we have to return back to jihad'. Through jihad, it is believed, 'Islam will be supreme throughout the world'. The mujahidin are promised that with the launching of the global jihad against all the unbelieving oppressors of the world, 'The day is just round the corner when Islam will prevail in this earth'.

Jihad has its more mundane benefits, too. Thus, it is also said to be indeed, 'the way that solves financial and political problems'.India is a special target for the Markaz's mujahidin. According to the amir of the Markaz, 'The jihad is not about Kashmir only. It encompasses all of India'. Thus, the Markaz sees the jihad as going far beyond the borders of Kashmir and spreading through India as a whole. The final goal is to extend Muslim control over what is seen as having once been Muslim land, and, hence, to be brought back under Muslim domination. Thus, at a mammoth congregation of Markaz supporters in November 1999, shortly after the Kargil debacle, Hafiz Muhammad Sa'eed declared, 'Today I announce the break-up of India, Inshallah. We will not rest until the whole of India is dissolved into Pakistan'. On the same occasion, Amir Hamza, senior Markaz official and editor of its Urdu organ, ad-Da'wa, thundered: 'We ought to disintegrate India and even wipe India out'. Those who take part in this anti-

Indian jihad are promised that 'Allah will save [them] from the pyre of hell', and 'huge palaces in paradise', it is said, await those who are killed in fighting the disbelieving enemies.

This project for the disintegration of India, followed by its take-over by Pakistan and then the establishing an Islamic state, is sought to be justified by an elaborate set of arguments that use the rhetoric of liberation. Thus, instances of human-sacrifice, untouchability and infanticide among the Hindus, the cruel oppression of the 'low' castes by the Brahmins and the suppression of women in Hinduism are described in great detail, and on this basis it is sought to be shown that such a religion as Hinduism should not 'be allowed to flourish'. This is a theme that Gilani does refer to in some of his writings, but he does not go beyond offering Islam as an alternative to Brahminical Hinduism. In Markaz literature, the mass slaughter of Muslims by Hindu chauvinist groups, often in league with the Indian state and its agencies, and the growing wave of attacks on other marginalized groups in India such as the 'low' caste Dalits, Shudras and Christians, are presented in stark colours, and the point forcefully made that such a country 'where non-Hindus are not allowed to exist' should be destroyed. The Markaz presents itself as a champion of not just the oppressed Muslims of Kashmir or India but even of the 'low' caste Shudras and Dalits. It sees itself as having a divinely appointed mission of saving the 'lower' castes from Brahminical tyranny. Thus, it says, 'It is incumbent upon us to save the Shudras of India [...] from the clutches of Brahmins'. Although it claims that its jihad is aimed only against 'the tyrannical government and the army' and that 'nowhere do the mujahidin target non-Muslim or innocent people', there is ample evidence to show the involvement of Lashkar militants in the killing of numerous Hindus in the Kashmir valley, Jammu, neighbouring Himachal Pradesh and elsewhere in India.

The success of the efforts of the Islamists in shifting the terms of debate in which the Kashmir struggle for political self-determination has sought to present itself has had to do with a host of internal as well as external factors that have been touched upon in this chapter. This clearly suggests that the Islamization of the Kashmiri struggle was neither necessary nor inevitable. It may, however, be, and, indeed, it actually does seem, that the Islamist attempt at hegemonizing the terms of discourse in which the Kashmiri liberation struggle has expressed itself has been only partially successful, at best. It can be argued that the apparent influence of the Islamists is deceptive, for while they have indeed marginalized the JKLF in military terms, owing, of course, to liberal patronage received from Pakistan, they enjoy little support among the Kashmiri masses themselves for their eventual political agenda. Despite its present low profile, the Kashmiri nationalist camp still seems to reflect the aspirations of the vast majority of Kashmiri Muslims. The stern Wahhabism of groups like the Markaz, based on an unremitting hostility towards and Sufism, religious liberalism and laxity, is bound to be unpopular among many Kashmiris, for whom Sufism is the normative expression of their faith and Islamic commitment. In other words, the radical Islamist rhetoric, to a considerable extent, represents an external agenda that is being sought to be imposed on Kashmir, and one that seems at odds, in several respects, with the internal conditions in Kashmir itself. Many Kashmiris might support radical Islamists in their ability to take on the Indian armed forces, but not all, or even most, are likely to enthusiastically welcome their ultimate political project. Meanwhile, rivers of blood continue to flow and the vexed problem of Kashmir shows no sign of moving towards an eventual resolution.

IS KASHMIR JIHAD OVER?

On September 30, President Asif Zardari met Kashmiri leader Mirwaiz Umar Farooq on the sidelines of the United Nations General Assembly session in New York and told him Pakistan would continue its political, moral and diplomatic support for the Kashmiri struggle for self-determination. But the Mirwaiz, who heads the moderate faction of the Hurriyat Conference, may still be disappointed with Pakistan.

No one is talking about the Kashmir jihad in Pakistan these days, not even those who once thrived on it. Gone are the days of the funerals-in-absentia for those killed fighting the Indian

Army in the valley. Donation boxes, walk chalking, and recruitment banners featuring Kalashnikovs have disappeared.

Jihadis of the past are now building new identities as philanthropists. They talk about charity and relief work now. February 5, which was once a day of expressing solidarity with the Kashmiri fighters, is now a lackluster affair. Jamaat-e-Islami, once the biggest proponent of the Kashmir jihad, now celebrates the day using Jamaatud Dawa's platform.

Relations between India and Pakistan are improving, and there is talk of trade and visa liberalization. Even the Pakistani military establishment seems to be changing its policy. Is the Kashmir jihad over?

Ershad Mehmood, an Islamabad-based researcher of Kashmiri origin, says Pakistan Army used to help jihadi infiltration into Kashmir by such measures as shelling on the Line of Control.

This 'cooperation' does not exist any more. "India has fenced the border and crossing the LoC is impossible, recruitment centers and training camps have been banned in Pakistan, and the entire infrastructure has been dismantled."

Delhi-based analyst Dr Ajai Sahni disagrees. "The Indian government continues to feel that Pakistan has not done enough to dismantle the infrastructure of terrorism," he said. "There has been a tremendous weakening and loss of support on the ground, although it is substantially the result of external factors, particularly Pakistan's preoccupation with internal difficulties and pressures and the Afghan campaign," said Sahni, who is the executive director of the Institute for Conflict Management. "Consequently, while there is satisfaction at the dramatic drop in violence in Kashmir, there is little cause for complacency. The general consensus is that the Pakistani intent has not substantially changed."

He said there was hope in India that there had been "a significant constituency in Pakistan that is increasingly opposed to the export of terrorism. This constituency needs to be cultivated and expanded to secure an enduring peace in the region."

Fazlur Rehman Khalil, chief of the defunct Harkatul Mujahideen that now operates as Ansarul Ummah, said the

Musharraf regime was a 'black era' for Kashmir jihad. "Musharraf betrayed the Kashmiris," he said, adding that President Asif Zardari's policies had been even worse for jihad in Kashmir. "He played Holi with the blood of the Kashmiris by granting India the Most Favored Nation status and forging trade ties with our eternal enemy," Khalil said in religiously charged idiom.

Pakistan reportedly sheltered 37,000 Kashmiris who had taken up arms against the Indian rule in Kashmir. As support from the Pakistani government dwindled, more than 500 of them went back to their homes via Nepal, many taking advantage of an amnesty announced by India in February this year.

But Hizbul Mujahideen, the largest Kashmiri jihadi outfit, wants the struggle to continue. "Our thinking has not changed," said Saleem Hashmi, a spokesman for the group. "It was the armed struggle that made Kashmir the flashpoint." India's recent confidence building measures were a conspiracy to freeze the issue, he said.

Hashmi said the people who had surrendered "were migrants, not Mujahideen" and numbered in thousands. "But our fighters are still present in the valley. The proof of that is the presence of 700,000 Indian soldiers in Kashmir."

Syed Salahuddin, the chief of Hizbul Mujahideen, was a politician before taking up arms. But he does not qualify for an amnesty.

"A separatist constituency remains in existence in Kashmir, but it has enormously weakened. It is believed that it would take extraordinary circumstances to revive violence to earlier levels," said Dr Sahni. "While anti-India sentiments are still in evidence in pockets, pro-Pakistan sentiments have virtually vanished. There is a broad disillusionment with the politics and patterns of terrorism emanating from Pakistan."

Hizbul Mujahideen makes a different argument. "This is not just an issue between India and Pakistan. Kashmiris are also a party to it," Saleem Hashmi said. He said his group wanted a plebiscite in Kashmir in line with the UN resolution, and would honor the result. "The Hizb will not oppose an independent

Kashmir if that is what the Kashmiris want." Hashmi admitted Pakistan was no longer supporting the militants. "We agree that Pakistan has its own problems, but it can never give up Kashmir," he said. "Giving up Kashmir is like giving up Pakistan."

Some analysts believe an end to the conflict may hurt stakeholders on both sides. And that is why they say there are so many Indian troops in Kashmir although militancy has weakened.

"The Kashmir conflict has corrupted the Indian Army and police to bones," Ershad Mehmood said. "They are paid more in conflict zones. They can sell weapons, ammunition and petrol to militants. They are paid protection money by Kashmiri traders and citizens. They can arrest anyone on charges of terrorism and release them for a bribe. And that is why they would never want peace with Pakistan."

KASHMIR ISSUE AND FIGHT FOR IT

The bitterness was palpable among the young fighters squatting on the floor of a dingy, cold room in their hideout outside Muzaffarabad. Some of them had just returned from a guerrilla operation on the other side of the Line of Control, dividing the disputed state. They looked frustrated and exhausted with their dishevelled beards and dirty clothes. Some of them were quiet while others talked about their future plans.

It was the most testing of times for the veterans of the 14-year-long guerrilla war after Musharraf had assured India that Pakistani territory would not be used for cross-border operations. Most of them were visibly frustrated and resigned to the fact that their jihad might well be coming to an end. 'We have no choice but to return to our homes,' said 30-year-old Mohammed Ashfaque, in a voice choked with emotion. A resident of Srinagar in Indian-controlled Kashmir, he had left his home and joined the guerrilla struggle some ten years ago after his brother was killed by Indian forces. However, others sounded more defiant and vowed not to lay down their weapons.

Meeting on the sidelines of the South Asian Regional summit in Islamabad, in January 2004, Musharraf and Indian Prime Minister Atal Bihari Vajpayee, had agreed to start a peace process to resolve all outstanding issues, including the Kashmir dispute, through bilateral negotiations. Musharraf was more categorical this time in his pledge to switch off the tap for Kashmiri militants. He had promised to curb the jihadists before, but in the past he had hedged his bets, ordering only a temporary halt, in the hope that India would reciprocate by sitting down for talks.

With India back to the negotiating table and after two assassination attempts on him involving jihadist groups, Musharraf had more reason than ever to crack down on his home-grown militants. He could not allow the militants to take over the country. His tone became increasingly conciliatory towards India and he hinted that he was willing to drop Pakistan's long-standing demand that a plebiscite be held in Kashmir under the 1948 UN resolution to determine its status as long as India was equally forthcoming.

Musharraf's peace overtures had angered the militants, who accused him of having conceded too much ground to India by reversing Pakistan's long-standing aggressive Kashmir policy. The jihadists saw the war in ideological and civilizational terms. Any concession to the 'enemy' was therefore a very serious matter. Many Islamist leaders described the peace process as the beginning of the end of the Kashmir jihad.

Islamabad's policy shift was also driven by external factors. Musharraf's change of tack had also placed him on the horns of a serious dilemma. Islamabad's new role as a key US ally in the war on terror was no longer compatible with Pakistan's use of those proxies, which underscored its Kashmir policy. Yet, while Musharraf was quick to abandon support for the Taliban, he was reluctant to break ties with the militants waging 'a holy war' in Kashmir.

In fact, Musharraf had sought to use his country's broad cooperation with the United States to gain some leeway for continuing Pakistan's proxy war in the disputed Himalayan state. He tried to draw a fine line between what he described as 'freedom fighters' and terrorists. But America was not interested in such distinctions.

For more than half a century, the Kashmir cause had been almost the raison d'e^tre for Pakistan's existence – not to mention for the role of the armed forces in the politics of the state. Musharraf's assumption of power had alarmed India at the time, as he was known for his aggressive stance on Kashmir. Once in power, however, Musharraf displayed the pragmatic tendencies which would later cause him to disappoint fighters like Mohammed Ashfaque so bitterly. The first sign of a thaw came in June 2001, when the two countries agreed to a ceasefire along the 1,000-kilometre Line of Control, dividing the Indian and Pakistani sides of the disputed territory. That helped to ease tensions and cleared the way for the first high level government contact between the two countries. In July 2001, the Indian Prime Minister, Atal Bihari Vajpayee, invited Musharraf for talks after dropping his precondition that Pakistan should first put an end to the infiltration of militants into Kashmir. That put the onus on Musharraf to come up with some offer to defuse tensions.

Musharraf was under tremendous strain when he proceeded to Delhi for talks with the Indian leader. Closely watched by both hardliners and peaceniks, often with contrary agendas, General Musharraf walked a political tightrope. He was under scrutiny, not only by the conservative, militant Islamic groups, but also by the hardline generals. The Jamaat-i-Islami and Islamic militant groups had warned him not to deviate from a single point of the Kashmir agenda. His own future was at stake, and dependent on the outcome of the most crucial diplomatic mission he had ever undertaken. His hardline generals were opposed to any concession on Kashmir. The officers, a number of whom had served in the ISI, argued that it was the 'success of jihad' that had forced India to come to the negotiating table. They wanted Musharraf to continue supporting the Islamic militants fighting the Indian forces.

Although he had appeared stronger with his ascension to the presidency, Musharraf continued to face growing domestic opposition to the perpetuation of military rule. The pressure on Musharraf not to let the talks fail was enormous, as Pakistani leaders had constantly been calling for a negotiated settlement of disputes with India. However, any room to manoeuvre was restricted by the long-standing, thorny Kashmir issue, which was the major cause for the festering conflict in the region.

While the summit was made possible largely because of strong international pressure, it had created its own dynamics. There were strong internal pressures forcing both countries to start a dialogue. For Musharraf, in order to prevent Pakistan from economic collapse, it was important to ease tension with India. A few weeks before his departure to India, in an interview on Pakistan state television, he had declared that Pakistan's economy was not compatible with its defence capability. A de-escalation was necessary, to win the support of the international community and to restart the flow of foreign aid.

On the very first evening of the summit, Musharraf gave a speech which seemed to push all the right buttons: 'The legacy of the past years was not a happy one ... blood has been spilt, precious lives have been lost.we must not allow the past to dictate the future,' he declared in his speech at the Indian President's dinner. Musharraf's call for peace changed the atmosphere and set a positive tone for the summit. The General seemed to have established a good rapport with the ageing Indian Prime Minister. Unlike any other summit, the Agra summit had no prior agreed-upon agenda and most of the meetings were one-on-one.

Inevitably though, the summit ended in a stalemate on 16 July 2001, with the two leaders unable to agree on the wording of the declaration. The deadlock did not come as a surprise. The final breakdown came when India refused to accept the centrality of the Kashmir issue and insisted on including the question of 'cross-border terrorism' in the declaration. Pakistan also showed its reservations over the reference to the Agra process as a continuation of the Simla and Lahore declarations. Both sides blamed each other of intransigence, but the reality was that neither leader was prepared to resist pressure from their respective hardliners.

Musharraf's position certainly didn't leave much room for compromise in negotiations. Never before had a Pakistani leader brought Kashmir to the centre of the summit table as forcefully as he did. His blunt talk with the Indian media editors on 16 July, which was televised by several networks, was also used by the Indian hardliners to obstruct an accord. The mood on the Indian side turned visibly bitter when Musharraf declared there should not be any illusion that the main issue confronting the two countries was Kashmir. 'I will keep saying it whether anyone likes it or not,' he said.

All was not lost, however. Musharraf and Vajpayee bade each other goodbye with a promise to meet again and pick up the threads from there. Despite the acrimony and bitterness that marked its closure, the Agra summit had broken the ice and revived the process of dialogue which had frozen after the Kargil conflict in the summer of 1999. The Indian Prime Minister accepted Pakistan's invitation for a return visit to Islamabad. It was also agreed to hold summit meetings between the Indian and Pakistani leaders once a year, and biannual talks at the foreign ministerial level to discuss issues relating to peace, security, confidence-building measures, Kashmir, narcotics and terrorism.

Not surprisingly, the stalemate at Agra was hailed by extremists in both India and Pakistan, who hoped to thrive in an atmosphere of tension. Islamic militant groups like LeT intensified suicide attacks in Kashmir and vowed to extend attacks inside India. Musharraf had provoked the ire of Islamic fundamentalists when he warned them against religious terrorism and militancy and tried to restrict the activities of militant groups, many of whom were fighting in Kashmir. Even more disturbing was the resumption of the exchange of artillery fire along the Line of Control, breaking the eight-month-old ceasefire. With the intensification of guerrilla attacks, India stepped up efforts to get Pakistan branded as a terrorist state. But this attempt to isolate Pakistan received a setback, as Musharraf's decision to support the US-led war in Afghanistan, improved Islamabad's international standing.

The 11 September terrorist attacks and their aftermath had changed the entire regional security scenario and triggered a rapid downslide in India-Pakistan relations. Worried with Pakistan's role as a key US strategic ally, India lost no time in urging Washington not to forget its sufferings from 'Pakistani-backed cross-border terrorism'. New Delhi tried to use the 'war on terror' to its advantage. It portrayed the Kashmir problem purely as a matter of combating terrorism and made the case that it also had the right to pursue militants from Pakistani- controlled Kashmir, exactly as the USA hunted down al-Qaeda and the Taliban in Afghanistan.

The tension mounted further in October 2001, following the LeT suicide attack by militants on the Kashmir assembly building in Srinagar which claimed 36 lives. The incident occurred as US forces were in the last stages of preparation to launch an attack on Afghanistan. Indian leaders and military commanders warned of 'hot pursuit', sending troops into Pakistani-controlled Azad Kashmir to destroy militant camps there. Musharraf denounced the attack as an act of terrorism, but that failed to pacify India. Both countries traded accusations, backed by an 'ominous troop build-up' along the border.

The situation raised serious concerns in Washington. Fearing that a fire could break out at any time in the base camp of its anti-terror campaign, the USA rushed its Secretary of State, Colin Powell, to India and Pakistan. The Bush administration, which had initially chosen to distance itself from the Kashmir conflict, showed greater enthusiasm to defuse tensions. Powell succeeded in persuading India and Pakistan to exercise restraint, but it was only a matter of time before the situation flared up again. A terrorist attack on the Indian Parliament on 13 December renewed the threat of war.

India quickly blamed two Pakistani-based Islamic militant groups, JeM and LeT, for the attack.This audacious raid on the symbol of Indian power brought the two newly nuclear-powered nations once again to the brink of war. India retaliated by severing diplomatic relations and cut rail and air communications and put Pakistan on notice to rein in the militant groups or face the consequences of war.

The gravity of the terrorist attack and the post-9/11 global security environment provided India the excuse to consider military action, to stop what it described, as cross-border terrorism. Meanwhile, India demanded that Pakistan hand over 20 'most wanted terrorists', including Masood Azhar, Ahmed Omar Saeed Sheikh and five other men involved in the December 1999 hijacking of an Indian Airlines plane. The new Bush doctrine of pre-emptive strikes against the source of terrorism and the changes in the international rules of engagement afforded India the chance to engage Pakistan in brinkmanship.

In the third week of December, India launched 'Operation Parakaram' (Valour), which constituted the heaviest Indian troop mobilization since the 1971 war. It was a deliberate move by New Delhi, amidst the war on terror, to threaten Pakistan with military strikes if Islamabad did not stop sponsoring cross-border terrorism. There was every indication that India would not shy away from going to war. With Pakistan's counter-mobilization, nearly one million troops sat eyeball to eyeball across the India-Pakistan border. Both countries moved ballistic missiles and troops close to their shared border. There was a considerable risk of nuclear escalation.

The threat of war, coupled with US pressure, forced Pakistan to take action against the Islamic militant groups. On 12 January 2002, Musharraf banned LeT and JeM, which were blamed by India for the 13 December attack. He promised not to let Pakistani territory be used for cross-border terrorism. Some two thousand activists of banned extremist groups were detained in a nationwide crackdown. Musharraf, however, made it very clear that the measures against the Islamic extremist groups did not change his position on Kashmir. 'Kashmir runs in our blood. No Pakistani can afford to severe links with Kashmir. We will continue to give all diplomatic, political and moral support to the Kashmiris,' he declared.

India reacted positively to Musharraf's 12 January speech and subsequent moves to curb the militants. Nevertheless, it kept its military on high alert and in forward positions. The Indian leaders wanted to see whether Musharraf's pledge was translated into practice. They refused to resume negotiations and normalize relations with Pakistan until all their conditions were met, including their extradition demands. Musharraf's 12 January speech drew domestic as well international, support. But the measures taken by his government were insufficient against the activities of the jihadist groups. The ban was not applied to Pakistani-controlled Kashmir, or the semi-autonomous tribal areas bordering Afghanistan, which enabled militant organizations to shift their infrastructure and cadres to these regions. Hundreds of Islamic militants, returning from Afghanistan after the collapse of the Taliban regime in December 2001, had moved to the Pakistani part of Kashmir and were ready to join the armed struggle on the other side of the border. Most of these militants belonged to the three outlawed Islamic groups.

It became apparent that, while promising to curb Islamic extremism and sectarianism, Musharraf was still not willing to completely de- link Islamabad's connection with the Kashmiri militants. Meanwhile, India's refusal to pull back troops from advance positions and resume negotiations with Pakistan also tied his hands. Cross-border infiltration of militants into Indian-controlled Kashmir slowed down, but never completely stopped. Most of the militants detained following the 12 January declaration, were released. On 20 March 2002, the CIA chief, George Tenet, told the United States Senate Armed Services Committee that the chances of war in the region were the highest since 1971. In the midst of the military stand-off with India, Musharraf decided to hold a referendum to extend his term in the office of President. In his address to the nation in March 2001, Musharraf declared his intent to enter politics and stay at the helm, a far cry from the 'reluctant coup- maker' of October 1999.

With a feeling of de'ja' vu in the air, Musharraf announced that he was seeking public approval for an extension of his tenure in office, for an additional five years beyond the three-yearperiod stipulated by the Supreme Court. The General also announced plans to introduce a new political formula, which he claimed was in conformity with the country's requirement for progress and stability. He declared that the military would continue to play a dominant role in the new political system, which was to emerge after the parliamentary elections scheduled for October 2002. Predictably, Musharraf received more than 90 per cent of the votes in a highly rigged referendum held in April 2002. The dubious polls not only dented Musharraf's credibility, but also sharpened the political polarization as the country braced for a possible war.

A series of suicide attacks by militants on a bus and in the residential quarters of an Indian army camp in Kaluchak in Kashmir on 14 May 2002 killed 35 people, mainly women and children, and brought the region closer to the nuclear precipice. Free of Islamabad's control, the militants had tried to push the two countries towards a military conflict. India quickly moved its forces to forward positions on war alert. It also expelled Pakistan's ambassador, closing the last line of direct communication with Islamabad. With missiles and heavy weapons in place, an Indian attack appeared imminent between 29 and 31 May. Nuclear signalling from both sides reminded the world of the gravity of the situation. Some Pakistani leaders openly warned of using nuclear weapons to counter India's overwhelming conventional military superiority. In the third week of May, Pakistan tested a series of nuclear-capable ballistic missiles and stepped up its nuclear weapons programme.

As the world faced perhaps its tensest nuclear stand-off since the Cuban missile crisis in 1962, the USA and Britain launched frantic diplomatic efforts to defuse the situation. President Bush and Colin Powell called the Indian and Pakistani leaders several times, urging them to pull back. On 28 May, the British Foreign Secretary, Jack Straw, visited Islamabad and asked Musharraf to take tougher measures to counter cross-border terrorism. He reminded Pakistan that as a UN member it had the responsibility to bear down 'effectively and consistently on all forms of terrorism, including cross-border terrorism'. In Delhi the next day, Straw called on the Indian leaders to exercise restraint. He also told them that Musharraf had promised to close down 'terrorist camps' operating in Pakistani-administered Kashmir and curb infiltration into India. Serious strains had emerged in relations between Washington and Islamabad after reports that the ISI was still linked with the militant groups. On 31 May, Colin Powell publicly accused Pakistan of continuing infiltration across the Line of Control, despite Musharraf's assurance that it would be halted. The following day, Musharraf told the BBC that he had issued instructions to end the crossing and stop all militant activities. But the statement did not satisfy the Bush administration which had demanded that Pakistan shut down cross- border infiltration permanently. 'When and if, it does stop, it must also stop permanently,' Colin Powell retorted. International patience was clearly running out with Musharraf's game of deception.

Musharraf was firmly wedged between a rock and a hard place. He sincerely wanted to prevent a war, but at the same time did not want to be seen as the leader who gave up his country's 'sacred' cause: Kashmir. He badly needed a face-saving device if he was to take further steps backward to meet the expectations of the international community. Musharraf tried desperately to maintain his balancing act. His 'blow hot, blow cold' posture accurately reflected the difficulties he faced at home, where he was, once again, taking a controversial position on a sensitive issue.

On 1 June, the USA, Britain, France, Canada, Japan, Australia and some other countries, issued travel advisories asking their citizens to leave India immediately and warning others against travelling to the country. Pakistan was already on the 'travel advisory' list after 9/11. The warning led to the exodus of thousands of businessmen, visitors, tourists and diplomatic personnel from India. This threatened the closure of foreign and multinational companies and caused much annoyance in Delhi, which perceived the advisory as an attempt to pressure it against launching an attack on Pakistan.

Once again, intensive US intervention was the key to walking both sides back from the brink. On 6 June, the US Deputy Secretary of State, Richard Armitage, arrived in Islamabad to build on Straw's visit and hammer out a deal between India and Pakistan. A former wrestler and a veteran diplomat, Armitage was known for his blunt talking. He had met Musharraf several times in the past and appeared to have developed a good rapport with the Pakistani military leader. Armitage had one critical objective when he arrived for talks at the sprawling presidential secretariat at the Margala foothills on the afternoon of 6 June: to extract an assurance from Musharraf that would satisfy India and remove the threat of a potential nuclear war.

Musharraf had previously pledged to stop the infiltration of Islamic militants into Kashmir, but Armitage wanted him to go one step further. The talks between the two men had stretched to two hours, when Armitage put the critical question: 'What can I tell the Indians?' he asked. He wanted to know whether Musharraf would agree to a 'permanent end' to the cross-border terrorist activity long accepted by Pakistan. 'Yes,' Musharraf replied. An elated Armitage flew to Delhi the next morning to brief the Indian leaders on his talks with Musharraf. Musharraf's agreement to the word 'permanent', backed by US assurances to India that he would keep his word, immediately led to the easing of tension. It was a hugely significant foreign policy victory for India, which, for more than a decade, had sought an end to the cross-border terrorist attacks. Indeed, Musharraf had no other option, as his refusal to concede would have had disastrous consequences. 'If Pakistan had not agreed to end infiltration, and America had not conveyed that guarantee to India, then war could not have been averted,' Vajpayee told an Indian newspaper a week later.

The Musharraf-Armitage agreement was a turning point in Pakistan's long-standing policy of using militancy as an instrument for its proxy war in Kashmir and paved the way for a new relationship between two nations long divided by a bloody, tense history. In return for his concession, Musharraf received private assurances from US officials that they would stay involved. On 5 June, President Bush had called Musharraf and gave his firm commitment that his administration would remain engaged to resolve the Kashmir conflict. Musharraf told Armitage that he expected an early and substantial response from the Indian side to make his action sustainable.

Within days of Armitage's departure, a thaw was evident. India responded to Musharraf's steps to curb cross-border terrorism by moving its naval fleet back to its base and allowed commercial overflights. It also announced the revival of diplomatic relations with Pakistan. That effectively ended the longest military standoff between the two countries. Pakistan's military and the ISI had always kept a fairly tight control on their militant clients and the restrictions resulted in an immediate drop in the infiltration of militants into Kashmir. But it never completely stopped. Some militant groups were not prepared to toe the new Pakistani line and continued to send their men into Kashmir. Pakistani officials argued that it was impossible to completely seal the LoC. For Musharraf, the major challenge was how to rein in the powerful militant groups. Predictably, his decision to stop cross-border infiltration, evoked angry reactions from the militant groups who, for more than a decade, had fought Pakistan's proxy war.

The atmosphere in the room was grim. A sense of unease gripped the two dozen guerrilla commanders, who had come to meet with a senior ISI officer at an army base in Muzaffarabad in the last week of May. The capital of Pakistani-controlled Azad Kashmir had long been the headquarters of more than a dozen Kashmiri militant groups. Some two hundred kilometres from Islamabad, the city was at an equal distance from Srinagar, the capital of Indian-administered Kashmir. 'We don't have a choice given the tremendous pressure on Pakistan,'

Major-General-Khalid Mahmood told them. 'So, you have to stop all cross-border operations.' Several of the guerrilla commanders leapt to their feet, shouting that Pakistan should not surrender to Indian and American pressure. 'After ditching the Taliban, Musharraf has now betrayed the Kashmiri cause,' said a senior commander belonging to HuM, one of the largest Islamic militant groups involved in the separatist war in Kashmir. 'How can we accept this?' The commanders were bitter and vengeful, and left the meeting declining the officer's invitation to join him for lunch.

This outburst of anger towards Musharraf and his policies appeared logical. Thousands of militants had perished fighting Pakistan's war in Kashmir. Islamic militant leaders, who had depended for over a decade on the active support of Pakistan's army for their cross- border guerrilla actions, viewed Islamabad's move as a betrayal of the Kashmiri freedom struggle. 'We have lost so many friends, brothers and relatives in the Kashmir struggle. What was that for?' asked Amiruddin, a veteran Kashmiri guerrilla fighter. He reflected the sentiments of thousands of jihadist cadres trained and armed by the Pakistani military establishment. 'We are not going to sit quietly.'

The orders came as hundreds of fresh guerrillas were waiting at their base camps in Azad Kashmir to cross the border. It was generally at that time of the year that infiltration took place. 'The volunteers are becoming increasingly upset over the delay. They have not been informed about Pakistan's ban,' said the commander. He complained that the communication link between the guerrilla fighters inside Indian Kashmir and their base on the Pakistani side had been cut off and that training centres inside Azad Kashmir had been closed down. 'Many of our colleagues are stuck across the border without reinforcements and supplies,' he said.

Pakistan's decision to withdraw support had caused a setback to the militancy, but did not bring it to an end. The militant infrastructure remained intact and outlawed groups continued working, either under new banners, or merged into others. Hundreds of Pakistani fighters who were inside Kashmir at that point had continued their jihad, ignoring Pakistan's policy shift. Most militant leaders hoped that the restrictions were temporary and still had faith in the army. 'The army will always be our ally,' a senior militant commander told me. Facing down the jihadists was not going to be an easy task for Musharraf. Since an indigenous insurrection against Indian domination broke out in Kashmir in 1989, some 10,000 fighters had crossed the border to help their Kashmiri brethren.

They were not prepared to give up the cause on Islamabad's orders. As an inevitable consequence of Pakistan's policy of using jihad as an instrument of covert war, some elements within the intelligence agencies had been radicalized by the Islamists. The handlers had become coloured by the ideology of the militants. They were unhappy with Musharraf's decision to support America's war on Afghanistan's Islamic regime, which they had helped install. But even deeper was the resentment on the reversal in Kashmir. There was a strong anti-American feeling in the military ranks. Many officers believed that western countries, particularly the USA, had not come to Pakistan's support when it faced the threat of war from its nuclear rival.

Once again Musharraf was walking a tightrope. His position had become even more tenuous after he ordered his troops to stop the infiltration. He had come to the conclusion that there was now a conflict of interest between the militants and the military. But it was not clear whether other army officers agreed with him. There was a strong feeling in the army that India was trying to humiliate them by dictating terms for peace.

Some hardline retired generals, who had been responsible for organizing the Kashmiri 'jihad', warned Musharraf that there was a limit to how far the army would go along with a policy of using force against those who were seen as fighting for Pakistan's interest in Kashmir. Lt.-General Hamid Gul, a former ISI chief and a fiercely anti-American former commander, accused Musharraf of 'going too far in appeasing the west' and taking a 'step back' on the Kashmir issue. 'By calling those attacking the Indian forces, terrorists, General Musharraf is only echoing the Indian position,' he declared. Despite military de-escalation, there was a wide gap between what the Indian leaders demanded and what Musharraf could deliver. India's mistrust of the Pakistani military leadership had thwarted all moves by the international community to bring the two sides to the negotiating table. It was only after the relatively peaceful polls for the Kashmir state assembly in October 2002, that Delhi and Islamabad opened secret back-channel diplomacy. Beginning in April 2003, Vajpayee's Principal Secretary, Brajesh Mishra, and Musharraf's top aide, Tariq Aziz, held several meetings in London, Dubai and Bangkok exploring avenues to begin a peace process.

A seasoned bureaucrat, Tariq Aziz was a college-mate of Musharraf's and had worked as his principal secretary after the military takeover. A former income tax officer, he was more into political wheeling and dealing and had no experience of diplomacy. However, being Musharraf's closest aide, he was considered the best man for this secret and extremely delicate job. Even the foreign ministry was kept out of the loop. Facilitated by the USA, this was the first senior official contact between the two countries for nearly two years.

Tariq Aziz was later appointed secretary of the National Security Council. In April 2003, the Indian Prime Minister extended a 'hand of friendship' to Pakistan during a public address in Srinagar. Pakistan's Prime Minister, Zafarullah Khan Jamali, responded by speaking to Vajpayee and invited him to visit

Islamabad. In yet another highly symbolic gesture, India announced the resumption of bus links with Pakistan. The twice-weekly coach service between Delhi and Lahore had been abruptly suspended 18 months earlier, after Islamic militants had attacked the Indian Parliament in Delhi. The bus service, which started in February 1999, had significant symbolic value. Vajpayee had travelled to Lahore by the inaugural coach for his historic meeting with Pakistan's then Prime Minister, Nawaz Sharif.

Given their deep-rooted mistrust of each other, the process remained a slow diplomatic dance, with the two governments circling one another warily, each making tentative offers. The efforts at that stage were largely aimed at de-escalation and the restoration of the situation that existed prior to the military standoff, rather than any great leap forward.

Pakistan moved very cautiously, given its traditional suspicion of its much bigger, and militarily powerful, neighbour. It was reluctant to open its airspace to Indian planes and remove all trade barriers. Pakistan feared that lifting the overflight ban could provide India with an opportunity to establish close trade links with, and consolidate its influence in, Afghanistan. There were strong apprehensions in Islamabad that the emerging process could prove to be another false start if India raised the size of the table, rather than picking up the thread from previous talks.

Kashmir remained the thorniest issue as the two countries moved towards a rapprochement. The events of May and June a year before had indicated how quickly the situation could escalate into a fully fledged conflagration, with both countries appearing all too willing to engage in nuclear sabre-rattling. There was no sign of flexibility yet on the Kashmir issue on either side. While India was eager to demonstrate that the Kashmir violence was totally Pakistani sponsored, Pakistan appeared equally adamant to keep up the pressure on Delhi.

Although Musharraf had agreed to clamp down on militant groups, the situation on the ground did not change much. Pakistan's promise of a complete halt to support for the Islamic militants did not seem credible at that stage. Pakistani military officials contend that a total turnaround in Pakistan's policy could not be possible without some reciprocity from India, for example, reduction of troops and an end to human rights violations in the state. 'We will lose all leverage if we just pull out our support to the Kashmiris without any show of flexibility by India,' said a senior Pakistani official.

'In the absence of any light at the end of the Kashmiri tunnel, it would be hard for the government to sell any proposal for peace with India to its own people.' It was quite apparent that the military-backed administration was not ready to put the Kashmir issue on the backburner.

The military officers, who stood by Musharraf when he moved away from Pakistan's long-standing policy of supporting the conservative Taliban regime in Afghanistan and joined the US-led coalition against terrorism, were not likely to maintain their loyalty towards him if he had decided to make a radical shift on the Kashmir issue.

With India agreeing to resume peace talks, Pakistan faced increasing pressure to come down hard on Islamic guerrilla groups and destroy militant infrastructure. A serious international concern was that Pakistan's inability to contain militancy could continue to be a significant obstacle to the normalization of relations between the two countries. While acknowledging that there had been a decrease in infiltration and that the level of violence in Kashmir had declined, Washington was not fully satisfied with the situation.

The situation then took a most dramatic turn in January 2004, when Vajpayee came to Islamabad to attend the seven-nation South Asian regional summit. Few had expected any breakthrough when the aged Indian Prime Minister went to pay a 'courtesy call' on Musharraf at the imposing presidential palace on 5 January. Although there had been hints of a possible meeting, nobody was sure until it actually happened.

The outcome of the 65-minute parley between the two leaders went beyond anybody's expectations. Not only were some significant decisions taken to move the process of normalization forward, but a road map for further interaction was also clearly stated.

Most importantly, Musharraf pledged to prevent the use of the territory under Pakistan's control 'to support terrorism in any manner'. It was the first direct commitment of this nature since the Pakistani- backed armed insurgency in Kashmir began in 1989. The joint statement also declared that both leaders were 'confident' of reaching a peaceful settlement of all bilateral issues, including Kashmir. It was a great leap forward in the relations between the two countries, which had been on the brink of nuclear war just a year before.

The outcome of the Islamabad meeting was not the result of a sudden surge of goodwill. The script was prepared after intensive back-channel diplomacy between Brajesh Mishra and Tariq Aziz. From 1 to 4 January, the two officials were in regular contact. Mishra also met with the ISI chief, Lt.-General Ehsan ul-Haq. Those interactions remained secret, even from Pakistani foreign ministry officials. Only the President's Chief of Army Staff, General Hamid, and Tariq Aziz were involved in the preparation of the joint communique'. Foreign Secretary, Riaz Khokar, was handed a copy just a few hours before the summit meeting. Musharraf's change of course on the Kashmir policy indicated that the Pakistani military establishment had finally acknowledged that support for militancy could not dislodge India from the disputed land. But there had also been concern that, in the absence of such pressure, India would not agree to a negotiated settlement of the Kashmir dispute. Vajpayee's agreement on a composite dialogue on all bilateral issues, including Kashmir, gave Musharraf some leeway to convince his generals of the need for peace with India.

Musharraf went one step further when he declared his readiness to consider all possible alternatives for the Kashmir solution. In November 2004, he outlined a step-by-step approach towards resolving the decades-old dispute, which involved making some parts of the disputed territory independent or placing them under joint Indian-Pakistani control. Indeed, the suggestion to identify the region, demilitarize it and change its status, signified a radical shift in Pakistan's Kashmir policy.

Though premature, the proposal indicated a significant come-down from Pakistan's traditional hardline position of holding a plebiscite, under the 1948 UN resolution that required Kashmiris alone to decide their political future. For the first time, a Pakistani leader had suggested making the territory a joint protectorate.

Finding a solution acceptable to both sides had always been a difficult task, even in the best of circumstances, as Kashmir has been so deeply intertwined with India and Pakistan's perceptions of national security and identity.

Domestic political compulsions had made the issue more complex. What had made securing peace even more difficult was the past baggage of mistrust and suspicion the two nations continued to carry. It had been such an accident-prone relationship that any incident could derail the whole process.

Musharraf's turnaround divided the separatist movement in Indian- administered Kashmir. The moderate elements supported his peace initiatives. For them, militancy could not provide the solution to the festering problem and it was time for the political parties to play their roles for a negotiated settlement of the issue. Once dismissed by the Pakistani military establishment as 'weak links', the moderate Kashmiri leaders became Musharraf's new allies. Mirwaiz Umar Farooq, a charismatic young Kashmiri leader, remembered his first meeting with Musharraf in New York in September 2001, when the Pakistani military leader accused him of being 'cowardly' for suggesting a non-militant course towards the solution of the Kashmir problem. 'The meeting ended on a bitter note,' Mirwaiz recalled when I met him in his heavily guarded house in Srinagar in April 2005.

The mood had completely changed when the two met again in Holland three years later, following the Indo-Pak rapprochement. 'It was I this time asking him to go slow on the peace process. Musharraf sounded too enthusiastic about the prospect of reaching a settlement,' Mirwaiz said.

The Kashmiri leader was thrown into separatist politics as a teenager after the death of his father, Mirwaiz Maulvi Farooq, in 1989. As a prayer leader at Srinagar's Jamia Masjid, he wielded considerable spiritual and political influence in the disputed state. He led the moderate faction of the All Parties Hurriyat (Freedom)

Conference (APHC), a loose coalition of more than 32 organizations, that wanted militancy to give way to political struggle. 'Militancy has played an important role in drawing international attention to the Kashmir issue, but now we should concentrate on a political struggle,' he declared. The moderates were also concerned about the struggle falling into the hands of the extremists.

The resumption of the Indo-Pak talks was fully backed by the moderates, though Musharraf's change of tack shocked the hardliners who had been fighting for the annexation of the entire disputed state with Pakistan. Their bitterness was palpable when the bus service between Srinagar and Muzaffarabad was restored on 7 April 2005, after a 57-year hiatus. It was a momentous occasion when the new Indian Prime Minister, Manmohan Singh, waved off the first bus with its 19 passengers. Described as the mother of all confidence-building measures between India and Pakistan, the bus link reunited divided Kashmiri families. But for the militants it was a betrayal of their cause. In an attempt to derail the peace process, the militants attacked the Tourist Reception Centre in Srinagar, where the passengers of the inaugural bus were kept under strict security.

'This is not what we have sacrificed thousands of lives for,' Syed Ali Shah Geelani, the head of his own faction of APHC, told me when we met at his Srinagar residence, a day after the bus had left for Muzaffarabad.

The 70-year-old, white-bearded Geelani was the chief of Jamaat-i-Islami in Kashmir, and had close links with the Islamic militants fighting Pakistan's proxy war. For his ardent support for Pakistan, he was often described as an ISI agent until Musharraf's turnaround. With Pakistan now betting on the moderates, Geelani felt isolated. But his loyalty to Pakistan was unquestionable. 'Musharraf is destroying Pakistan. Things will change once he is gone,' he said.

THE RENEWED TIDE OF JIHAD AGAINST INDIA

The first wave of Jihad against India occurred just a few years after Muhammad's (PBUH, for safety's sake) death in 632 CE and it continues to this day. Let's not forget that it took nearly *five hundred* years for the invading Turkish and Arab armies to establish an empire in Delhi, and another *two hundred* before the Mughal Empire took firm roots under Akbar. This holds an extremely significant lesson about the nature of Jihad: it is relentless and it goes on undaunted using any and all means available at the time, and it simply won't stop until its goal of total Islamization has been achieved.

Cut to the 20th Century. Pakistan launched *three* wars against us between 1947 and 1971, and all of them without any provocation from our side. Which normal nation does something like this? And let's also not forget the fact that Pakistan is a pretty tiny state compared to us, and it scores horribly on pretty much every index of human development that exists. So why does this do something apparently so stupid? The answer becomes clear when we look at the *motivation* behind such wanton and repeated aggressions. The motivation is Jihad against India at all costs.

And as to the question of why it has launched no full-scale war after 1971–I do not regard Kargil as a full-scale war–the answer is simple: change of strategy. It lies in the genius of Zia ul Haq, who realized that Pakistan could never win a war with India in a direct confrontation. And so the choice was clear: operate in stealth mode. The phrase "bleeding by a thousand cuts" became popular and was a result of his policy. Indeed Zia's policy was extremely farsighted and as we see now, became successful beyond his wildest dreams.

No columnist or newspaper worth his salt will tell you this: Pakistan views India as a *Hindu*nation; more correctly, a *kaffir* nation that needs to be blessed with the light of Islam through perfidy or violence or both. Equally, what no newspaper or analyst will tell you is also this: *the leaders of Pakistan have always held us in utter contempt.* They see themselves as the proud and rightful inheritors of the Mughal Empire, which had the whole of Hindustan under its foot, and where the Kaffir Hindus were their slaves. It's reflected in almost anything that has a Pakistani tinge–their missiles are named after Ghazni, Ghori, Tipu and other fanatical Islamic mass murderers, and their history textbooks preach hatred against Hindus. Actually there's some justification for their contempt apart from the Islam-fuelled one. It began with–who else?–that original nutjob Nehru who proudly declared that India was *not* a Hindu nation but failed to explain what exactly India was. *That* was the precedent set. And with his vile dynasty controlling this nation for over 50 years, are you still surprised how traitors like Fai's guests emerge?

But no, our analysts and policy superstars and nouveau think tanks talk about everything but the *real* basis of Indo-Pak hostility. It is in fact incorrect to even frame this as Indo-Pak hostility–it is a wanton, declared and demonstrated intent of aggression against India–demonstrated in both word and deed. The *real* basis like I said, is Jihad with the ultimate goal of Islamizing all of India. And a think tank eminence talks about something called the Pakistan's "military-Jihadi complex." But he doesn't explain *what* it really is. He only talks about how it works. You cannot have a Jihadi complex without having Jihad as your goal. And if you have Jihad as your goal, it logically means you need to look at the Koran and the Hadis. And that's the point at which the think tank's pants start to get wet. But it's only an illustration of how effective the taboo of critiquing Islam is: in this case, it prevents you from even criticizing the basis of an enemy nation's wanton and repeated assaults. And these analyst-policy-think tank complex wants to somehow transform India into a strong nation and formulate an effective Pakistan policy?

Pakistan in other words, has *always* been clear about its goal: Jihad against India. It's only India which continues to fool itself that Pakistan is a peace loving country but for "some rogue elements" and assorted crap. Even more shamefully, India recognized the Rogue of rogues, Musharraf as the President of Pakistan. And you *still* wonder why Pakistan treats us with contempt?

And were we clear about our goal for the same period? Oh yes we were. Utterly, completely, absolutely clear: first it was keeping Madam happy and then her son, and now her daughter-in-law and that dolt of a grandson. And keeping Madam happy meant several things, a significant one of which was keeping the minorities *extremely* happy. They throw a tantrum? Give them chocolate. They create a ruckus? Give them dole. They take out*violent* protests? Just give them that damn thing, whatever it is. Here's a question: had the Golden Temple been a Mosque, would Indira Gandhi have ordered military action? And by extension, the same question applies to the subsequent terrorism that erupted–had it been a demand for a separate Muslim state, where would place your bets vis a vis the Congress regime?

Meanwhile, something else was also occurring. Pakistan was growing from strength to strength. It began to vigorously implement Zia's policy of waging stealth Jihad. Back home, successive Dynastic rulers in India kept doing what they know best: *one,* they fragmented India mostly on communal lines, and *two,* they wreaked havoc on our institutions. As a result, the greatest victory that Pakistan continues to enjoy over India is the manner in which they're playing Kashmir like a harp. Indeed, the mass murders and exodus of Pandits from Kashmir were achieved in a relatively short period.

And now, cut to the present. Communal fragmentation was the most essential device for the Congress to stay in power. Nothing is more valuable than the Muslim vote. Not even the nation. And so, what at one time used to be mere appeasement of Muslims has now metamorphosed into open submission. On the eve of Independence, India's sworn enemy was Pakistan, and Pakistan's was India. After successive Congress regimes, it's clear that we lack spine with respect to Pakistan but Pakistan is sure where *it* stands–five dead Indian soldiers on August 6. The Congress has met the most outrageous demands and indulged the worst excesses by Muslims for over five decades. Indeed, the Creative Directors in the Congress party have in some cases, *anticipated* newer and newer forms of appeasement and have squandered enormous taxpayer money on such doles. Even if we dismiss this as vote bank gimmicks, what explains the fact that our defence minister defended *Pakistan* when its army men mowed down five of our soldiers in a flagrant violation of the LOC? Whose side is AK Antony exactly on? As a result, the inevitable consequences have inevitably occurred: India is now slowly passing into a dangerous grip of a Jihad, the signs of which have become starkly visible especially over the last two years.

SECOND SUNRISE OF INDIAN JIHAD

"You who have ruled India for eight hundred years, you who lit the flame of the one true God in the darkness of polytheism: how can you remain in your slumber when the Muslims of the world are awakening?" the al-Qaeda ideologue Asim Umar asked India's Muslims last summer. "If the youth of the Muslim world have joined the battlefields with the slogan 'Shari'a or Martyrdom,' and put their lives at stake to establish the Caliphate, how can you lag behind them? Why is there no storm in your ocean," Mr. Umar demanded to know.

Last week's arrests of key Indian Mujahideen operatives have led to speculation that India's most feared terror group — responsible for savage serial bombings in major cities, including the 2006 attacks on Mumbai's suburban train system — may be disintegrating. Tehseen Akhtar, its key recruiter, is now in prison; so is Muhammad Zarar Siddibapa, its operation chief.

For investigators though, these breakthroughs have brought forth disturbing new evidence that Mr. Umar, and other propagandists like him, are succeeding in calling a new army into being — an army born in Indian towns and cities scarred by communal warfare and hardened in the battlefields of Pakistan's north-west.

The dusk that shrouds the Indian Mujahideen heralds, the evidence suggests, the coming of its second sunrise.

THE NEW *JIHADIS*

Karachi residents Muhammad Fahim and Muhammad Abdul Walid, held by the Uttar Pradesh police last week, told investigators that they had first been recruited by the Lashkar-e-Taiba, and then broke with it to make their way to a Taliban training camp in Afghanistan's southern Helmand district. Then, they were led by the fugitive Pune *jihadist,* Mohin Chaudhury to the Indian Mujahideen's Karachi-based chief, Riyaz Shahbandri. Faisalabad-based bombmaker Zia-ur-Rahman, Mr. Akhtar's recently arrested deputy, served with Taliban groups in Pakistan's Punjab before volunteering to serve with the Indian Mujahideen fighting across the border.

Meanwhile, new *jihadist* cells have sprung up within India. The recruits include young people, their minds fired by Internet Islamism, as well as veterans once linked to the proscribed Students Islamic Movement of India (SIMI). Fugitive Ranchi resident Haider Ali, the National Investigation Agency (NIA) says, raised volunteers from both these groups for the bombing of the revered Buddhist shrine at Bodh Gaya last year, as an act of vengeance for communal violence against Myanmar's Rohingya Muslim minority.

Mr. Ali's cell, only loosely connected through him to the Indian Mujahideen, followed up that attack with an attempt to assassinate Gujarat Chief Minister Narendra Modi at a rally in Patna, surprising the organisation's leadership in Karachi.

In Tamil Nadu, volunteers at a Chennai college even signed up to serve with *jihadists* in Syria — recruited by local Islamists, and financed by a Singapore-based executive.

Key commanders of the Indian Mujahideen, meanwhile, remain active in Karachi, most important of them being Riyaz Shahbandri, his brother Iqbal Shahbandri and Abdul Subhan Qureshi. There are a host of second-rung leaders still at large, like Mirza Shadab Beg, Shahnawaz Alam, Muhammad "Bada" Sajid, Alamzeb Afridi, Zulfikar Fayyaz "Kagazi," Rahil Sheikh and Ariz Khan. The man who financed them all, ganglord Amir Raza Khan, is also at large.

The Western Storm

From Internet chats between Mr. Shahbandri and Mr. Siddibapa, recovered by the NIA, we know that several of those men have sought combat training with *jihadists* in Pakistan's north-west, and in Afghanistan, developing skills the Indian Mujahideen's cadre never had.

It has long been evident that the gathering storm of violent Islamism in Pakistan would lash India, too. In 2010, al-Qaeda released a posthumous audio message from Egyptian *jihadi* Said al-Masri, claiming responsibility for the bombing of the German Bakery in Pune. "The person who carried out this operation was a heroic soldier from the Soldiers of the Sacrifice Brigade, which is one of the brigades of Qaedat al-Jihad [the al-Qaeda's formal name] in Kashmir, under the command of Commander Illyas

Kashmiri, may Allah preserve him." Mr. al-Masri's message was wrong on several details of the operation, but for investigators, news that elements of al-Qaeda had developed links with *jihadi* groups acting against India did not surprise anyone. David Headley, the Pakistani-American Lashkar operative now serving a life term for his role in the 26/11 attacks, had told the NIA of an anti-India "Karachi project" linked to global *jihadi* groups.

Driven by Communal Events

Following Pakistani military ruler General Pervez Musharraf's 2007 siege of jihadists holed up inside Islamabad's Lal Masjid, Mr. Headley told the NIA, that an ideological war broke out among Pakistan's*jihadis*. In spite of efforts by Pakistan's Inter-Services Intelligence, he said, the "aggression and commitment shown to *jihad* by the several splinter groups influenced many committed fighters to leave Kashmir-centric outfits and join the Taliban."

In turn, al-Qaeda became increasingly interested in India, as a means of competing for influence and legitimacy with traditional *jihadi* groups like the Lashkar, which were supportive of the Pakistani state. In the wake of 26/11, al-Masri himself released a statement warning India of attacks if it struck against Pakistan.

The renewal of a *jihadist* constituency within India shouldn't be a surprise: the rise of Mr. Modi, and the Hindu nationalist tendencies he represents, has unleashed existential anxieties among large numbers of Indian Muslims. Though the numbers of jihadi recruits are minuscule, the members of the new cells are also true to a familiar pattern. The earliest Indian *jihadist* formation, the Tanzim Islahul Muslimeen, was formed to protect Muslims against communal violence, and carried out its first strike, the 1993 bombings of inter-city express trains, to avenge the demolition of the Babri Masjid.

In interrogations, Indian *jihad* volunteers have repeatedly said they acted to avenge the Gujarat carnage of 2002. Feroze Ghaswala told police he had volunteered to join *jihad* training after witnessing the mass burial of 40 Gujarat riot victims. Peedical Abdul Shibly and Yahya Kamakutty, both successful computer professionals, are alleged to have prepared to carry out attacks in Bangalore.

Men from Kerala trained in the mountains of Jammu and Kashmir with the Lashkar-e-Taiba. Zabiuddin Ansari, from Maharashtra, famously ended up in the 26/11 control room.

Founded in April 1977, SIMI, the fountainhead of the modern Indian *jihadist* movement, was itself driven by the forces of communal violence. From the outset, scholar Yoginder Sikand has said "that Islam alone was the solution to the problems of not just the Muslims of India, but of all Indians and, indeed, of the whole world." It drew thousands disillusioned with traditional politics, Dr. Sikand has recorded, providing supporters "a sense of power and agency which they were denied in their actual lives."

From December 1992, following the demolition of the Babri Masjid, SIMI's language became increasingly aggressive. In a statement in 1996, it declared that since democracy and secularism had failed to protect Muslims, the sole option was to struggle for the caliphate. Soon after, it put up posters calling on Muslims to follow the path of Mahmood Ghaznavi, the 11th century warlord. In 2001, after the 9/11 attacks, SIMI activists organised demonstrations hailing Osama bin-Laden as a "true mujahid."

Early in the summer of 2004, a group of young men fed up with SIMI's inability to act on its own talk gathered in the small coastal town of Bhatkal in Mangalore — and founded what we now call the Indian Mujahideen.

The Jihadi *Tradition*

To understand the durability of the *jihad* within India, it is important to remember that its cadre are inheritors of a long political tradition. In a manifesto sent to the media after their September 2008 bombings in New Delhi, the group said the attacks were carried out "in the memory of two most eminent Mujahids of India: Sayyed Ahmed Shaheed and Shah Ismail Shaheed (may Allah bestow His Mercy upon them) who had raised the glorious banner of Jihad against the disbelievers." The historian Ayesha Jalal has shown that the notion of *jihad* was an important theme in both pre-colonial and colonial India. Syed Ahmad and Shah Ismail were killed battling Sikh troops in a failed *jihad* involving the tribes of Pakistan's north-west.

Historian Stephen Dale has observed that these ideas stretched to the south of India, noting the work of the Sixteenth Century author, Zayn al-Din al-Ma'bari, who chronicled the *jihad* against Portugal's intrusions into the Indian Ocean, hoping to "inspire the Faithful to undertake a *jihad* against the worshippers of the cross."

Each bombing the Indian Mujahideen carries out is a medium for a political message enmeshed with India's dystopic communal landscape: that democratic politics cannot defend India's Muslims. India's intelligence and police services deserve credit for the long war they have fought, but it is time for politicians to act to heal our fractured nation.

KASHMIR: AN ARGUMENT FOR THE MULTI-SCALAR APPROACH

My central argument in this chapter will be that the militancy in Kashmir is best understood through both levels of analysis : the relationship of the terrorists to the Indian state and the ways in which terrorists operate on a transnational level. In demonstrating how both levels of analysis are relevant, this chapter will also begin to explore one way of constructing such a multi-scalar approach that will be further elaborated upon in subsequent portions of the paper.

The chapter will be organized as follows: first, I explain the relevance of Kashmir to Islamist terrorism in India as a whole; second, I will provide a brief overview of the militancy; and third, I will apply the state-based and transnational approaches to the Kashmir conflict to demonstrate their limitations.

Relevance of Kashmir

The point of using Kashmir here is not to suggest that it is representative of Islamist terrorism in India as a whole. Rather, the use of Kashmir is two-fold. First, as the place which accounts for approximately 72% of attack attempts of Islamist terrorism in India (START 2011), it is worth understanding on its own merit. Second, Kashmir is increasingly becoming intertwined with terrorism in other parts of India, by virtue of the groups currently controlling the conflict and their broader ambitions (Swami 2003).

Thus, being able to study Kashmir through the best approach gets us a long way toward understanding much of Islamist terrorism in India.

Overview of Conflict

Kashmir has been a source of tension between India and Pakistan at least since partition (Varshney 1991), as well as the reason for two of their three wars (Bhatt 2007). India and Pakistan's battle over Kashmir is linked to their fundamentally divergent ideas of nationhood (Bhatt 2007). Muhammad Ali Jinnah, leader of the Muslim League and founder of Pakistan, argued that India and Pakistan should be two nations on the basis of religion (Bhatt 2007). His two-nation theory suggests that Kashmir, as a Muslim-majority area, is rightfully part of Pakistan. By contrast, India's ideal nation is a secular democracy, and for India, having Kashmir would affirm its own model of statehood (Bhatt 2007).

The insurgency, which began in 1989 against this backdrop of a struggle between two nations, was the result of both long-term precipitous factors as well as more proximate causes (Ganguly 1997). The long-term factors were increasing political mobilization and institutional failure which no longer made a political solution viable (Ganguly 1997). When Sheikh Mohammed Abdullah's Jammu and Kashmir National Conference took over, it had popular support but was not particularly democratic. The Conference's ability to govern was based on the personality of Abdullah, who was also the party's primary decision-maker (Ganguly 1997). The Indian government, for its part, was not concerned about the lack of democracy in Kashmir as long as its leaders didn't pursue secession (Ganguly 1997). There were only four elections in Kashmir in 54 years, three of which were tampered with in some way (Bhatt 2007). Despite the lack of democracy, however, economic development took place in Kashmir, consequently increasing political demands among citizens (Ganguly 1997).

While the failure of democratic institutions at the same time as political mobilization was already making Kashmir volatile (Ganguly 1997), the biggest proximate cause of the insurgency was the failure of the 1987 elections (Varshney 1991). The Congress-

National Alliance won a significant majority of the seats even though it did not even get half of the popular vote (Ganguly 1997). The election demonstrated to Kashmiris that state was no longer a feasible means of expressing their frustration. By 1989, the situation had turned violent (Behera 2006).

Led mostly by the Jammu and Kashmir Liberation Front (JKLF), the insurgency at this point sought an independent and unified Kashmir (Behera 2006). Before proceeding, it is important to slightly expand our understanding of Islamism. Initially, a component of the definition of Islamism was that it sought to establish an Islamic state. Of course, relative to other Islamist organizations, JKLF stands apart from this goal as a more secular group which wanted an independent Kashmir (Behera 2006). However, in the case of Kashmir, this delineation of an organization as 'secular' proves far more difficult, as there are significant ideological continuities between different groups (Swami 2003). Even the JKLF was involved in the expulsion of the Pandit minority (Swami 2003) and in this way is more than just a separatist organization. For the remainder of the paper, therefore, we will classify the JKLF rather loosely as an Islamist terrorist organization.

The general populous in Kashmir valley supported the JKLF as an extension of Kashmiri identity, and being able to fight was seen as a form of honor (Behera 2006). These young militants also had the support of Pakistan with regard to training and financial assistance (Varshney 1991). Even years later, Pakistan has retained its hand in the conflict as approximately three quarters of the groups fighting in Kashmir are funded by the ISI and other Pakistani organizations (Jamwal 2003). However, the JKLF stopped being the dominant group in the 1990s because it was marginalized by the ISI in favor of other, more radical terrorist organizations:

Where Pakistan was concerned, the "Kashmiri card" had served its purpose and, if allowed to reach its logical conclusion, might back-fire, especially since the JKLF's goal was "independence and re-unification of the divided Kashmir and not accession to Pakistan." (Behera 2006: 151)

One of the most prominent groups to rise after the decline of JKLF was Hizb-ul-Mujahideen (HuM) (Behera 2006). HuM and several other right-wing Islamist groups changed the discourse of the Kashmir struggle from one of secession to one of accession with Pakistan. Their strategy followed the "Afghan model" (2006: 154)—they intended to make holding on to Kashmir expensive for India, and did so by calling for Jihad. For example, a popular HuM slogan translates as 'It is neither a guerrilla war nor a national war: it is a holy war' (2006: 154).

Not only did HuM and the groups that followed it change the rhetoric behind the struggle, but in so doing, they also lost the local support that was such a big part of the initial stages of the movement (Behera 2006). Consequently, these more extremist groups struggled to radicalize significant numbers of Kashmiris, causing Pakistan to increase the number of foreign terrorists (Behera 2006). Whereas until about 1996, the terrorists taking part in the insurgency were mostly ethnically Kashmir (Swami 2003), as of 2002, an estimated fifth of the militants were foreign, about 90 percent of whom were Pakistani (Trehan 2002). Moreover, of the many active groups in Kashmir, only three are operating in Kashmir exclusively1—the vast majority are also operating elsewhere (Haleem 2004). Some of the largest terrorist organizations in the region are based out of Pakistan and simultaneously pursue objectives that are global in scope (Roy-Chaudhary 2003):

These groups are the JKLF, Harkat-ul-Ansar, and Al-Faran

In (the militants) world-view, the armed struggle in Kashmir is but one stage of a wider, indeed global, Jihad. Kashmir is not a territorial dispute between India and Pakistan, not even a clash between cultures, but nothing less than a war between two different and mutually opposed ideologies: Islam and kufr (disbelief). (Behera 2006: 157).

In addition to the more global goals of the organizations now dominating the violence in Kashmir, the conflict also has an international dimension because of the symbolic significance of Kashmir to groups like AQ (Rapoport 2006).

KASHMIR THROUGH THE STATE-BASED APPROACH

The application of the state-based approach to the Kashmir conflict would point out the radicalization of the JKLF as a response to the inability of the Indian state to address Kashmiri needs. Indeed, an explanation of why terrorism in Kashmir began when it did is intimately intertwined with the failure of the Indian state, both on a long term and with regard to the 1987 elections. Additionally, the tremendous amount of popular support for the terrorists among Kashmiris must be taken into account, and cannot be explained by analyzing the conflict on a transnational level. Data from the GTD supports the validity of the state-based approach in the initial stages of the conflict—the groups attacking most frequently were those in which ethnic Kashmiris fought and were otherwise supported (Behera 2006). A comparison of Chart C and Chart D shows that JKLF was much more dominant in the initial years of the conflict than HuM.

However, the state-based approach begins to fall short in explaining the most recent iteration of the conflict, which is increasingly being led by radical Islamist organizations with little local support (Behera 2006). HuM starts to increase its attack attempts by 2000. Although these are only two organizations, analyses of other organizations reveal the same pattern: more radical groups wanting Kashmiri accession with Pakistan have been the biggest perpetrators of violence in the region in recent years. Additionally, it is unclear how the foreign terrorists, as citizens of Pakistan and other countries, relate to the politics of the Indian state and its failures in Kashmir. Thus, the state-based approach is useful for explaining the origins of the conflict, but cannot explain how it has transformed since.

KASHMIR THROUGH THE TRANSNATIONAL APPROACH

Two aspects of the conflict lend support to the use of the transnational approach: first, the shift in the types of groups attacking, and second, the fact that Kashmir is becoming increasingly interconnected with Islamist terrorism outside of India. This latter point is facilitated by virtue of the fact that groups like HuM and LeT have much broader, non-local goals:

As the Jihad in Jammu and Kashmir has progressed, the notion of this conflict as a first battle in the war for the defense of Islam throughout India has been increasingly translated into action' (Swami 2003: 79).

Evidence from the GTD supports Swami's finding. Although some Kashmiri terrorist groups have made attack attempts in Bombay as early as 1990, the general number of average annual attack attempts outside Kashmir has been increasing significantly at the same time that the number of average annual attack attempts within Kashmir has been decreasing.

Thus, to describe the violence in Kashmir as it is today, the transnational approach is much more useful: the biggest perpetrators of terrorism have little in common with native Kashmiris and hold ambitions which extend far beyond Kashmir's borders. However, it is difficult to explain how the insurgency had such tremendous support in its initial stages without the state-based approach. Thus, each approach is well-suited for a particular period of time.

THE ARGUMENT FOR THE MULTI-SCALAR APPROACH

The statement that the Kashmir conflict started as a domestic struggle and became more international is hardly a new one. But it does demonstrate the number of different forces that can act upon Islamist terrorism in India. The Kashmir conflict has always had both domestic and international dimensions, yet during certain moments one or the other is more dominant. Consequently, neither the state-based nor the transnational approach alone can explain patterns of terrorism in the region. Although, as previously stated, Kashmir is not representative of Islamist terrorism in India as whole, it accounts for the overwhelming majority of all instances of Islamist terrorism in India. Additionally, scholars who look beyond the state tend to focus on Kashmir while those who use the Indian state as their level of analysis write about particular organizations like SIMI. However, it is becoming more apparent that the Kashmir conflict has extended its borders and has to be understood alongside changes happening in the rest of India.

By extrapolating from the case of Kashmir to look at Islamist terrorism in India as a whole, we can learn one more lesson. Time can act as one way to link the state-based approach to the transnational one.

BRIDGING THE GAP: BEGINNING TO THINK ON A MULTI-SCALAR LEVEL

The example of the Kashmir conflict demonstrates the limitations of taking each of the two approaches in isolation. The state-based approach is useful for explaining particular aspects of Islamist terrorism in India, such as the radicalization of the more 'indigenous' groups like SIMI and the IM. However, in only being able to account for a very small piece of the terrorist attacks that have taken place, its explanatory power is limited. The transnational approach to studying terrorism, unsurprisingly, has the opposite problem. It can explain much of the nature of contemporary Islamist terrorism and indeed the majority of attacks as a whole. However, the large-scale framework cannot account for the diversity in Islamist terrorism in India.

At this point we could just conclude that Islamist terrorism in India is simply both: it is caused by both domestic and international forces. It is both local and global. While this is likely true, the conclusion is very limiting. In order to construct the most effective counterterrorism policies, what is required is an understanding of *how* Islamist terrorism in India is shaped by these different factors. And in order to answer the question of 'how', it is necessary to connect these two approaches. My aim in this chapter is to explore some ways of constructing a multi-scalar approach to understanding Islamist terrorism in India.

As was previously stated, the argument made offers one mean of bridging connecting the transnational approach and the state-based approach. The approach that was best-suited to explaining the conflict in Kashmir changed over time. If we take the implications of the state-based approach and the transnational-approach without being confined by their framework and levels of analysis, it becomes possible to make a conceptual shift to thinking of domestic and transnational approaches as 'influences' instead. One way of constructing a multi-scalar approach, therefore, is to identify which sphere of influence, the domestic or the international, is more dominant at a particular moment of time. Indeed, empirical data from the GTD and the RDWTI suggests that there is significant variation in the number of terrorist attacks across time. Equally, the diversity in the spatial distribution of attacks suggests that a second-way of constructing a multi-scalar approach would be to identify which sphere of influence is more dominant in a particular location. Taking into account the temporal and spatial geographies of Islamist terrorism in India would not only allow for the construction of a multi-scalar approach, but would also bring an entirely new perspective to the literature. Indeed, both the literature in the state-based approach and the transnational approach tends to be quite static: they do not engage with transformations in the nature of Islamist terrorism in India.

Additionally, the gap between the state-based and transnational approach can be reduced by allowing one to inform the other. The first step, as discussed before, is to abandon these approaches as analytical frameworks and to think of them as co-existing spheres of influence. However, if we maintain that the state-based approach has the advantage of looking at the smaller-scale while the transnational approach has the advantage of painting a broader picture, we can still use both together. For example, by first looking at Islamist terrorism on a more aggregate level and identifying particular trends, either with regard to the groups attacking, the locations of the attack, or the timings of the attack, it is possible to identify particular clusters of attacks (the most prominent groups, or years with the most attacks, etc.) and then try to establish the more local specificities of those clusters. Conversely, it would be possible to take the small-scale studies of groups like SIMI and place them in a broader context. For example, SIMI might have radicalized after the events at Ayodhya but since radicalizing, how does it function operationally? How does SIMI relate the training and funding network of other Islamist terrorist organizations?

So while one method of constructing a multi-scalar approach is to identify whether the domestic or transnational is more relevant at particular times and in particular spaces, the other is to use the domestic approach to inform the transnational (and vice versa). There are likely also several other ways to link these different levels of analysis. The crucial point is to abandon each approach as a bounded framework and instead to think of them as factors which interact with one another.

ISLAMIST MILITANCY IN KASHMIR: THE CASE OF THE LASHKAR-I TAYYEBA

The emergence of radical Islamist groups in Kashmir over the last decade has added a new dimension to the ongoing conflict in the region. It has led to a rapid transformation in the terms of discourse in which the conflict is represented, by India, Pakistan and by many Kashmiris themselves.

The current stage in the Kashmir conflict can be dated to 1989, when the Jammu and Kashmir Liberation Front (JKLF) inaugurated an armed uprising against Indian rule. By the mid-1990s, however, the JKLF had been increasingly taken over by Pakistan-based Islamist groups.

The wiping out of many of its cadres in confrontation with the Indian armed forces, the withdrawal of Pakistani support and the growing realisation of the need for peaceful, as opposed to military, means for the eventual resolution of the Kashmir dispute, seem to be among the major reasons for the gradual decline of the JKLF as a military force in Kashmir, despite the fact that its goal of an independent Kashmir still commands the support of many Kashmiri Muslims. On the other hand, military and other forms of support from the Pakistani establishment, from private *jihad*ist groups in Pakistan and elsewhere, in addition to a passionate zeal for what is seen as a 'holy' cause, account, in large measure, for the gradual take-over of the armed struggle in Kashmir by militant Islamist groups, mainly based in Pakistan and led, for the most part, by Pakistani nationals.

Despite the active involvement of Islamist groups in the on-going struggle in Kashmir, little written has been written about them from a scholarly and detached point of view.

This article seeks to provide an account of the ideology, organization and development of one of the leading Islamist groups active in Kashmir today, the Lashkar-i Tayyeba. Of the several Pakistan-based Islamist groups active in Kashmir today, the Lashkar is, by far, the most well-organised, well-trained and heavily armed.

From the mid-1990s, this once little known group has emerged today as the most serious challenge to the Indian armed forces, being responsible for several attacks in Kashmir, killing a large number of Indian soldiers as well as civilians, both Hindu as well as Muslim.

This article looks at the emergence of the Lashkar as a key player in the present stage of the Kashmiri struggle. Owing to the relative paucity of published material, the article relies heavily on the official Internet web site of the Markaz Da'wat wa'l Irshad ('Centre for Invitation and Instruction'), of which the Lashkar is the armed wing.

This article is divided into three main sections. Part I looks at the origins of the Lashkar in the specific South Asian context, tracing its understanding of Islam and *jihad* to the emergence of the Ahl-i Hadith ('The People of the Prophetic Tradition'), an Islamic reformist movement, in the sub-continent.

We then look at the ideology of the Lashkar, seeing how it seeks to fashion armed *jihad* as a means for the 'liberation' of Muslims from what it sees as 'oppression' and to advance its own stated goal of establishing the 'supremacy' of Islam, as it understands it, as a global ideology. Part II examines the involvement of the Lashkar in Kashmir, seeing it as emerging out of a broader Islamist movement in the region, the roots of which go back to the early years of the twentieth century. The concluding section of the article looks briefly at how far the Lashkar has been able to actually establish itself among the Kashmiri Muslims. In assessing its ability to do so, a distinction is stressed between, on the one hand, its military engagements against the Indian armed forces, and, on the other, its ability to impose its own vision of Islam as the accepted version.

The Lashkar: Early Origins

The Lashkar is the military wing of the Markaz Da'wat wa'l Irshad, with its headquarters at the town of Muridke in the Gujranwala district in Pakistani Punjab. The Markaz was established in 1986 by two Pakistani university professors, Hafiz Muhammad Sa'eed and Zafar Iqbal.

They were assisted by the late 'Abdullah Azam' a close aide of Osama bin Laden, who was then associated with the International

Islamic University, Islamabad. Funds for setting up the organization are said to have come from Pakistan's dreaded secret services agency, the Inter Services Intelligence (ISI).

The Markaz is affiliated to the Ahl-i Hadith school of thought, a reformist Islamic movement, which had its origins in early nineteenth century north India.

The founders of the Ahl-i Hadith, men such as Maulana Nazir Husain (1805-1902), Nawab Siddiq Hasan Khan Bhopali (d1832-90) and Maulana Sanaullah Amritsari (1870-1943), believed that they were charged with the divine responsibility of purging popular Muslim practice of what they saw as 'un-Islamic' accretions and borrowings from their Hindu neighbours, regarding these as 'unlawful innovations' (*bida'at*), and as akin to *shirk*, the sin of associating anything with God.

They insisted that Muslims must go back to the original sources of their faith, the Qur'an and the Hadith, the Traditions of the Prophet, and abandon all beliefs and practices not sanctioned therein. They called for Muslims to abide strictly by the Islamic law (*shari'ah*) and to abandon 'imitation' (*taqlid*) of the traditional schools of Islamic jurisprudence (*mazhab*. pl. *mazahib*), attempting to refashion the worldwide Muslim community in the mould of the Companions of the Prophet.

The '*ulama*of the Hanafi *mazhab*, representing the vast majority of the Muslims of South Asia, entered into bitter conflict with the Ahl-i Hadith on the matter of *taqlid*. The latter defended their opposition to *taqlid* on the grounds that the schools of jurisprudence had developed more than two hundred years after the death of the Prophet, and that, therefore, the Companions of the Prophet did not follow *taqlid*.

Since, they argued, Muslims should follow the model of the Companions, there was no need for them to 'blindly follow' the schools of jurisprudence, for this would be tantamount to 'personality worship' of the founders of the *mazahib*, a heinous sin. Further, they claimed, the Hanafis had fabricated numerous *hadith* to prove the claims of their *mazhab*, and quoted a *hadith* to the effect that 'he who fabricates *hadith* shall be thrown into hell-fire'.

Besides attacking the Hanafi *'ulama*, the Ahl-i Hadith directed their attention to bitterly critiquing Sufism, which they saw as a 'wrongful innovation', for, they argued, it had no sanction in the practice of the Prophet and his Companions. Every 'wrongful innovation', they insisted, was a heinous sin, the punishment for which was damnation in hell. They stiffly opposed the adoration of the Prophet as a superhuman being as well as the devotion to the saints and the cults centred on their shrines that are an integral part of popular Sufi tradition in South Asia, seeing this as a deviation from the practice of the Prophet and the early Muslims. Faith in the powers of Sufi preceptors and the widespread belief in the Sufi saints as intermediaries with God were condemned as akin to polytheism. So, too, was the belief in the supernatural powers of the Prophet and of his being ever-present and all-seeing.

Given the immense popularity of the Sufi traditions and the influence of the Hanafi 8*ulama* among the Muslims of South Asia, it was hardly surprising that the Ahl-i Hadith faced stiffed opposition, being banned from worship at mosques and condemned as apostates and enemies of Islam. For their part, the Ahl-i Hadith appeared to have revelled in controversy, not losing any opportunity of attacking their Muslim opponents for what they branded as their 'un-Islamic' ways.

Engaged in constant conflict with other Muslims, drawing clear lines of division between themselves as the only truly Muslim group and the rest, seems to have played a crucial role in the development of a separate Ahl-i Hadith identity.

Confrontation with other Muslim groups created an atmosphere conducive to militancy, and the Ahl-i Hadith saw themselves as carrying on in the long tradition of *jihad*, which they accused other Muslims as having abandoned.

The founders of the Ahl-i Hadith claimed the legacy of the early nineteenth century jihad movement led by Sayyed Ahmad Barelvi and Isma'il Shahid against the Sikhs in the Punjab.

In the failed revolt of 1857 against the British, several Muslim *ulama* associated with Ahl-i Hadith-style activism played a role in leading uprisings at some places.

After 1857, while some Ahl-i Hadith leaders accommodated themselves to British rule and devoted themselves to peaceful preaching, others continued to carry on violent struggles against the British in the North-West Frontier Province, till they were finally crushed by the end of the nineteenth century.

Although from the early twentieth century onwards the Ahl-i Hadith, as a whole, gave up the path of violence in the face of British arms, an Ahl-i Hadith scholar writes that they 'refused to accept the supremacy of the British and the Hindus', and vowed to carry on the struggle through other means to 'convert India into an abode of Islam (*dar-ul islam*) through *jihad*'.

While they desisted from entering into violent confrontation with the British, their opposition to Sufism and to the Hanafis brought them into conflict with many traditional Muslims, which sometimes took violent forms. However, they were doomed to a marginal existence owing to their vehement opposition to popular Muslim practice, and hence were not able to emerge as a mass movement. Rather, they remained an elitist group, characterised, as Barbara Metcalf writes, by a sense of 'moral superiority' and 'self-righteousness', tinged with 'a certain harshness', and with a small following among urban Muslims, particularly in north India.

LET ENTERS KASHMIR

Under the banner of LeT, foreign mercenaries were first introduced into Kashmir in 1993 and were dispersed within the mountainous regions. In this same year, the Islami Inqalbi Mahaz camp in Poonch District was established near the Line of Control (LOC) with the help of ISI and Pakistani military officers, and by 1994 LeT was ready to undertake major operations throughout the Kashmir Valley. At first, local militant groups were wary of LeT as its fighters were mostly foreign mercenaries and much more fundamentalist than the locals. Although this suspicion has subsided somewhat, it has not entirely evaporated as some indigenous groups question whether a mercenary-dominated LeT represents the interests of the Kashmiri people or Islamabad's foreign policy objectives. LeT's first mission was in October 1994 when a group of 50-60 militants ambushed an Indian army convoy and abducted and eventually executed five army personnel, including two officers. Since 1994, LeT has engaged in numerous attacks on not only Indian security forces in Kashmir, but also on Muslim and non-Muslim civilians. Further, *fidayeen* attacks such as the December 27, 1999, mission on the Indian Special Operations Group (SOG) headquarters have become a LeT trademark.

Even though LeT was in possession of considerable resources in the early 1990s, its successful establishment in Kashmir would not have been possible without ISI assistance. The construction of Islami Inqalbi Mahaz near the heavily fortified LOC would have required transport capabilities, smuggling expertise, and local contacts, all of which would have required a significant logistics capacity, something that LeT unlikely had in its possession. Stanley Bedlington, a former CIA official, supports this view and claims that ISI was intricately involved in LeT's initial development.

Although ISI was heavily involved in the early years of LeT, LeT clearly does not view itself as accountable to Pakistan any longer. Its involvement in the November 2008 Mumbai attack is testimony to this as it occurred at a very inopportune moment for Pakistan. At present, Pakistan is suffering from an economic crisis, surging inflation, a poorly-performing stock market, and considerable internal instability as a result of a myriad of militant groups. Rising tensions with India and the possibility of war would exacerbate all of these difficulties and strengthen the position of extremist groups in the country. None of this is in Pakistan's interest, and if LeT was overly concerned about maintaining favor with Pakistan its leadership would not engage in such a reckless operation.

Recruitment

LeT recruits and trains many more militants than it actually needs to fight in Kashmir at a given time, thus reducing its vulnerability to a massive strike and ensuring that the organization maintains an ample supply of reserves. LeT is also believed to be in possession of thousands of weapons including a substantial number of Chinese hand grenades and an unknown number of Chinese pistols. Most of LeT's recruits come from madrassas in

Pakistan, and even a few within India. Although some may find it hard to believe that LeT actually recruits Indian nationals to carry out attacks against their own country, the April 2, 2007, arrest of an ISI agent in Hyderabad is a clear demonstration that LeT does not view the Indian Union as inaccessible. The agent was detained for recruiting youth of behalf of LeT and JeM to engage in militant activity in Hyderabad and Gujurat.

The Student Islamic Movement of India (SIMI) was suspected of involvement in the July 2006 Mumbai train bombings (commonly referred to as the 7/11 bombings). It is alleged that they worked alongside of Pakistan-based LeT operatives and assisted them in illegally entering India. This home-grown militant group has gained power and influence over recent years and does not show signs of weakening. LeT experienced an increase in the recruiting of SIMI activists following the anti-Muslim riots in Bombay (Bombay was renamed Mumbai in 1995) in the 1990s and in Gujurat in 2002. However, Marwah, of the Institute for Defence Studies and Analyses (IDSA), India's key strategic think tank, believes that even though some Indian Muslims have begun to take a more anti-India stance, they have done so to increase pressure on New Delhi to give them more influence in the political system, but not necessarily because of Islamic extremist tendencies. Marwah's point is debatable. The fact that LeT now has operatives based in New Delhi, Mumbai, and other major Indian cities and was able to recruit Indian citizens to carry out attacks within India demonstrates that there exists some degree of sympathy towards their radical ideology, although the exact numbers are unknown.

Evidence has recently come to light that alleges that LeT has recruited thousands of mostly-Punjabi men ages 18 to 25 for operations in Iraq and that LeT hopes to send suicide bombers overland to Iraq through the porous Pakistan-Iran border. If accurate, this development is a clear demonstration of the increasing independence that LeT is exhibiting in its decisionmaking as it seeks to expand its scope of operations and possibly extend its influence outside the subcontinent. Further, by dispatching fighters to Middle Eastern conflict zones such as Iraq, LeT would be attempting to forge broader partnerships with like-minded militant groups, a move that would enhance LeT's operational capabilities and diversify its financial support base, thus further lessening its dependence on Islamabad and guaranteeing its continued existence in the medium term. However, it is of note that suicide bombings have not yet been used by LeT. Also, expect LeT to continue to prioritize South Asia while viewing the Middle East as a potential source of expert knowledge and funds.

LeT's India-centric recruitment efforts were not likely foreseen by many in Pakistan aside from the extremist elements within the government that were involved in the gradual evolution of the group. The initial decision to nurture and gradually introduce LeT into Kashmir was based on the premise that it would remain there at Islamabad's behest to carry out limited objectives vis-a-vis India but would not make any ill-advised moves that would escalate tensions to an unacceptable level. For nearly 2 decades, this analysis appeared to hold true until several international events and at least an official policy reversal by Pakistan regarding its support for irregulars prompted a dramatic revision in LeT's strategic thinking. This revision caused it to morph from a subservient proxy strictly following directives, while being careful not to harm Pakistani interests, to a group that is now overtly hostile to Islamabad and makes most of its own decisions. This lesson should not be lost in several capitals, namely Damascus and Tehran, and it must be recognized that when it comes to state sponsorship of terrorism or insurgency, no two actors have identical interests; and long-established ties do not mean that they are permanent or not subject to a review or even outright reversal by either party. However, by this time the nonstate actor has often developed an intimate knowledge of the society, economy, and governance structure of its former patron, thus allowing it to target the patron with increased lethality and effectiveness.

6

India's Home-Made Jihadi Threat

Unknown before 2008, the Indian Mujahedeen (IM) has emerged as a well-organized jihadi terrorist group in India, claiming responsibility for a number of terror attacks perpetrated in various urban centers of India during 2007-2008. Even though the exact moment of IM's formation is not known, the recent arrest of a number of IM operatives has revealed its possible existence and involvement in terror strikes in India as far back as late October 2005. The name "Indian Mujahideen" was reportedly conceived at a terrorist conclave attended by top leaders of the Lashkar-e-Taiba (LeT) and Harkat-ul-Jehadi Islami (HuJI) in Pakistani-administered Kashmir in early May 2008 (Rediff.com, July 29, 2008).

The well-concealed rise of the Indian Mujahedeen as a home grown jihadi organization is not a good omen for India's security. IM came into the open for the first time in November 2007, when simultaneous bomb blasts targeted lawyers in court premises in three Uttar Pradesh cities—Varanasi, Faizabad (Ayodhya), and Lucknow (NDTV, November 23, 2007). IM described the attacks as "Islamic raids" and justified them as revenge against lawyers who had allegedly assaulted a couple of Jaish-e-Muhammad terrorist suspects. IM also alleged that the lawyers had refused to take cases involving other alleged terrorists, including suspected HuJI leader and Phulpur-based Islamic cleric Muhammad Waliullah, the alleged mastermind of the March 2006 Sankatmochan temple blasts in Varanasi. In IM terror strikes, email messages have typically been sent out to the media prior to the attacks, describing IM viewpoints on issues such as the Babri mosque demolition, the Mumbai riots, the communal violence in Gujarat that followed the 2002 torching of a train carrying Hindus, and various atrocities against the Muslim community in Gujarat and beyond. IM cites these incidents as reasons for their Islamic Jihad. IM's email manifestos shed some light on its objectives. The group calls for spreading Islam in India and waging Jihad against the "infidels" (non-Muslims, i.e. Hindus) and establishing "God's government" according to Quranic tenets.

After prolonged investigations, Indian intelligence agencies have corroborated that members of IM are mainly drawn from proscribed outfits such as the Students Islamic Movement of India (SIMI), the Pakistan-based LeT and the Bangladesh-based HuJI. IM's email statements indicate their ties with SIMI when they put forward demands for the release of SIMI cadres under detention or serving jail terms. However, the newly emerged IM continues to deny any connection with Pakistan, Bangladesh, or any of their agencies (e.g. Pakistan's Inter-Services Intelligence [ISI] and Bangladesh's Directorate General of Forces Intelligence [DGFI]). It also denies any links with terrorist groups such as LeT and HuJI.

The Indian Mujahideen has been trying to garner support from India's teeming Muslim population, often by raising indigenous issues in its manifestos. Since the Uttar Pradesh Court attacks, IM, as a home-grown jihadi outfit, has claimed responsibility for at least four major terror strikes in 2008 that targeted civilians. Each attack came with prior emails to media citing a list of anti-Muslim atrocities in the country. The group justifies the violence by tagging the terror campaign as the "rise of Jihad" and the "revenge of Gujarat."

THE INDIAN MUJAHIDEEN'S URBAN MAYHEM

Massive IM terrorist attacks occurred throughout India in 2008, all apparently designed to inflict maximum civilian casualties:

- May 13, 2008: Jaipur, the capital city of Rajasthan State, suffered nine bomb blasts that killed over 60 and injured scores of people. The explosions occurred in busy MARKET places, including Tripolia market, Manek Chowk and Johri Bazaar.

- July 25, 2008: IM struck again in India's IT capital, Bengaluru (Bangalore, Karnataka State), with eight simultaneous low-intensity blasts, in which at least two people were killed and seven injured. The explosions occurred near the Madivala check point in Hosur Road, the Adugodi area, a place near the Mallya Hospital, and another site near the Rashtriya Military School.
- July 26, 2008: A series of over 16 synchronized bomb blasts hit Ahmadabad (Gujarat State), in which as many as 38 people were killed and more than 100 others injured. Most of the blasts occurred in crowded places like Hatkeshwar, Bapunagar, Narol, Ishanpur, Saraspur, Sarangpur, and L.G. General Hospital in Maninagar.
- September 13, 2008: The national capital, New Delhi, was hit by a series of five bomb blasts that killed nearly 30 people and injured over 100 others. The explosions took place in the crowded Karol Bagh area, the busy Barakhamba Road, the MARKET place at Greater Kailash, and the Central Park in Cannaught Place area.

After widespread mayhem in these vital urban centers, the organization was subject to a stepped-up counterterrorist crackdown on its operatives and hideouts across the country. At least six senior IM leaders are reported to have fled to Pakistan or Bangladesh after the Delhi serial blasts.

They were identified by Mumbai's Crime Branch as Riyaz Bhatkal, Amir Reza, Iqbal Bhatkal, Muhammad Khalid, Shahzad Ahmed, and Ariz Khan.

After months of investigations it is widely believed by intelligence agencies in India that the IM was created by Pakistan's ISI to operate beyond Kashmir. However, no conclusive evidence has been gathered to implicate the ISI in such an alliance. The alleged Pakistani connection has not been supported by the large number of arrests of Indian operatives after the recent terrorist attacks.

Terror Tentacles

Though many details of IM's organization remain unclear, some facets of the mystery were unraveled during the interrogations of arrested cadres, documented in the 1,809-page charge sheet filed by the Mumbai Crime Branch. 21 IM members have been charged for conspiracy, damaging a place of worship with intent to insult a particular religion, collecting arms for waging war, and waging war against the country.

Most of the accused are from Azamgarh in Uttar Pradesh and are well-qualified professionals (The Hindu, February 18). Among the 21 suspects is Muhammed Saif, who was involved in the September 13, 2008, New Delhi serial blasts and was later captured during the controversial October 19, 2008, Batla House raids, in which two suspects were killed.

Since his arrest, Muhammad Saif has provided details of the IM organization and its countrywide activities. According to his confession, the Indian Mujahedeen has four wings, each wing having a distinct responsibility for spreading terror in India with the LeT's active assistance (Bangalore Mirror, February 18; Rediff.com, February 10):

(1) Shahabuddin Ghouri Brigade: Headed by Amir Raza; responsible for planning and executing attacks in southern India, headquartered in Kerala

(2) Muhammad Ghaznavi Brigade: Responsible for planning and executing terror strikes in northern India

(3) Shaheed-al-Zarqawi Brigade: Responsible for targeting political and other important personalities of the country as well as organizing suicide attacks

(4) Media Wing: Headquartered in Pune, Maharashtra, the wing was responsible for email and print media communications/press release of manifestos before or after the blasts

The arrest of IM cadres from different locations demonstrates the geographical spread of a terror network that now spans the length and breadth of India—possibly even extending into neighbouring states.

Indian Mujahideen Who's Who

After months of speculation on the leadership hierarchy of IM, investigating agencies finally sketched a relatively clear picture of who's who in IM. Earlier, it had been speculated that the group's leader was Abdul Subhan Qureshi (a.k.a. Taqueer), a former SIMI cadre and software engineer by profession. However, instead the credit of founding the first home-grown Indian jihadi outfit goes to Sadiq Israr Sheikh of Azamgarh. A former SIMI member and an electronics engineer by profession, Sheikh has been identified as the co-founder and leader of the IM. Sheikh is alleged to have contacts with LeT in Pakistan through his brother-in-law, Mujahid Salim (The Hindu, February 22). The anti-terrorism squad of the Maharashtra police has been interrogating Sheikh regarding his role in the group's July 2006 serial train blasts in Mumbai. Sheikh has described how the group planted seven cookers filled with explosives on the train before getting off in advance of the blasts (Times of India, February 27). Sheikh's confession also indicates IM's hand in the March 2006 attack on the Sankat Mochan temple in Varanasi.

Riyaz Bhatkal (a.k.a. Ismail Shahbandri), who has eluded police so far, is the commander of the southern region. Iqbal Bhatkal, Riyaz's brother, has a senior position in the IM hierarchy, according to police sources. Riyaz Bhatkal was previously involved in organized crime in Mumbai as part of the infamous Fazlu Rehman gang (Chennai Online, September 27, 2008). Interrogation of arrested IM members revealed that Bhatkal was a key LeT operative in south India who had planned the Hyderabad, Bengaluru, Ahmadabad, and New Delhi serial blasts (Rediff.com, January 5). Abdul Subhan Qureshi, still on the run and formerly believed to be IM's leader, has now been confirmed as the IM second-in-command. Despite previously being named as one of the country's most wanted terrorist masterminds, Abdul Subhan's name did not appear in the recently filed chargesheet (Indian Express, February 19).

The most surprising revelation has been the many IT professionals found to be involved in IM's activities, including wealthy professionals Asghar Peerbhoy, Salman Kadar Shaikhand,

and Asif Bashiruddin Shaikh, who have played pivotal roles in generating FUNDS for the outfit and planning attacks. Peerbhoy, believed to have headed IM's media wing, reportedly worked for Yahoo.com before being arrested by the Mumbai Anti-Terror Squad in October 2008 (Indian Express, February 5, 2009).

INDIAN MUJAHIDEEN AND ITS DUBIOUS ORIGIN

For all the claims, the probing and prosecuting agencies have not come out with one individual who has a proven association with this so-called nationwide organization supposedly working at the behest of Lashkar e Toiba, Hizbul Mujahideen, Taliban and you name who, so how do we know IM really exists or is merely the figment of imagination of the IB/Saffron brigade happily lapped up by an already biased media?

But let us just glean through the official explanation. Wikipedia says, "Investigators believe that Indian Mujahideen is one of many groups composed of lower-tier SIMI members. According to the Indian Intelligence Bureau, SIMI took new titles because the top leadership of SIMI have been detained and would be available for interrogation. The change in name is believed to signal a change in tactics as SIMI affiliated militants attempt to garner more support from India's Muslim community rather than be seen as a group consisting of foreigners. Two days after the 13 May 2008 Jaipur bombings, the extremist group sent an e-mail to Indian media in which they claimed responsibility for the attacks and said they would "demolish the faiths (all religions apart from Islam) of the infidels of India". The biggest and boldest attack to date by the group was the 2008 Ahmedabad serial blasts, where it gained national notoriety with a casualty count towards 50."

Now who banned SIMI and when was it banned and on what grounds? First came the terror attack on the Indian Parliament on December 13, 2001, which is a grey area because of the apprehension of the whole exercise sponsored by the then NDA-led government and specifically the Union Home ministry under the then Home Minister LK Advani. Soon thereafter Narendra Modi led Gujarat government patronized the pogrom of Muslims ostensibly to avenge the burning down of kar sevaks in coach number S-6, in the Sabarmati Express on February 27, 2002, just two months after the Parliament attack. Those who don't suffer from a memory loss remember the whole charged atmosphere created by Advani-Modi and Jaitley combine against the Muslim youth in preparation of bringing in POTA and to justify POTA SIMI was banned just a little before POTA was conceived. While announcing the ban Advani held a press conference in North Block and distributed to the media some SIMI posters in Urdu, none of which carried any seditious material. All these were expressions of anger and frustration over the Gujarat pogrom and the inability of anyone to counter Modi.

So what is wrong in saying that IM is an outcome of Gujarat pogrom? When did IM come into prominence and how? The official version says, "Two days after the 13 May 2008 Jaipur bombings, IM sent an e-mail to the Indian media in which they claimed responsibility for the attacks and said they would "demolish the faiths of the infidels of India". The biggest and boldest attack to date by the group was the 2008 Ahmedabad serial blasts, where it gained national notoriety when 56 people were killed in those serial blasts." This is the official version.

Who according to the official version are prominent leaders of IM:

1. Abdus Subhan Qureshi, alias Ali Tauqeeer a Gujarati software engineer from Mumbai
2. Safdar Nagori from Indore
3. Qayamuddin Kapadia, a TRADER from Vadodra
4. Usman Agarbattiwala, a PG diploma holder from Vadodra
5. Alazeb Afridi, a jobless youth from Ahmedabad
6. Abdul Razzzak Mansuri, an embroidery unit owner from Gujarat
7. Mujib Shaikh, a stone polishing artisan from Gujarat
8. Zahid Sheikh, a mobile repair owner from Ahmedabad
9. Amil Parvaiz, a native of Ujjain. These were the original IM men according to the IB along with just one Mufti Abu Bashir from Azamgarh. Later after the Batla House incident of Delhi, according to the investigative agencies it had also

spread its tentacles in UP as well, and in particular in Azamgarh district.

But then stating the obvious becomes a crime and the BJP cries hoarse attacking poor Shakeel Ahmad while the Congress always lacking spunk, hurriedly withdraws what with the Heir Apparent in the ruling party advising everyone not to irritate BJP/Modi too much and so poor Shakeel has to shut up.

THE CHANGING THREAT TO THE "IDEA OF INDIA"

For most of India's history, dissenting parties to its founding idea—at least the ones that also pose threats of secession and violence—have metastasized in the form of separatist insurgencies. The majority of terrorist incidents in India have been the work of these insurgencies. Therefore, India's original counterterrorism strategy has been, in fact, a counterinsurgency strategy. For example, the Rashtriya Rifles, a specialized counterinsurgency force, was created to fight small-scale, low-intensity conflicts in Jammu and Kashmir, and the Indian army learned to integrate former insurgents, called*ikhwani*s, into cohorts that gather local intelligence in conflict zones. The government also provided civilian support and development assistance to insurgency areas in Punjab and Mizoram, addressing socioeconomic issues like unemployment, wealth disparities, and lack of education that exacerbate local tensions. But terrorism in India is no longer relegated to the mountains of Kashmir or the valleys of Manipur, and the culprits are not poor locals but rather well-trained urban soldiers.

Terrorism in India is no longer relegated to the mountains of Kashmir or the valleys of Manipur, and the culprits are not poor locals but rather well-trained urban soldiers.

Insurgencies employ terrorism for short-term tactical gains, but their preferred modus operandi is ideological indoctrination. Many terrorists, however, favor indiscriminate violence aimed at GENERATING feelings of insecurity and provoking harsh responses by the targeted governments. Terrorism in India has moved away from the ideological cast of insurgency. The indiscriminate nature of Indian jihadist violence today is evident in the terrorist attacks conducted over the last three years by radicalized members of the Students Islamic Movement of India (SIMI) and the Indian Mujahideen (IM), a prominent and well-networked Indian terrorist organization. In July 2006, SIMI militants detonated seven bombs on the suburban Mumbai railway system, killing two hundred commuters.

Then, in 2008, the cities of Jaipur, Bangalore, Ahmedabad, and New Delhi were all sites of IM bombings whose casualties were all civilians. This is distinct from separatist operations, which tend to target security personnel. The IM and rogue members of SIMI are based domestically, and their attacks are intended to target major urban and suburban areas in order to inflict heavy civilian casualties. Not only are their motives fundamentalist and pan-Islamist, but the groups are also fueled by domestic grievances, such as ethnic riots, religious discrimination, and opposition to Hindu nationalist politics.

The IM, an umbrella organization that includes members of SIMI and other smaller groups, networks Indian terrorists across the country and organizes attacks. Its leaders, Riyaz Bhatkal and Abdul Subhan Usman Qureshi, both former engineers raised in middle-class families in Mumbai, have built a network of young radicals (including former software engineers and small businessmen) to manufacture bombs and attack India's largest cities.

Consider the July 2008 bombings in Ahmedabad. The IM prepared for these attacks in a highly coordinated, albeit decentralized, manner. Atif Amin, an IM commander, led the assault team, which planted the bombs, while a computer graphics designer, Qayamuddin Kapadia, provided safe houses and logistical support. At the same time, Bhatkal designed the bombs, and Qureshi coordinated the entire operation. A few days before their mission, three IM operatives took a train from New Delhi to Ahmedabad to conduct reconnaissance, finding unsecured wireless Internet sites for use during the bombings. Based in several cities, including Ahmedabad, Mumbai, New Delhi, and Mangalore, these terrorists used CELL PHONES, Wi-Fi, and GPS to run a sophisticated and efficient operation that was difficult to track in real time.

In an e-mail entitled "The Rise of Jihad, Revenge of Gujarat," sent by the IM following the Ahmedabad bombings, the terrorists invoke distinctly political tones in their tirade against Hindu nationalist organizations such as the Bharatiya Janata Party (BJP), the Rashtriya Swayamsevak Sangh, and the Vishwa Hindu Parishad, calling for Gujarati Muslims to take revenge for the 2002 Hindu-Muslim riots in their state. The e-mail also lashes out at counterterrorist police forces in several states for their alleged religious profiling and at the Indian government in general for its discrimination and "harassment" of Muslims. Finally, the e-mail concludes with a request "to Lashkar-e-Toiba and other organizations, for the sake of Allah, not to claim the responsibility for these attacks." Indeed, the IM and similar domestic jihadists are distinctly Indian groups with Indian goals, but they have become allies of convenience with Pakistan and Pakistani operatives.

The Pakistan Question

Indian Muslim radicals expose India's cultural and religious fissures and fault lines, just as Sikhs, Tamils, and Nagas have in the past. The terrorists attempt to redress their grievances through acts of violence and propagate the notion that minorities—especially Muslims—cannot live peacefully in the Hindu-dominated Indian democracy. This is an image that Pakistan takes advantage of for its own strategic interests in Kashmir and for Indian-Pakistani relations in general.

Just as India used counterinsurgency strategy in the past to contain domestic separatists, it will have to create a new counterterrorism strategy to deter domestic jihadists.

Many analysts argued that the three-day siege of Mumbai in November 2008 by LeT only confirmed Pakistan's internal instability and inability to control expanding jihadist threats. Even the U.S. Joint Forces Command referred to Pakistan as a possible "failed state." Quite the contrary: Pakistan's strong military, which keeps Pakistan from failing, appears to dictate the country's internal and external decision-making for its own strategic interests. In the context of the geopolitical duel between Pakistan and India, which is underlined by their conflict of founding ideas, LeT's operations and Pakistan's inaction toward them make sense. LeT is simply another operative in Pakistan's quest to corrode the idea of India, and as LeT's proxy war raises tensions on the border, the Pakistani military can also shift focus away from a difficult mission in the tribal areas of Baluchistan and the North West FRONTIER Province. Even though Pakistan fights the same Islamists at home, the benefit provided by their operations in India makes the Pakistani choice more complex than it appears. Yet, Pakistani attempts to chip away at the idea of India are nothing new.

In the late 1980s and early 1990s, Punjabi Sikh militants who were part of the Khalistan independence movement, which advocated for the creation of a separate Sikh state, engaged in a series of riots, assassinations, and bombings across India. During this time, Pakistan and its Inter-Services Intelligence (ISI) provided FUNDING, refuge, and training sites for these militants. Since then, the leader of the International Sikh Youth Federation, Lakhbir Singh Rode, who has been accused of "arms smuggling and conspiracy to attack government and political leaders in Delhi," has been allowed to live in and work from Lahore. Apart from the Sikh movement, Pakistani militants supported by the ISI have sponsored and conducted attacks in Jammu and Kashmir. LeT, for example, has conducted the majority of its operations in the disputed region, with eighteen attacks between September 2001 and October 2004.

New evidence also shows that LeT has been able to conspire with Indian separatist groups that did not previously associate with radical Islamists. In Northeast India, the United Liberation Front of Assam, the National Democratic Front of Bodoland, and other militants have worked with jihadist groups in their latest attacks. In what the Jamestown Foundation calls "ethno-Islamist" terrorism, there were, for the first time, "tell-tale signs of collaboration between ethnic-separatist militants and Muslim jihadi groups with a strong cross-border reach." After more than a decade of calm, it also appears that Pakistan has begun to renew its support for Sikh militants fighting for an independent Khalistan—this time with the support of LeT and Jaish-e-Mohammad, another

Pakistan-based jihadist group. In each of these cases, from the Khalistan movement to the Mumbai shootings, the involvement of LeT and Pakistani operatives only reflects the increasing internationalization of the jihadist threat in India. The threat is still rooted domestically, under the leadership of Indian Muslim jihadists, but both Pakistan and LeT have been able to take advantage of the vacuum in which these jihadists operate in order to pursue their own strategic goals, whether they are geopolitical gains or global Jihad. Just as India used counterinsurgency strategy in the past to contain domestic separatists, it will have to create a new counterterrorism strategy to deter domestic jihadists.

The State of Indian Muslims

The increasing radical activity of Indian Muslims—especially those of the urban middle class—poses questions: Do Indian Muslims in general buy in to the "idea of India"? Is domestic terrorism reflective of wider sentiment among the Indian *ummah*, or are these attacks merely outliers conducted by disillusioned rogues acting irrationally and excessively?

The World Values SURVEY asks subjects to respond to a series of questions about cultural and national identity, trust, and happiness. It is possible to tabulate these responses based on religion. In the case of India, not only are Indian Muslims equally as happy and proud to be Indian as Hindus, they tend to be apolitical and broadly respectful of democracy. Approximately 90 percent of Indian Muslims and Hindus express pride in being Indian, assert the importance of democracy, and are willing to fight for their country. According to the survey, Muslims are also slightly more active in religious practice (90 percent versus 80 percent) and less trusting of others (71 percent versus 61 percent) than Hindus, but they believe almost as strongly as Hindus that society should not be radically changed (85 percent to 86 percent).

Anecdotal evidence adds further confirmation of Muslim integration. Muslims play prominent roles in Indian popular culture and political life. Three of the country's most famous and widely adored Bollywood actors are Muslims named Khan (Salman Khan, Shah Rukh Khan, and Aamir Khan). The award-winning song by Muslim composer A. R. Rahman, "Jai Ho," from the blockbuster *Slumdog Millionaire* (which itself features a successful Muslim protagonist), became this year's campaign theme song for India's Congress Party. And in politics, A. P. J. Abdul Kalam was elected the first Muslim president of India by the parliament in 2002. Muslims are underrepresented in politics at the national level, but not significantly; they hold 8 percent of the seats against their national population share of 13.4 percent.

Evidence from the World Values SURVEY and examples of Muslim integration in Indian popular culture appear to support the idea that Muslims are not inherently excluded from the country's identity. Nevertheless, as a report by the Prime Minister's High Level Committee (the Sachar Commission) on the status of India's Muslims shows, there are still significant discrepancies between the socioeconomic status of Muslims and other Indians. By some measures, Muslims rank near the "untouchable" Scheduled Tribes and Scheduled Castes.

While Hindus had a literacy rate of 80.5 percent in 2004-2005, the rate for Muslims was 59.9 percent. Higher education graduation rates are also significantly disparate, with only 4.5 percent of Muslims between the ages of twenty and thirty having degrees at the tertiary level in 2004-2005, as opposed to 18.6 percent of Hindus aged twenty to thirty. As the report states, "In urban areas, Muslims are falling behind not only vis-a-vis 'All Other [Minorities],' but also Scheduled Castes and Scheduled Tribes in several states."

Despite the presence of Muslims in prominent political and cultural spaces in India, the majority of Indian political and economic power still rests in the hands of Hindus, both secular and orthodox.

Compared to the national average, a larger proportion of Indian Muslims work in the informal sector of the economy or are engaged in "small proprietary enterprises." Yet, as the Sachar Commission report notes, "the access of Muslims to bank credit... is low and inadequate," and the share of banking facilities is much lower in villages where the percentage of the Muslim population exceeds 50 percent.

Discrimination against Muslims is also evident in civil society, in which segregation continues to be the rule rather than the exception. In 2006, Muslims made up only 4.9 percent of all government employees and 3.2 percent of all civil service officers. It is also important to note the vast underrepresentation of Muslims in the Indian army: out of 1.1 million soldiers, only 29,000 (2.6 percent) are Muslims.

In addition to social rifts, the ongoing religious and political tug-of-war between certain Hindu and Muslim factions could exacerbate extremism. Three events in modern Indian history—the destruction of the Babri Mosque in 1992, the 2002 riots in Gujarat, and the 1986 Shah Bano case—have dictated these tensions. The first two events, cases of religious violence between Hindu and Muslim fanatics, are of importance because of their human toll in addition to their impact on political debate. In 1992, a group of Hindu nationalists destroyed a sixteenth-century mosque in the town of Ayodhya, claiming that the mosque was built on the birthplace of the Hindu god Ram. A riot spread following the destruction, in which two thousand Indians, mostly Muslims, were killed. In 2002, more than one thousand people perished in riots in Gujarat following an arson attack on a train of Hindu pilgrims. Once again, the majority of victims were Muslims, and the BJP-led state government was widely criticized for its failure to respond to the pogrom.

The origins of these riots still evoke debate among members of the BJP, secular Hindu politicians, and Muslims in fear of a reprisal. The Hindu-Muslim conflict also hinders political discourse by prioritizing ethnic and religious divisions over critical social and economic issues. For example, in the latest election campaign, BJP candidate Varun Gandhi—an estranged member of the Nehru-Gandhi political dynasty and grandson of former prime minister Indira Gandhi—was arrested after making disparaging remarks about Muslim parliamentary candidates and telling supporters at a rally that he would "cut the hands" of anyone who "raised a finger towards Hindus."

The other turning point, the Shah Bano case of 1986, reflects discrepancies in the legal and institutional status of Muslims versus those of other Indians. In 1986, Shah Bano, a sixty-two-year-old Muslim divorcée, filed a suit to claim alimony from her husband, claiming that she had no means to support herself and her children. While orthodox Muslims felt that alimony was unacceptable according to *sharia* law, the Supreme Court ruled in her favor, invoking the Indian Code of Criminal Procedure. Following the ruling, an organization of Muslim community leaders and intellectuals successfully lobbied the government to overrule the court's decision. The government's appeasement was derided as "pseudosecularism" by its opponents, and it set a precedent for Indian Muslims that has made room for self-imposed compartmentalization and isolation from mainstream society.

Despite the presence of Muslims in prominent political and cultural spaces in India, the majority of Indian political and economic power still rests in the hands of Hindus, both secular and orthodox. As the primary owners of the country's political and economic capital, these Hindus should be conscious of their implicit responsibility to prevent calamities like the Babri Mosque destruction and the Gujarat riots and to bolster the social and economic inclusion of Muslims in the country.

But there is also an onus on the leaders of the Indian Muslim community to reconcile Muslim identity with Indian identity and address Indian Muslims' radicalization and social segregation. The ability of external forces, regardless of their strength, to influence the Muslim community is limited, compared to the capacity of Muslims themselves to address these issues. The Shah Bano case is an example of self-imposed isolation that hinders ethnic and cultural integration and compromises the secular nature of the Indian polity, which, as the World Values SURVEY shows, is not contrary to wider Muslim sentiment.

Conclusion

There is no easy path to prevent middle-class Indian Muslims from radicalizing and attacking their fellow citizens. But before addressing the problem, the Indian government must understand the roots of domestic jihadism and its implications for India's long-term strategy. As Angel Rabasa et al. write, " t the strategic level, the Mumbai attack underscores the imperative of addressing the transnational sources of Islamist terrorism in India. How to do this is an extraordinarily difficult question that will require the reassessment of basic assumptions concerning policy toward Pakistan by members of the international community."

Nevertheless, the transnationalization of Islamist terrorism in India is rooted in the growing strength and scope of domestic Islamist terrorism, as evidenced by the increasing frequency and magnitude of attacks in urban areas of India. The attacks in Mumbai were merely one more step down a road that organizations such as the IM have been paving for more than a decade.

For more than six decades, Indian governments, despite occasional domestic pressures from the far right and left wings, have remained steadfast in their commitment to preserving the "idea of India." The threats to this idea continue to exist, but they have changed significantly. In a "post-11/26" world, preserving Nehru and Gandhi's vision of a secular and pluralistic democracy will require more than just a tough stance across the Indian-Pakistani Line of Control. It will require a reassessment of counterterrorism and counterinsurgency at home and a renewed focus toward the integration and assimilation of minorities, specifically Muslims, into the expansive definition of India.

THE NEW JIHADIS

Karachi residents Muhammad Fahim and Muhammad Abdul Walid, held by the Uttar Pradesh police last week, told investigators that they had first been recruited by the Lashkar-e-Taiba, and then broke with it to make their way to a Taliban training camp in Afghanistan's southern Helmand district. Then, they were led by the fugitive Pune *jihadist*, Mohin Chaudhury to the Indian Mujahideen's Karachi-based chief, Riyaz Shahbandri. Faisalabad-based bombmaker Zia-ur-Rahman, Mr. Akhtar's recently arrested deputy, served with Taliban groups in Pakistan's Punjab before volunteering to serve with the Indian Mujahideen fighting across the border.

Meanwhile, new *jihadist* cells have sprung up within India. The recruits include young people, their minds fired by Internet

Islamism, as well as veterans once linked to the proscribed Students Islamic Movement of India (SIMI). Fugitive Ranchi resident Haider Ali, the National Investigation Agency (NIA) says, raised volunteers from both these groups for the bombing of the revered Buddhist shrine at Bodh Gaya last year, as an act of vengeance for communal violence against Myanmar's Rohingya Muslim minority.

Mr. Ali's cell, only loosely connected through him to the Indian Mujahideen, followed up that attack with an attempt to assassinate Gujarat Chief Minister Narendra Modi at a rally in Patna, surprising the organisation's leadership in Karachi.

In Tamil Nadu, volunteers at a Chennai college even signed up to serve with *jihadists* in Syria — recruited by local Islamists, and financed by a Singapore-based executive.

Key commanders of the Indian Mujahideen, meanwhile, remain active in Karachi, most important of them being Riyaz Shahbandri, his brother Iqbal Shahbandri and Abdul Subhan Qureshi. There are a host of second-rung leaders still at large, like Mirza Shadab Beg, Shahnawaz Alam, Muhammad "Bada" Sajid, Alamzeb Afridi, Zulfikar Fayyaz "Kagazi," Rahil Sheikh and Ariz Khan. The man who financed them all, ganglord Amir Raza Khan, is also at large.

The western storm

From Internet chats between Mr. Shahbandri and Mr. Siddibapa, recovered by the NIA, we know that several of those men have sought combat training with *jihadists* in Pakistan's north-west, and in Afghanistan, developing skills the Indian Mujahideen's cadre never had.

It has long been evident that the gathering storm of violent Islamism in Pakistan would lash India, too. In 2010, al-Qaeda released a posthumous audio message from Egyptian *jihadi* Said al-Masri, claiming responsibility for the bombing of the German Bakery in Pune. "The person who carried out this operation was a heroic soldier from the Soldiers of the Sacrifice Brigade, which is one of the brigades of Qaedat al-Jihad [the al-Qaeda's formal name] in Kashmir, under the command of Commander Illyas Kashmiri, may Allah preserve him."

Mr. al-Masri's message was wrong on several details of the operation, but for investigators, news that elements of al-Qaeda had developed links with *jihadi* groups acting against India did not surprise anyone.

David Headley, the Pakistani-American Lashkar operative now serving a life term for his role in the 26/11 attacks, had told the NIA of an anti-India "Karachi project" linked to global *jihadi* groups.

Driven by communal events

Following Pakistani military ruler General Pervez Musharraf's 2007 siege of jihadists holed up inside Islamabad's Lal Masjid, Mr. Headley told the NIA, that an ideological war broke out among Pakistan's*jihadis*. In spite of efforts by Pakistan's Inter-Services Intelligence, he said, the "aggression and commitment shown to *Jihad* by the several splinter groups influenced many committed fighters to leave Kashmir-centric outfits and join the Taliban."

In turn, al-Qaeda became increasingly interested in India, as a means of competing for influence and legitimacy with traditional *jihadi* groups like the Lashkar, which were supportive of the Pakistani state. In the wake of 26/11, al-Masri himself released a statement warning India of attacks if it struck against Pakistan.

The renewal of a *jihadist* constituency within India shouldn't be a surprise: the rise of Mr. Modi, and the Hindu nationalist tendencies he represents, has unleashed existential anxieties among large numbers of Indian Muslims. Though the numbers of jihadi recruits are minuscule, the members of the new cells are also true to a familiar pattern. The earliest Indian *jihadist* formation, the Tanzim Islahul Muslimeen, was formed to protect Muslims against communal violence, and carried out its first strike, the 1993 bombings of inter-city express trains, to avenge the demolition of the Babri Masjid.

In interrogations, Indian *Jihad* volunteers have repeatedly said they acted to avenge the Gujarat carnage of 2002. Feroze Ghaswala told police he had volunteered to join *Jihad* training after witnessing the mass burial of 40 Gujarat riot victims.

Peedical Abdul Shibly and Yahya Kamakutty, both successful computer professionals, are alleged to have prepared to carry out attacks in Bangalore. Men from Kerala trained in the mountains of Jammu and Kashmir with the Lashkar-e-Taiba. Zabiuddin Ansari, from Maharashtra, famously ended up in the 26/11 control room.

Founded in April 1977, SIMI, the fountainhead of the modern Indian *jihadist* movement, was itself driven by the forces of communal violence.

From the outset, scholar Yoginder Sikand has said "that Islam alone was the solution to the problems of not just the Muslims of India, but of all Indians and, indeed, of the whole world." It drew thousands disillusioned with traditional politics, Dr. Sikand has recorded, providing supporters "a sense of power and agency which they were denied in their actual lives."

From December 1992, following the demolition of the Babri Masjid, SIMI's language became increasingly aggressive. In a statement in 1996, it declared that since democracy and secularism had failed to protect Muslims, the sole option was to struggle for the caliphate. Soon after, it put up posters calling on Muslims to follow the path of Mahmood Ghaznavi, the 11th century warlord. In 2001, after the 9/11 attacks, SIMI activists organised demonstrations hailing Osama bin-Laden as a "true mujahid."

Early in the summer of 2004, a group of young men fed up with SIMI's inability to act on its own talk gathered in the small coastal town of Bhatkal in Mangalore — and founded what we now call the Indian Mujahideen.

THE JIHADI TRADITION

To understand the durability of the *Jihad* within India, it is important to remember that its cadre are inheritors of a long political tradition. In a manifesto sent to the media after their September 2008 bombings in New Delhi, the group said the attacks were carried out "in the memory of two most eminent Mujahids of India: Sayyed Ahmed Shaheed and Shah Ismail Shaheed (may Allah bestow His Mercy upon them) who had raised the glorious banner of Jihad against the disbelievers." The historian Ayesha Jalal has shown that the notion of *Jihad* was an important theme in both pre-colonial and colonial India. Syed Ahmad and Shah Ismail were killed battling Sikh troops in a failed *Jihad* involving the tribes of Pakistan's north-west.

Historian Stephen Dale has observed that these ideas stretched to the south of India, noting the work of the Sixteenth Century author, Zayn al-Din al-Ma'bari, who chronicled the *Jihad* against Portugal's intrusions into the Indian Ocean, hoping to "inspire the Faithful to undertake a *Jihad* against the worshippers of the cross."

Each bombing the Indian Mujahideen carries out is a medium for a political message enmeshed with India's dystopic communal landscape: that democratic politics cannot defend India's Muslims. India's intelligence and police services deserve credit for the long war they have fought, but it is time for politicians to act to heal our fractured nation.

THE MUMBAI BLASTS AND THE INDIAN MUJAHIDEEN

On Wednesday evening, bombs tore through three separate parts of Mumbai over a 15 minute period. They spanned Dadar West, Zaveri Bazaar, and Opera House. Early estimates of the injury and death toll suggest that this is more lethal than the February 2010 bombing of a bakery in Pune, which killed 14, but much less severe than the November 2008 commando-style raids that killed nearly 170.

Mumbai, as the commercial capital of India, has long been a target of foreign and domestic jihadi groups. For residents, these explosions will trigger terrible memories of a series of blasts in 1993 that killed 250. Those attacks were the first acts of mass casualty terrorism on Indian soil, and the first jihadi (as opposed to, say, separatist) attacks against India outside Kashmir. After a lengthy gap, a pair of CAR bombs killed 50 in 2003, and seven bombs against trains killed 209 in 2006. Since 1993, roughly 700 people have been killed in Mumbai.

THE INDIAN MUJAHIDEEN

Indian sources have indicated, though tentatively, that the Indian Mujahideen (IM) may be responsible. This is an opaque group about which relatively little is known. It first claimed responsibility for serial bombings in multiple north Indian cities in 2007, and came to prominence after attacks in Ahmedabad in 2008. It has also claimed responsibility for numerous other attacks, including those in Jaipur, Bangalore, and Delhi.

Indian TELEVISION channel NDTV noted in 2008 that "investigators say the Indian Mujhadeen is a front for groups operating out of Pakistan most likely the [Pakistan-based group] Lashkar-e-Taiba [LET]". This is almost certainly a severe oversimplification of the group's origins.

The IM is principally the product of the Student's Islamic Movement of India (SIMI). SIMI formed in 1977 within India itself, as a student wing of the Jamaat-e-Islami-i-Hind (though the latter has condemned terrorist attacks, including the 2008 Mumbai attacks). In 1986 SIMI called for the 'liberation' of India's Muslims and, at some point in the 1990s, evolved into a militant organisation with (ongoing) ties to LET.

SIMI then evolved into IM from 2001 after increasing numbers of the group acquired a violent pan-Islamic, but India-focused, agenda (many other members wished to remain non-violent). Praveen Swami, an Indian journalist and expert on Indian jihadi groups, describes IM as 'a loose cluster of semi-autonomous SIMI-linked cells' rather than an independent and separate organisation.

Indian intelligence also claims that elements of the pan-Islamic Harkat ul-Jihad-e-Islami (HUJI, whose operational commander, Ilyas Kashmiri, was recently killed in Pakistan) and a separate criminal-jihadi network led by Aftab Ansari contributed to the formation of IM.

Home-grown terrorism

SIMI's (and, thereafter, IM's) distinguishing characteristic was that it was, essentially, home-grown. Its activists and leaders are virtually all Indian. It recruited lower and middle class Indian Muslims, as well as a smaller number of educated professionals.

Key members of the network were motivated by the 2002 anti-Muslim pogroms in the Indian state of Gujarat; that horrific event proved a boon for wider recruitment too. IM's training was reportedly in places like Kerala and Gujarat, not primarily on Pakistani soil. Core leaders hailed from the Indian state of Uttar Pradesh (UP).

This is quite unlike that GENERATION of groups who cut their teeth on the anti-Soviet Jihad, later shifted to Kashmir with the assistance of the ISI, and today form ad hoc groupings of inter-operable or cooperative networks across Pakistan.

This is crucially important, because it greatly lessens the likelihood that these attacks will precipitate an India-Pakistan crisis, as with the major standoff that occurred during 2001-2.

INDIAN MUHAJIDEEN AND LASHKAR-E-TAIBA

This is not to say that Pakistani intelligence plays no role. SIMI and IM have extensive ties to Pakistan-based groups like LET and HUJI. The general secretary of SIMI, Safdar Nagori, after his arrest in 2008, claimed that the ISI had provided FUNDS to the group. Captured members of LET have also described a broad funding, training, and operational interface between that group and IM.

Indeed, far from being a self-contained group, 'LET serves as a provider of logistical and ideological infrastructure to the regional jihadist movement'-including IM. Christine Fair, a professor at Georgetown, notes that 'SIMI/IM appears to be an important vector of LET infiltration and cultivation of Indian leaders and cadres'.

Interrogations of David Coleman Headley, the Pakistani-American member of LET with a major role in the 2008 Mumbai attacks, pointed to the existence of a 'Karachi Project'. This was a scheme, overseen by the ISI, to mobilise Indian Muslims for attacks on Indian urban targets, moving them to Pakistan via third countries like Bangladesh or Nepal.

Vikram Sood, the former head of India's foreign intelligence service, argues that this heralds 'a new phase of terrorism within India, where international terrorist groups like LET and HUJI (and through them Al Qaeda), are likely to exert influence on a small and diffused group of individuals to take up arms against the state in the name of religion'. The devastating 2006 attack on multiple Mumbai targets was, according to some ACCOUNTS, a LET operation implemented through SIMI or IM. This indicates the depth and strength of ties between these ostensibly discrete groups. In turn, LET is closely connected to the ISI.

Although THE DEGREE of granular ISI control over LET operations is contested, most authoritative accounts are in agreement that, at the very least, the state determines the parameters in which the group can operate. Christine Fair, for instance, notes simply that 'for Pakistan, LET is an existential asset in the same way that it is an existential enemy for countries like India and even the United States'.

Although the semi-indigenous character of IM undercuts repeated Indian claims that Indian Muslims are not a meaningful part of jihadi terrorism, this should not be understood as diminishing the major problem of Pakistani state sponsorship and de facto protection of militant organisations. Although it is important to remember that SIMI and IM would not vanish were Pakistan to become cooperative, their operational capabilities and underlying strength would suffer serious damage.

Implications for the India-Pakistan Relationship

But SIMI and IM, unlike LET or Jaish-e-Mohammed or other such groups, are perceived to be outside the direct control or immediate influence of the Pakistani state. One officer involved with the investigation at Zaveri Bazaar did observe that this "attack is very different from the one we had in 2008... here there is no Pakistani involvement it is very clear from the early evidence we have collected."

This will limit not just Indian demands for retaliation against Pakistan, but also persuade influential states, and the US in particular, that Indian action would not be warranted. Moreover, the use of explosives rather than *fedayeen* (commando) tactics lessens the prolongation of the attack and therefore the theatrical effect. This, too, lessens the prospect of a forceful response.

Indian investigators have not yet made any conclusions about responsibility. The absence of an email claiming responsibility, the usual practice of IM hitherto, is strange. Moreover, a series of arrests by Indian security officials since 2008 had weakened the group's operational capability. In December 2010, Indian authorities claimed that four LET members had entered Mumbai with the intention of carrying out an attack.

It remains possible that these attacks were carried out by (1) LET, under the supervision of the ISI (perhaps to deflect attention from the Pakistani military's travails at home); (2) LET, without the supervision but with the cognizance of the ISI; (3) LET, with neither the supervision nor cognizance of the ISI; (4) a separate but affiliated Pakistan-based group; (5) by IM, acting in close concert with Pakistani affiliates; (6) IM, acting in relative isolation.

These (non-exhaustive) possibilities are not all equally likely. Prior attacks suggest that scenario (5) is the most plausible, though it is crucially important to stress that this assessment is purely speculative. The Indian authorities' praiseworthy reticence in apportioning blame indicates that the evidence is still ambiguous.

If IM turns out to have been at the front-line of the attack, this is almost certainly enough to guarantee that India-Pakistan relations will remain stable. India's prime minister, Manmohan Singh, is suffering serious domestic political difficulties. He has staked large amounts of political capital on the resumed dialogue with Pakistan, which was scheduled to convene later this month, and has been perceived as relatively successful by both parties.

If, however, LET's role is prominent, then the situation is far more unpredictable-options will quickly appear. In the longer-term, it is imperative to understand *both* the domestic factors enabling the consolidation of SIMI and IM *and* the thicket of cross-border links on which they rely for their operational potency; ignoring either of these will simply allow the stream of such killings to continue apace.

APPROACHES TO ISLAMIST TERRORISM IN INDIA

In this chapter, my objective is to briefly outline the two main approaches to understanding Islamist terrorism in India, as well as their advantages and disadvantages as they pertain to the scope of analysis. Subsequent chapters will expand on these overviews to outline the implications of these approaches with regard to their conclusions. The term 'approach' as it is used in this chapter does not refer to a particular research methodology (e.g. case study, discourse analysis), but rather to a paradigmatic framework. An 'approach', in this context, establishes particular conceptual parameters and understands Islamist terrorism within this lens. Each approach also tends to have a certain level of analysis.

Scholars who take the state-based approach view Islamist terrorism in India in relation to the Indian state. Their level of analysis tends to be much smaller as their studies rely on the examples of particular terrorist organizations. These small-scale studies are advantageous as they provide a more nuanced understanding of Islamist terrorism. Additionally, they can contextualize the rhetoric of 'global Jihad' and 'the global war on terror' to explain its relevance (and often lack thereof) to India. The primary disadvantage of the state-based approach is that the claims it makes, based on the examples it uses, tend not to be representative of Islamist terrorism in India as whole. While studies that are not representative can still be informative, it is a limitation when considering that the goal of this chapter is to identify the best approach to understanding Islamist terrorism in India as a whole.

The transnational approach mainly uses "large-n" studies, focusing on broader trends instead of specific examples. Scholars who pursue this approach look beyond the Indian state for explanations of terrorism, and often at the relationship between India and Pakistan. Perhaps unsurprisingly, many advantages of the transnational approach are disadvantages of the small-scale state-based approach, and vice versa. The transnational approach is much more useful for understanding the majority of Islamist terrorism in India but it often does so using the post-9/11 discourse, and consequently is not poised to identify the ways in which the Indian context is idiosyncratic.

A third key component of this chapter is not an approach, but a type of evidence, which is incorporated into subsequent chapters. As indicated in my methodology section, I have used empirical data from the GTD and the RDWTI. This type of data has rarely been applied to the study of Islamist terrorism in India, and therefore offers a unique perspective but is also subject to numerous limitations. The GTD collected information about attack attempts from 1990-1997 as they were occurring, but collected information retrospectively for attack attempts between 1998 and 2007. Therefore, evidence of a greater number of attacks from 1990-1997 compared to 1998-2007 could partly be due to data collection errors as certain publications are no longer around. Additionally, the GTD has a category in its datasets called 'guncertain,' which allows the user to differentiate between an attack in which a perpetrator is unconfirmed but suspected and an attack in which the perpetrator has been verified by a non-government analyst.

In analyzing the data, I did not differentiate between the two categories as a key feature of Islamist terrorist organizations is that they tend not to claim responsibility for an attack (Devji 2005). And while the GTD does attempt to verify its information, my inclusion of both categories of attacks does pose a problem because the number of actual confirmed attacks attributed to each organization could be different.

A second major limitation of this data is that I had to use my own judgment in determining whether an act of terrorism was specifically an act of *Islamist* terrorism. Given all the assumptions I made through the process described in the previous methodology chapter, it is very possible that someone else would have slightly different numbers than the ones stated in this chapter. However, the groups which make up the majority of discussion in the paper, such as Lashkar-e-Taiba (LeT), the Students Islamic Movement of India (SIMI), the Indian Mujahideen (IM), are viewed as Islamist terrorist organizations by the scholars included in this chapter.

ISLAMIST TERRORISM AND THE INDIAN STATE: THE STATE-BASED APPROACH

On December 6, 1992, the state of Uttar Pradesh was the site of one of the most significant moments of religious conflict in India's history. Approximately 200,000 people were demonstrating in Ayodhya when 'Hindu nationalist militants climbed a sixteenth century mosque, the Babri Masjid, and with pick hammers, pipes and sticks, battered the sacred structure to the ground' (Bacchetta 200: 255)

On the anniversary of the mosque demolition, Jalees Ansari, a former resident of Uttar Pradesh and a graduate of Maratha College at Nagpara (Swami 2003), set off serial bomb blasts in Jaipur in retaliation (The Times of India 2012). Ansari, who has only recently been convicted for his involvement in the Jaipur bombing, has already been serving life in prison for taking part in bombings in Mumbai (The Times of India 2012). Not originally a follower of radical Islam, Ansari felt discriminated against on the basis of his religion while attending Maratha College. Other instances of communal violence in India also shifted his beliefs:

Although Ansari claimed to have been a "secular-minded person", the massacre of Muslims during the Bhiwandi riots of 1985 transformed him completely. (Swami 2003: 80).

Ansari's story of radicalization problematizes the predominant post-9/11 terrorism discourse. Not only did Ansari join Jihad after having lived and studied in India, but he also joined on the basis of the nature of domestic politics *within* India. Indeed, Ansari's narrative supports the framework taken by scholars who argue that the Indian Islamist terrorism has to be understood as a response to the Indian state. The aim of this chapter is two-fold: first, it will demonstrate understandings of Islamist terrorism in India that are derived from the state-based approach and its key arguments.; second, it will analyze the advantages and limitations of the state-based approach.

Philippa Williams (2011) argues that the emphasis on 9/11 in the Indian context has ignored the fact that the majority of Muslim-Hindu relations in the country are peaceful. Additionally, when there was been violence, it has been a response to the state (Williams 2011). She furthers that religion is a 'marker of difference' in India because it corresponds to socioeconomic and political marginalization (Williams 2011). Irfan Ahmad (2009b: 33) also agrees that '...Islamist radicalisation should be seen as a political phenomenon... that... cannot be divorced from the practices and role of the State'. Ahmad (2009a) argues that the Indian state and its transformations are crucial to understanding the radicalization of the Students Islamic Movement of India (SIMI). SIMI, originally a moderate, educational organization, began to advocate Jihad in response to the activities of Hindutva and its Ayodhya campaign of the 1980s (Ahmad 2009a). During this time there was a significant amount of violence and rioting that resulted in the death of many Muslims, in addition to rhetoric and slogans that alienated the Muslim community (Ahmad 2009a). Indeed, a key component of Hindutva has been the portrayal of Muslims as the enemy:

> *'The Muslim' as an object of insecurity in the Hindutva discourse inhabits the levels of the personal, local, national, and international. 'The Muslim' is discursively constructed as a site of fear, fantasy, distrust, anger, envy, and hatred, and thus generating desires of emulation, abjection and/or extermination. (Anand 2005: 207)*

The impact of Hindutva, and its heightened and conflict-ridden presence leading up the mosque demolition, played a significant role in the radicalization of SIMI. The leader of SIMI at Aligarh Muslim University Student Union at the time, did not just see Indian Muslims as the victims but Islam itself as being 'under attack' (2009a: 173). Struggles abroad in places like Palestine were equally not seen as nationalist ones but as an attack on Islam (Ahmad 2009a). While SIMI did protest international events before, politics and Jihad were not priorities until the rise of Hindutva (Ahmad 2009a). It is also telling that the first clear Islamist terrorist attack outside of Kashmir was the 1993 Mumbai blasts (Devji 2011), a year after the mosque demolition.

Fair (2010) also supports Ahmad's and William's analysis, arguing that Islamist terrorism in India is mostly a domestic phenomenon, although her study more exclusively looks at the nature of SIMI and the Indian Mujahideen (IM), instead of making claims about how we can understand Islamist terrorism as a whole. In addition to issues of communal violence, IM's motivations for terror, Fair argues, also have to do with a general socioeconomic marginalization of Indian Muslims:

> *IM, in its manifestos, seeks to cultivate support among members of India's large Muslim population that harbour, to varying degrees, grievances regarding access to public—an—private-sector jobs, development, educational opportunities, the rising tide of Hindu nationalism, and anti-Muslim violence, among other issues.(Fair 2010: 112)*

She acknowledges operational linkages between SIMI, IM, and international terrorist organizations, but states that Jihad in India is ultimately domestic because these organizations need the support of local people to exist. This claim might be somewhat problematic because it conflates passive support with active support for Jihad, but what we see in Fair's analysis is the assertion that Islamist terrorism is intertwined with the Indian state and its treatment of Muslims.

Thus at the heart of the state-based approach is the idea that the Indian state, owing in part to the activities of the right-wing Hindu nationalist movement, has marginalized Indian Muslims. A second argument of the state-based approach is that Indian Muslims are radicalized on the basis of grievances they have about a lower socioeconomic status. This approach is useful because it can situate Islamist terrorism in India in its longer history of religious conflict. The very framework of the approach, which places the Indian state at the centre, also demonstrates the ways in which the Indian context challenges the dominant post-9/11 discourse that portrays Islamist terrorism as a global phenomenon. But can we understand all of Islamist terrorism in India in this way?

An analysis of the empirical evidence on attack data in India over time indicates significant limitations to applying the state-based approach more broadly. Chart A shows the five Islamist terrorist groups which have been responsible for the most attack attempts according to the GTD. Although SIMI is on this list, it has only been involved in 13 attack attempts, or 4.2% of the total (START 2011).

Data from the RDWTI on the total number of attacks is shown in Chart B. SIMI is not among the five groups responsible for the most attacks, and actually is only listed for one attack in the database (RDWTI 2008). The IM, which has been involved in 3.2% of attack attempts according to the GTD (START 2011), is among the five most significant groups and has been responsible for 12.1% of attacks according to the DWTI (RDWTI 2008). The discrepancy in the number of total attacks could be due to the databases' different methodologies and understandings of terrorism. Nevertheless, it is clear that the terrorist groups which very clearly did respond to the events of the Indian state, SIMI and the IM, cannot explain the entirety of Islamist terrorism in India.

The two groups that have been involved in the most attack attempts according to the GTD, HuM and LeT (START 2011), as well the two groups that have committed the most attacks according to the RDWTI, LeT and Harkatul Jihad-e-Islami (RDWTI 2008), are based in Pakistan (Sreedhar and Manish 2003). LeT, is under the umbrella of Markaz Dawal-ul-Irsahd (MDI), a group with many members who fought the Soviet invasion in Afghanistan (Sreedhar and Manish 2003). Both LeT and Harkatul Jihad-e-Islami also have financial and other operational ties with Pakistan (Sreedhar and Manish 2003). Thus, the groups responsible for the most attacks according to both databases do not fall within the explanations of the state-based approach, as they originated outside of India.

In addition to the lack of representativeness, the state-based approach is also problematic because despite being a response to discourse that homogenizes Islamist terrorism and its aims, it curiously homogenizes 'Indian Muslims'. They are discussed as a singular entity that experiences a singular Indian state in the same way. In reality, of course, Muslims in India also relate to the Indian state and Indian society upon the basis of several other markers of identity such as caste, class, and gender (Alam 2003). These cleavages within "the" Muslim community are hardly acknowledged by scholars taking the state-based approach, yet are important because talking about Muslims as a singular category is not without normative implications. As with the Hindu right movement, upper-caste and upper-class Muslims in India have tended to emphasize religious identities and speak of a singular Muslim community as a political tactic (Alam 2003). The state-based approach, in doing the same, might be conflating the politics of religious identity with the lived experiences of Muslims in India.

Thus, the state-based approach, while being able to highlight the uniqueness of the Indian experience with Islamist terrorism, presents significant limitations. It is unable to explain the majority of Islamist terrorist attacks in India, which are committed by groups lacking a personal relationship to the Indian state. The state-based approach also problematically assumes that Indian Muslims experience the Indian state in the same way, not acknowledging divisions within the Muslim community.

ISLAMIST TERRORISM AND THE INTERNATIONAL ARENA: THE TRANSNATIONAL APPROACH

On November 26, 2008, ten terrorists from Pakistan came by sea to Mumbai and orchestrated a terrorist attack in which over 172 people died over the course of 60 hours (Rabasa et al. 2009). The attack took place in the Indian cultural centre of Mumbai but targets of the attack included American and British citizens, as well as the Jewish Chabad centre (Rabasa et. al 2009). Although hardly the first instance of Islamist terrorism on Indian soil, the event has repeatedly been referred to as 'India's 9/11' (Rabasa et al. 2009). The use of this label could be partly be due to the magnitude of the attacks, as well as the fact that the attackers are not Indian by nationality. Indeed, while Jalees Ansari was radicalized on the basis of very local reasons, it is curious that the perpetrators of the most high-profile terrorist attacks in India have still been non-Indians (Neyazi 2009). This trend is in stark contrast with countries in the West, where homegrown terrorists committed the recent London and Madrid Islamist terrorist attacks (Neyazi 2009).

This feature of high-profile attacks in India, along with many others, has led scholars to argue that Islamist terrorism in India needs to be understood by looking outside of India's borders (Chellany 2001; Mann 2001). In this chapter, we will outline the arguments of the transnational framework, as well as discuss its advantages and limitations. Using terms like "cross-border terrorism," transnational studies tend to focus on ideological and operational linkages between groups in India and groups elsewhere, especially those based in Pakistan.

Brahma Chellany (2001) argues that Afghan war veterans have been responsible for many of the terrorist attacks in the 1990s and that there are instances of attacks happening in India before similar attacks are carried out against the West. He furthers that terrorism in India and the rest of South Asia can be understood as a historical product of the Cold War era:

The spread of militancy and terrorism in southern Asia is linked to the Afghan war of the 1980s and the U.S. and Saudi funnelling of arms to the anti-Soviet guerrillas through Pakistan's Inter-Services Intelligence (ISI) agency. (Chellany 2001: 96)

Chellany's point regarding Pakistan's ISI is an especially significant theme relating Islamist terrorism in India to Pakistan. Poonam Mann (2001) views the ISI and its support of terrorist groups over the years as the key source of terrorism within India. Indeed, Pakistan has previously been involved with the training and aiding of Sikh separatists as early as the 1970s (Mann 2001).

Created in 1948, the objectives the ISI would take on 10 years later are still maintained today: '...(a) to safeguard Pakistan's interests, (b) to monitor political opposition, and (c) to sustain military rule in Pakistan' (Gregory 2007: 1014). When America decided to support Afghan rebels after the Soviet invasion, it used Pakistan's ISI, giving the intelligence agency full-reign over how the war would be fought, as well as control over rebels and weapons, consequently allowing it to shape events in Afghanistan (Gregory 2007):

The willingness of the CIA to agree to these terms, at least for the early years of the war, enabled the ISI to hijack U.S. money and arms for its own purposes in Afghanistan and for Pakistan interests more broadly. (2007: 1016).

More specifically, these interests manifested themselves through support for pro-Pakistan groups among the rebels, especially those practicing Sunni Islam. The ISI also began training young students to help fight and according to Gregory (2007), 'this is the moment at which Pakistan began to promote the idea of pan-Islamic Jihad for its own geostrategic interests' (2007: 1017).

This practice by the ISI not only marginalized the secular rebel forces in Afghanistan (a pattern seen again in the case of Kashmir), but also eventually led to the training of key members of Al Qaeda (AQ) and the Taliban. Many of these links between Pakistan and international terrorist organizations still exist. For example, after 2001, many AQ terrorists shifted to Pakistani cities of Karachi and Peshawar (Krondstat 2003).

Thus, not only has Pakistan's ISI been responsible for terrorism in India, but it also has links to transnational terrorist groups like AQ. Actual direct links between AQ and terrorism in India appear to be limited. Evidence that Islamist terrorist organizations find India ideologically significant is more apparent. Osama bin Laden and other key members of AQ have made many statements against the country (Riedel 2008), and Kashmir and Palestine are seen as symbolic battlegrounds (Rapoport 2006).

The transnational approach uses the international arena as its level of analysis. Although this approach is consistent with the dominant post-9/11 discourse that portrays Islamist terrorism in India as an external threat, it does differ by linking Jihad with the geopolitics of South Asia. As mentioned earlier, the transnational approach provides a better framework for explaining the groups that most frequently attack, as these groups do indeed have international origins. The transnational approach also appears to have the advantage of explaining the recent counter-terrorism behaviour of the Indian government, which suggests that it too views Islamist terrorism as an external threat. After the attack on the Indian Parliament in December 2001, for example, India started increasing its international cooperation efforts with regard to counterterrorism strategies (Roy-Chaudhury 2003). The perpetrators of the attack are believed to be from Pakistan and the two countries were nearly at the brink of war as a result (Roy-Chaudhury 2003).

At this point it is important to note that while disengaged from domestic politics within India, the transnational approach, like the state-based approach, is not apolitical. Discourse has a productive role, and creates certain 'truths' about a subject through the way in which it discusses it (Carabine 2001); the discourse pertaining to terrorism is no different. Jones (2009) writes about how the Indian government has adopted American discourse by defining the enemy terrorist as outside the realm of modernity and yet connected to particular places from where terrorism originates. In doing so, India is able to justify more aggressive counterterrorism policies (Jones 2009). For example, India undertook construction of a fence on its border with the predominantly Muslim Bangladesh (Jones 2009).

While Jones (2009) views this use of the discourse by the Indian government as linked to the normative implications of the 'global war on terror', Ashis Nandy (2003) notes a much longer history of the import of Western discourse of terrorism. He argues that historically, terrorism was not part of mainstream politics in India. Insurgencies in places like Nagaland, for example, were understood as local conflicts (Nandy 2003). But once terrorism came to the forefront, we see '..the import of concepts, styles of management, and technologies of counter-terrorism from countries which Indians see as 'advanced', democratic polities' (Nandy 2003: 135). On the one hand, therefore, the transnational approach to study of Islamist terrorism in India is helpful because it is consistent with the dominant policy perspective of the Indian state. However, for this same reason, the transnational approach is also problematic because it cannot disentangle the political use of terrorist discourse through this framework from realities of the Indian experience.

Among the biggest realties left out of the transnational approach is that Islamist terrorism in India is quite heterogeneous. Indeed, one major limitation of the transnational approach is that it assumes Islamist terrorism in India to be homogenous, which simply is not the case for at least three reasons. First, groups engaging in Islamist terrorism in India hold a range of ideological positions. SIMI was the only group to march in Delhi in celebration of the Iranian revolution, which saw the rise of a Shia'a leader Iran (Ahmad 2005). Other Islamist organizations in India, predominantly Sunni, did not support the revolution due to its ideological tilt (Ahmad 2005). Additionally, groups like LeT and Jaish-e-Mohammad, which while being very much outside the realm of domestic Indian politics, are also outside the realm of global Islamist ideology which demands a caliphate. These groups have the objective of fragmenting South Asia into separate states:

Whatever its genealogy, however, the Lashkar's utopia, with its nostalgia for the colonial past, is worlds removed from the Islamic emirates and universal caliphates that serve as models among many of its peers. (Devji 2011: 288)

This heterogeneity in the ideology of Islamist terrorist organizations operating in India suggests that there is merit to studying them on a smaller scale, and limits to making broad generalizations. The transnational approach rarely differentiates between terrorist organizations on the basis of ideology as nation states, and not the groups themselves, are the focus of its analysis.

Second, the diversity in the goals and actions of these terrorist organizations indicates that they have a degree of autonomy not accounted for by theories which describe them as puppets of Pakistan. This autonomy, as well as the relationship between the ISI and terrorist groups, has changed over time. Ganguly and Kapur (2010) describe Islamist terrorism in India as a 'sorcerer's apprentice' problem: while Pakistan might be responsible for the birth of Jihad, it no longer has the same control over it. For example, the Taliban now has aspirations of gaining power within Pakistan. Though Pakistan would benefit from Taliban elements being powerful in Afghanistan, Pakistani government forces have been fighting the Taliban within their borders (e.g. South Waziristan). The lack of control of the Pakistani government over terrorist organizations operating within its borders brings into question the value of thinking of Islamist terrorism as just a function of South Asian geopolitics.

Third, empirical evidence suggests a broad spatial distribution of attacks over time. According to both data sets, the most attack attempts (outside of Kashmir) have taken place in New Delhi and Mumbai (START 2011), which is not surprising considering that the two are major cities and high-profile targets. There also appear to be more attack attempts in some places, such as Tripura and Karnataka, than others (START 2011). This distribution could be due to a number of factors, and analyzing how targets are selected is beyond the scope of this chapter. However, what the distribution does suggest is that Islamist terrorism in India has a spatial, and perhaps local, element. The fact that Islamist terrorism is experienced to different degrees in different places could partly be explained by domestic factors and most certainly is not explained by large-scale transnational approaches. Thus, the transnational approach cannot account for the diversity of Islamist terrorism in India. However, it does have some explanatory power: operational linkages between Islamist terrorist groups exist, as does historically, at least, a connection between the groups and Pakistan's ISI.

Additionally, although groups like LeT, which have been responsible for a significant number of attacks, have ideological dissimilarities from other Islamist organizations, their origins in Pakistan suggest that the transnational approach is much better equipped to understand them than the state-based approach. The transnational approach is in the opposite position of the state-based approach: it can account for much of Islamist terrorism in India but ignores its diversity.

The state-based approach, by contrast, creates a framework that is not helpful to explain the vast majority of Islamist terrorism in India, but is much more telling of the idiosyncrasies of Islamist terrorism in India. While the two approaches are not mutually exclusive, in practice we tend to see a focus on just one or the other. Consequently, there are major gaps in the terrorism literature in terms of being able to highlight *how* more global trends *interact* with local realties on the ground. What is necessary, then, is a multi-scalar approach that combines the merits of the transnational and state approach, and links them together. Indeed, the Kashmir conflict cannot be understood without it.

7

Terror War in South Asia

THE GLOBAL WAR ON TERROR

Using the opportunities therefore afforded by the global war on terror, the Pakistani security services systematically eliminated many sources of sectarian violence within two years of the campaign's initiation, even though they have been unable to conclusively eradicate the cancer of sectarian bloodshed within Pakistan itself. In part, this is due to the selectivity of Musharraf's antisectarian campaign. But the continuing fragmentation of these violent groups; their links to the wider networks of international terrorism now resident in Pakistan, various foreign sponsors abroad, and the flourishing madaris within the country; and the continuing utility of their gun- toting membership to different political parties and occasionally to governmental organs themselves imply that sectarian threats will be impossible to extinguish so long as "state policies of Islamisation and [the] marginalization of secular democratic forces" continue to persist in Pakistan.

The second set of groups, the terrorist outfits operating with Pakistan Army and ISID support against India in Kashmir, was treated in a remarkably different way compared with the anti-national sectarian militants inside Pakistan. These groups, such as the Lashkar- e- Toiba, the Jaish- e- Muhammad, and the Harkat-ul- Mujahideen, for example, were the long lances in the Pakistani campaign to wrest the disputed state of Jammu and Kashmir from India. Since the late 1980s, the Pakistani military has financed, trained, armed, and launched these cadres on their murderous missions into Kashmir and elsewhere inside the Indian union. Because the struggle for control over the disputed Himalayan state was fully under way by the time the global war on terror was inaugurated, these terrorist groups were more or less exempted from Musharraf's domestic campaign against violence and extremism.

This exclusion was justified both on the strategic rationale that Pakistan's participation in the war on terror was intended, among other things, to protect its freedom of action in Kashmir and on the repeated, though fraudulent, assertion that these groups, far from being terrorists, only personified the legitimate Kashmiri struggle for self- determination against India. In fact, of all the Pakistani- sponsored Deobandi terrorist groups operating against India in Kashmir and elsewhere, only one entity— the Hizbul Mujahideen— began life as an indigenous Kashmiri insurgent group; the others, including the most violent organizations such as the Lashkar- e- Toiba, the Jaish- e- Muhammad, and the Harkat- ul- Mujahideen, are all led, manned, and financed by native Pakistanis.

This reality notwithstanding— and perhaps because of it— Islamabad continued to sustain the operations of these groups against India but, in an effort to maintain the consistency of its commitments to the global war on terror, now began to emphasize that its support took only the form of moral, and not material, encouragement.

This charade was rudely interrupted by the December 13, 2001, terrorist attack on India's parliament when, in response to New Delhi's subsequent military mobilization, Pakistan was compelled by U.S. diplomacy to initiate a series of measures to restrict the activities of its terrorist clients. The implementation of these actions, however, was at best halfhearted and inconsistent.

Far from seeking to extirpate these terrorist groups permanently, Musharraf sought mainly to defang India's threats of military action and to alleviate Washington's fears of an inconvenient Indo- Pakistani war. His overarching objective consisted of protecting these terrorist assets to the extent possible because they represented national investments— a "strategic reserve" —in Islamabad's subconventional war against New Delhi.

Consequently, to this day, Musharraf has not sought to eliminate the Deobandi terrorist groups operating against India in Kashmir and elsewhere; he has instead sought only to modulate their activities, depending on the extent of satisfaction he derives from the prevailing state of diplomatic relations with New Delhi and the progress secured in the ongoing Indo- Pakistani peace process.

Although the Pakistani- supported infiltration of terrorist groups into Kashmir— but not into the rest of India— appears to have abated in recent years, most observers conclude that this phenomenon is linked either to Musharraf's desire not to provide India with any excuses to abandon the generally fragile peace process or to domestic crises within Pakistan. In any event, it is agreed that Musharraf simply has not made the decisive decision to abandon or eliminate the terrorist groups operating against India in the manner witnessed, for example, in the case of the more virulent anti- national sectarian entities operating within Pakistan.

The third group relevant to the Pakistani decision to join the U.S.-led coalition against terrorism consisted of the Taliban, that is, the Pashtun remnants of the regime ejected from power in Kabul as a result of the initial success of Operation Enduring Freedom. After their defeat at the hands of the Northern Alliance, the Taliban cadres hastily returned to the regions whence they originated.

Many in the rank and file withdrew to their villages in the southern Afghan provinces of Helmand, Kandahar, Oruzgan, and Zabol as well as along the border areas on the western side of the Durand Line separating Afghanistan from Pakistan, that is, in the eastern Afghan provinces of Paktika, Paktia, Khowst, Nangarhar, and Konar. Given their significance as high- value targets, the core Taliban leadership— along with those Pakistani Pashtuns who had joined their movement— crossed over the Afghanistan-Pakistan border into the relative safety of the FATA.

Because most of the Taliban's fighters originally mobilized by the Pakistani ISID were drawn from the Ghilzai confederation of

Pashtuns, which dominates eastern and southeastern Afghanistan, and from the other Pashtun tribes inhabiting the FATA, their return to these ancestral lands was not surprising. In fact, all the evidence relating to the incidence of terrorist attacks since 2001 suggests strongly that the war- fighting cadres of the Taliban continue to remain bivouacked in these areas.

The exact location of the supreme leadership of the Taliban movement, however, cannot be established with any self- evident clarity. Irrespective of where the rahbari shura (leadership council) centred on Mullah Omar and his closest associates found shelter in the immediate aftermath of their defeat, Afghan military and civilian intelligence officials as well as NATO commanders today believe that this coterie eventually found refuge in Quetta, the largest city and capital of Pakistan's Baluchistan Province, from where they continue to operate to this day.

As Col. Chris Vernon, NATO's chief of staff for southern Afghanistan, declared forthrightly, "The thinking piece of the Taliban [operates] out of Quetta in Pakistan. It's the major headquarters— they use it to run a series of networks in Afghanistan."

These networks, in turn, are judged to be directed by four subsidiary shuras based in Quetta, Miran Shah, Peshawar, and Karachi: the first three actually control or coordinate most of the ongoing terrorist operations occurring, respectively, along the southern, central, and northern "fronts" in Afghanistan, whereas the fourth is believed to connect the Taliban with the logistics, financial, and technical assistance conduits emanating from the wider Islamic world. The pattern of terrorist attacks occurring in Afghanistan from 2002 to 2007, again corroborates this judgment.

Because the Pakistani state was most intimately involved in the creation of the Taliban before their fall, Musharraf's antiterrorism campaign after September 11, 2001, deliberately avoided any concerted targeting of this group and, in particular, its senior leadership. No other explanation is consistent with the fact that, although Pakistani military, intelligence, and paramilitary forces apprehended scores of al- Qaeda operatives, including numerous key individuals in the al- Qaeda hierarchy, the senior

Taliban leaders killed or captured in southern Afghanistan or in the FATA have numbered literally a handful in comparison.

This asymmetry in seizures is all the more odd because, prior to Operation Enduring Freedom, Pakistani military and ISID liaison elements were deeply intertwined with all levels of the Taliban mand structure and its war fighters in the field. In contrast, the Pakistani intelligence relationship with al- Qaeda in Afghanistan was more tenuous, yet Pakistan's military forces were able to apprehend far more al- Qaeda cadres than Taliban operatives.

These successes in regard to al- Qaeda have invariably been attributed by Pakistanis, including General Musharraf, to the fact that it was always easier to identify the ethnically alien al- Qaeda elements along the frontier in comparison with the Taliban who, being ethnically Pashtun, were able to disguise their identities by assimilating into the larger tribal population.

While this explanation is only partly true— non- native fighters have lived in and become amalgamated into the social structures of the Afghan- Pakistani frontier since at least the anti-Soviet jihad of the 1980s— it is also disingenuous because the Pakistani ISID was not only deeply involved in the recruitment, training, arming, and operations of Taliban fighters at multiple bureaucratic levels, but it also maintained an intense liaison relationship with the Ghilzai tribes whose population has been disproportionately represented in the Taliban. Since protecting these relationships was deemed to be especially critical for Pakistan's national security interests in the aftermath of the Northern Alliance victory in Kabul, the large number of Taliban foot soldiers who made their way into the FATA were largely ignored by Pakistani counterterrorism operations so long as they did not engage in any untoward activities that either called attention to their presence or magnified the troubles confronting the Pakistani state.

All told, then, the Taliban network, just like the Pakistani-aided terrorist groups operating in Kashmir and elsewhere in India, was deliberately permitted to escape the wrath of General Musharraf's counterterrorism operations in the initial phase of the war on terror. Such an approach, however, could not be extended to the fourth group, al- Qaeda, which had also taken up sanctuary in the FATA, particularly in South Waziristan initially. Although al- Qaeda continued to have sympathizers within the extreme fringes of Pakistani society even after the terrible events of September 11 were conclusively attributed to its operations, the Pakistani military establishment did not enjoy the luxury of slackening its campaign against this target because of the consequences for U.S.-Pakistani relations at a time when bilateral ties were just recovering after a decade of U.S. disfavor and when Washington had just embarked on a ferocious campaign against al- Qaeda worldwide.

Most senior Pakistani military officers at the corps command level were also genuinely horrified by the destruction that al-Qaeda wreaked in New York and Washington and, fearing for their country's own future in the face of the monster now present in their midst, supported Musharraf's decision to engage and destroy this terrorist organization of global reach.

Pakistan's military, accordingly, began to prosecute the war against al- Qaeda with great vigor, if not always with finesse, through multiple instruments. These included providing the United States and its military with facilities and access for the prosecution of Operation Enduring Freedom in Afghanistan, and conducting various law enforcement and internal security operations (sometimes in cooperation with their U.S. counterparts) aimed at interdicting terrorist financing and apprehending and rendering terrorist targets for prosecution abroad.

Most important, however, the Pakistani military initiated Operation Al Mizan, a large- scale effort that involved moving major military formations from the Army's XI Corps and elite Special Services Group (SSG) battalions into the FATA, an area where regular army units had not ordinarily been deployed for decades.

These infantry forces joined the Frontier Corps regiments—the paramilitary formations usually located in the region— as a show of force in order to both reassert the strong state presence that historically was lacking and apprehend the al- Qaeda elements that had taken shelter within the area.

This military campaign, which took the form of a gigantic cordon- and- search operation, had several consequences. First, it resulted in the capture of numerous al- Qaeda and other extremist operatives— some 700 at last count— who have since been turned over to the United States.

Because these individuals are mostly foreigners— non–South Asian arrivals living in what are essentially Pashtun lands— detecting their presence, while not easy because of the local support they receive from the natives for ideological reasons and sometimes simply out of greed or fear, was certainly easier.

Second, it forced some though by no means all senior al-Qaeda operatives— for example, Khalid Sheikh Muhammad and Ramzi Binalshibh— to leave the relatively secure FATA sanctuary and disperse further inward into Pakistan, where their insertion into less ideologically congenial surroundings and their need to rely on more complex means of communication increased their susceptibility to detection and arrest.

Third, the dramatic irruption of the Pakistani state into the FATA, through a significant military presence of the kind not seen in more than a century, resulted in making conditions sufficiently inhospitable for al- Qaeda such that its senior leadership and cadres were compelled to relocate under fire from South to North Waziristan and beyond, where they operate to this day.

This forced displacement, which unfortunately remains at continuous risk of reversal, nonetheless had the beneficial effect of disrupting many planned terrorist operations, but the dispersal of the organization's leadership in the northern FATA, especially in the Bajaur Agency where the terrain is inhospitable, the population is violently pro- Taliban, and the presence of the Pakistan Army is thin, has inadvertently made the task of destroying the al- Qaeda core all the more difficult.

In any event, these outcomes suggest that although Pakistan began as a reluctant entrant into the global war on terrorism, it has since become an active participant in the struggle. More than 85,000 Pakistani troops remain garrisoned along the Afghanistan-Pakistan border— a deployment that predates the initiation of the global war on terror. A significant fraction of these forces, however, is engaged today in counterterrorism operations in the border areas, and more than 600 soldiers have already sacrificed their lives in this effort.

Further, Islamabad itself has now become a victim of terrorism as a variety of groups, ranging from those previously nurtured and now discarded by the Pakistani state, such as the al-Alami faction of the Harkat- ul- Mujahideen, to more distant beneficiaries of past Pakistani policies, such as al- Qaeda, seek to wreak an orgy of revenge against institutions and individuals whom they had previously counted among their sponsors and friends.

That Pakistan has made significant contributions to defeating various terrorist groups is therefore undeniable, yet its larger campaign against terrorism has also been conspicuously selective and perhaps self- serving. While it has secured major gains in eradicating some domestic anti- national sectarian terrorist groups and has contributed disproportionately to the ongoing campaign against al- Qaeda, it has been much more reluctant to conclusively eliminate those terrorist entities operating against India in Kashmir and elsewhere and against Afghanistan both in the FATA and in transit back and forth to the southern and eastern Afghan provinces. Further, the protection of the terrorist infrastructure that supports these groups has produced undesirable blowback because the actors traditionally involved in perpetrating terrorism in Kashmir increasingly either coordinate with or directly assist the Taliban and al- Qaeda in operations against not only Afghanistan but also the United States and even Pakistan itself.

Clearly, strategic and geopolitical calculations play an important part in accounting for this segmented Pakistani response. Islamabad, for example, has long viewed the terrorist groups operating in Kashmir and now in other Indian states as useful instruments for executing its policy of "strategic diversion" against New Delhi. For this reason, Pakistan has been reluctant to target and eliminate these groups conclusively, preferring instead to alternately tighten and loosen control over their operations depending on how much satisfaction it receives from India at any given moment.

The decision to avoid targeting the Taliban was born of similar calculations. Initially, it was owed simply to the inclinations of senior Pakistani military commanders who were just not prepared to add insult to injury by physically eliminating the very forces they had long invested in, especially because they had now suffered the ignominy of having to consent to their client's defeat.

Over time, however, the reasons for protecting the Taliban only grew stronger: India's growing prominence in Afghan reconstruction, its increased influence and presence in Afghanistan more generally, the weakening of the Hamid Karzai government in Kabul, the progressive souring of Pakistani- Afghan relations (including those between Karzai and Musharraf personally), and the disquiet about a possible U.S. exit from Afghanistan (a prospect inferred from the mid-2005 announcement that the United States would divest full command of Afghan combat operations to NATO) once again increased Pakistan's paranoia about the prospect of a hostile western frontier.

It was exactly the desire to avert this outcome that led to the initial Pakistani decision to invest in sustaining the Taliban. And with fear of the wheel turning full circle gaining strength in Islamabad since at least 2005, the temptation to hedge against potentially unfavorable outcomes in Kabul— by protecting the Taliban as some sort of a "force- in- being"—only appeared more and more attractive and reasonable to Pakistan.

Although Pakistan's discriminative approach to fighting terrorism was shaped and implemented by General Musharraf in his dual capacity as president and previously chief of army staff, it would be erroneous to conclude that this prevailing strategy is owed simply to the whim of one man.

This is particularly relevant today when Musharraf's hold on power has become progressively weaker and the future of his political status and effectiveness increasingly clouded. Rather, Musharraf's decisions in regard to counterterrorism strategy since 2001, although publicly perceived as personal dicta, invariably reflected the consensus among the corps commanders of the Pakistan Army and, hence, represent the preferences of Pakistan's military- dominated state.

In other words, even if Musharraf were to suddenly exit the Pakistani political scene at some point, Islamabad's currently disconsonant counterterrorism strategy would still survive so long as the men on horseback continue to be the principal guardians of national security policy making in Islamabad.

Because it is unreasonable to expect that the uniformed military will give up its privileges in this regard anytime soon— even if a civilian regime were to return to the helm in the future— the internally segmented counterterrorism policy currently pursued by Pakistan will likely persist for some time to come.

Even if it could be imagined that a civilian dispensation could wrest some control of Pakistan's national security policy from the military, it is not at all certain that the current strategic direction would change dramatically: a civilian regime would probably have greater incentives to combat all sectarian terrorist groups more evenhandedly, but that too is uncertain. After all, both the Pakistan People's Party led by the late Benazir Bhutto and the Pakistan Muslim League led by Nawaz Sharif have had problematic Islamist political allies in the past and, depending on the political exigencies of the moment, could harbor incentives to give even sectarian or otherwise radical entities a breather from prosecution, although that would likely be justified as only a temporary expedient.

Both civilian parties historically also permitted the Pakistani military and intelligence services to aid, abet, and arm the terrorist groups operating in Kashmir and elsewhere in India, sometimes because they were simply powerless to prevent it but at other times with their full knowledge and consent.

It also ought not to be forgotten that even a radically atavistic Islamist group such as the Taliban was raised, promoted, and unleashed by the civilian government of the late Benazir Bhutto (during her second term in office from 1993 to 1996) with the full collaboration of the Pakistani military and intelligence services— and that the Taliban continued to receive complete moral and material support under her civilian successor, the then prime minister, Nawaz Sharif.

INTER-STATE COUNTER-TERRORIST COOPERATION IN SOUTH ASIA

Terrorism was noticed as a new phenomenon in India only since the mid-1980s after Prime Minister Indira Gandhi s assassination by her police guards on October 31, 1984. India then created new Central anti-terrorist forces to help the state police in meeting terrorism which had raged in Punjab after Indian forces stormed the Sikh religious shrine in June 1984 to flush out militants. From 1989 onwards Kashmir related terrorism gave a new dimension to the problem while the Babri Masjid demolition by Hindu zealots on December 6, 1992 extended it to the rest of India. Communal strife gave way to Jehadi terrorism. However Indian Police did not evolve a holistic strategy to tackle terrorism since information on terrorist activities was scattered in different wings of the Security machinery. The March 12, 1993 serial blasts in Mumbai, which killed 257 in 13 "serial" explosions, were considered as the first manifestation of externally sponsored terrorism in the "rest of India". It was not so. Indian security forces forgot that an earlier externally sponsored attempt to spread strife to South India with similar *modus operandi* by bombing various targets including the Madras Stock Exchange. This series of attacks failed due to the chance arrest of the Toronto based Lal Singh on July 16, 1992. The Central Bureau of Investigation which took over investigation from the local police in August 1992, failed to inform others of this methodology of serial bomb blasts-much like the failures of US authorities prior to September 11 where interrogation reports were not shared. Consequently the then Bombay Police Commissioner told the media that he suspected LTTE s hand immediately after the March 1993 blasts in which the Bombay Stock Exchange was also bombed.

The lack of a holistic understanding of the inter links between terrorists adversely affects not only the internal counter-terrorist operations within a country but also the countering of global terrorism. I first underlined the importance of understanding how terrorists operated trans-nationally during a lecture at the Seminar on Terrorism organized by the National Advisory Council on South Asian Affairs, Washington DC on June 19, 2003. It was the chance arrest of Noor Sikander by Mumbai Police in May 2003, who was responsible for the March 2003 serial Mulund blasts, that revealed Aftab Ansari – deported from Dubai to India in February 2002 – was involved in the January 2002 shooting of the Kolkata American Centre in Calcutta, and as the mastermind of the kidnapping for ransom of Partha Burman (Kadim shoes, Kolkata) in July 2001. The ransom (reportedly US$ 600,000 or $830,000) was sent through "Hawala" channels in Hyderabad or Dubai to Saeed Omar Sheikh of Jaish-e-Mohammad (the killer of Daniel Pearl) who forwarded it to Mahammed Atta before September 11. In other words the Kolkata ransom wholly or partially funded September 11 attacks. We came to know about this only in 2003. No state police with inherent handicaps would have learnt about this in advance since criminal activities spanned several states/ countries.

Counter-terrorist cooperation between different countries usually depends on bilateral political relations. If bilateral relations warm up there is some movement in cooperation as we see with India and Bangladesh. The present Bangladesh Government has handed over several fugitives of Unit ed Liberation Front of Assam (ULFA), a regional terrorist group hiding in Bangladesh. However by and large there has been no satisfactory cooperation among South Asian countries due to historical factors.

Despite reaching the "SAARC [South Asian Association for Regional Co-Operation] Regional Convention on Suppression on Terrorism" since 1987 no concrete steps have been taken by the signatories to establish intelligence sharing or arrest of fugitive terrorists. Sometimes even when political relations are normal such exchanges do not result in prompt action. Early in October 1994 Indian intelligence came to know LTTE preparations to assassinate Gamini Dissanayaka, one of Sri Lanka's brightest politicians. Sri Lankan authorities were immediately alerted through diplomatic channel. However this was lost in the bureaucratic chain and Gamini Dissanayaka was killed in a suicide bomb attack near Colombo on October 24, 1994 much like former Indian Prime Minister Rajiv Gandhi who was killed on May 21, 1991.

Studies of the Indo-Pakistani relations indicate that temporary groundswell of good dialogue is not translated into policy correction. The "Hawana Declaration" (September 16, 2006) between President Pervez Musharraf and Prime Minister Dr. Manmohan Singh on intelligence exchange was a non-starter. The bonhomie witnessed during SAARC Interior Ministers Conference (Islamabad, June 2010) and the warm sound bites between Indian and Pakistan Interior ministers during bilateral parleys, which also saw the first ever meeting between both countries Chiefs of Intelligence Bureaus, did not in fact result in any forward movement to implement "SAARC Convention on Mutual Assistance in Criminal Matters". Indeed, the verbal pyrotechnics witnessed later between both countries on Kashmir stone throwing and police action have almost wiped out the possibility of any movement by Pakistan pursuing the case against November 26 conspirators which were purely as a result of external pressure.

What is the way out?

It will be futile to imagine that relationship between some South Asian countries would improve in the near future to enable active counter terrorist cooperation to European standards. However, experience reveals that activities of scattered extremist modules in different countries pose threats not only to home countries but also to the rest of the world. Experience during the last thirty years has revealed that terrorism is not a conventional foreign intelligence problem. Yet most nations still entrust their foreign intelligence agencies with collection of intelligence on terrorism and liaison merely because terrorists usually live outside their national boundaries. Most intelligence agencies are organized on the basis of lessons learnt from World War II to support their foreign offices. They share the same professional culture and outlook, and often undertake intrusive and at times coercive operations under cover of diplomacy. Because of this they suffer from mutual distrust. In contrast, terrorism based on transnational religious extremism is a new phenomenon that uses organized crime's tradecraft. It is more of a policing problem than a foreign intelligence service problem. In this context it is useful to remember the main recommendation of the "John Major Enquiry Report" on the 1985 Air India Kanishka aircraft bombing. He advised the CSIS to upgrade their intelligence collection to the level of MI5 or ASIO in producing intelligence that can be used as evidence.

It is a generally accepted fact that police organizations enjoy better credibility even between less friendly nations since their activities are governed by national criminal laws supervised by courts. That is not the case with intelligence agencies, which are often suspected to be working against other countries or whose work are not subject to be tested in a court of law. It is for this reason why national crime investigating agencies like FBI or Australian National Police have foreign relations posts. Even New York Police and Los Angeles Police Departments have foreign liaison posts in view of the complex problems of terrorism originating from abroad. To make South Asia more effective in countering transnational terrorism, "Police Attaches" should be appointed to liaise with local police authorities where they are needed.

RELIGION, TERROR AND SACRIFICE

To disenchant terrorist discourse also means, in a multi-religious and multicultural society, the necessity of disenchanting the state and public rhetoric. The turn to talk of religion and spirituality, that talk of re-enchantment and desecularization, not only serves to act as public space for religious diversity to state their claims of communal legitimacy, it also provides a public space for the religion of terror and terror discourse. To disenchant is not to dismiss the various religious claims or affiliations, but to effectively seek to secularize them into the realm of privatism. Yet in order to do this we need to be also aware of the claims of the sacred, especially in claims of sacrifice and transgression that *exist still* within our society – and which are repositioned into the public sphere by acts of terror.

Georges Bataille offers a provocative take on the challenges of sacrifice and transgression, in which the sacred unleashes itself in acts of passion which are contrary to reason. He notes the links of horror, terror and the sacred and how, in the contemporary world, with the reduction to symbolic passion in our religion we have attempted to domesticate our fascination with death and destruction that sits at the heart of religion. This is the basis of the *religare* of terror – our fascination with death as *sign and symbol* of the sacred. Therefore the challenge of terror is the return of the sacred as transgressive in a world seeking to limit and contain it, to reduce it. The problem is that we fail to see acts of terror as acts of exaltation and intoxication in the sacred, failing to acknowledge Bataille's claim for the transgressive eroticism of terror:

> The inner experience of eroticism demands from the subject a sensitiveness to the anguish at the heart of the taboos no less great than the desire which leads him to infringe it. This is religious sensibility, and it always links desire closely with terror, intense pleasure and anguish.

This is why terror has become the new global religion. It reflects and provides the religious sensibility in the contemporary world – it transgresses the space given to religion in the postmodern turn and rejects both the restraints of controlled plurality and the turn away from plurality in the turn back to a new modernity. Today, terror is a religion that acts as transgression and taboo to *both* modernity and postmodernity. In a sense, following the Nietzschean nihilism of *Beyond Good and Evil* we now exist in a world of taboo and transgression, a world of sacred violence.

As Bataille notes: "the transgression does not deny the taboo but transcends and completes it". In this we need to now view the transgression of terror as that *which transcends and completes* both taboos – those of death and of religion/sacred in public space – in the modern world.

As "the taboo is there to be violated" and is "at the very least...the threshold beyond which murder is possible", our taboos on public death and public religion are in fact those which paradoxically issue a form of demand *for* the transgression of terror – and the terror of transgression. In effect, notes Bataille, for our profane world to exist we require the complementary acts of transgression that exceed its limits but do not destroy it: "the profane world is the world of taboos. The sacred world depends on limited acts of transgression".

This means that acts of terror are acts of transgression for the expression of the reality of the sacred world. In other worlds, acts of terror are a form of sacrifice. What the act of sacrifice does is not a killing but rather a relinquishing and a giving. What is sacrificed is what is useful – it "restores a lost value by relinquishment of that value". As bin Laden would have it:

When you talk about the invasion of New York and Washington, you talk about the men who changed the face of history and went against the traitors....These great men have consolidated faith in the hearts of believers and undermined the plans of the crusaders and their agents in the region. Terrorism against America deserves to be praised because it was a response to injustice, aimed at forcing America to stop its support for Israel, which kills our people.

The acts of terror are, from a religious viewpoint, acts of sacrifice: they give up what is useful – the life of the terrorist, the life of the believer, the sacrifice of people in the profane world – in a manner of transgressive action that seeks to transcend the taboo on violence, death and the sacred. As Bataille notes: "The sacrificer declares ...I call you back to the *intimacy* of the divine world, of the profound immanence of all that is...".

The spectacle of terror is therefore on one level the intimacy of sacrifice in the intimacy of our daily lives, in the intimacy of our living rooms, in the intimacy of our public and private spaces. It is on one level, as Bataille states of sacrifice, "the communication of anguish". So what is this anguish?

Perhaps it is as Slavoj Zizek notes, the cry of anguish of sacrifice, of terror, of violence. Furthermore, that our transgressive avidity for these is our passion for the "Real" – that which he notes Alain Badiou as claiming is "the key feature of the twentieth century".

This passion for the Real is what sits at the heart of Loos' call for the overthrow of unnecessary ornamentation; this passion for the Real sits at the heart of the Futurist worship of the cleansing effect of technology, war and death; this passion for the Real is what lies in modernity's rejection of transcendence – and in Postmodernity's rejection of modernity's secularity. In effect, the dualistic battle in modernity between what is seen as order and what is seen as chaotic *is* this battle over what is Real and where the Real is located. Violence, taboo, transgression and sacrifice are those acts that serve as both statements of the Real – and the rejection of what is perceived to be non-Real. Acts of terror, made possible by the space given in postmodernity for the articulation of varieties of transcendent "Real", are an act of the rejection of these possibilities in a challenge of what is seen as the Real. Yet in their symbolic intention, they participate in the postmodern spectacle as an attempt to evangelize by effect. The passion for the Real and the attempt to represent it are actually transgressive to modern world where we attempt to keep the Real controllable by not confronting it. The response to the rise of transcendence as the location of the Real was not to confront it but rather to seek to splinter it by postmodern tolerance. Yet all this did was to give consent to those who sought to destroy even the possibilities of competing Reals.

In effect, contemporary terrorism is the Real of modernity (a battle beyond good and evil, of order and chaos) confronting itself with the non-reality of terror and spectacle that act as transgressive to that which we seek to hold as Real. The effect is not concerned with the reality of the chaotic act, but rather with the chaos that is the response to the reality of the act. In effect we say "we cannot believe this act has occurred" and this stating of our inability to believe in the Real is the chaos that the act of terror seeks. We then search to ascribe a meaning to the event that may mean *we claim to see the reason behind the act*, the "cry of anguish" that caused this act. To ascribe meaning to the act is to order it, in effect to attempt to "make it real" – and in making it Real paradoxically giving a form of inverted value and meaning to the actions and beliefs of those who undertook it.

Yet often what happens in response is the turn away from the liberal tolerance of dissenting beliefs that (perhaps) marks off a Western sense of the Real: a form of order that exists by ordering chaotic elements within pluralism. Yet the act of terror is a rejection of Western liberal pluralism, a rejection of the type of Western order that secularizes its taboos and transgressions.

DEVELOPING STRATEGIC LEADERS FOR THE 21ST CENTURY

It is remarkable how the scope and focus of American national security policy have changed since September 11, 2001 (9/11). The United States has fought two major wars in Afghanistan and Iraq and is engaged in the daunting challenges of post-conflict stability operations in both countries. The "war on terrorism" continues both here in America as well as throughout the globe. Policymakers remain engaged with the challenges of globalization, international trade, the spread of AIDS, etc., that predate the 2001 terrorist attacks. Now, however, they must view these problems through a new lens and confront emerging challenges with Iran and North Korea. Finally, these conditions are not transitory—the nation must expect that the threat of multiple crises having an immediate effect on American security will continue indefinitely. The old adage that Washington is "a one crisis town" can no longer apply.

These events have changed how we think about "national security." They have dramatically expanded not only the number and scope of issues, but also the overall complexity of the process. Americans who felt safe at home and viewed security threats as distant from our shores no longer feel this way. The government that is supposed to protect us has also felt the winds of change. The requirement for interagency decisionmaking has accelerated, demands for greater policy flexibility have increased, and a process that was largely confined to a few agencies of the Federal government now involves a multitude of new players and allied states. Clearly, the sad and apparently unexpected aftermath of the Iraq War underscores the critical need for significant changes in the planning of military operations, preparation for post-conflict requirements, *and* oversight of their execution.

As the nation embarked on this new era at the turn of the century, the *2002 National Security Strategy* noted that we must "transform America's national security institutions to meet the challenges and opportunities of the 21st century." The Bush administration responded initially with the creation of the Department of Homeland Security, the largest change in the structure of the Federal government since the National Security

Act of 1947. But we must also transform existing institutions, the policy process, and how we "think" about the defense of the nation. Furthermore, as General Richard Myers, former Chairman of the Joint Chiefs of Staff, observed, this transformation cannot wait—"It must take place as we wage the war on terrorism."

Crucial to this effort is developing a system that places the right people in the right places in government at the right moment. The nation critically needs civilian policymakers who can manage change and deal with the here and now. This monograph will examine the development of career civilian leaders for strategic decisionmaking in the national security policy process. Such development must include the recruitment of high-quality personnel, experiential learning through a series of positions of increasing responsibility, training for specific tasks or missions, and continuous education that considers both policy and process. Consequently, it requires people who are not only substantively qualified and knowledgeable of policy issues, but also possessed of the leadership abilities to direct large complex organizations.

This monograph will first consider existing efforts in the Office of the Secretary of Defense (OSD), State Department, and Central Intelligence Agency (CIA) and then make appropriate recommendations for each. It will further consider what changes must be made to existing personnel management systems and development programs to encourage the creation of an effective cadre of civilian "national security" professionals for the policy process. Such recommendations may be applicable to other executive agencies as well. These three departments were selected since they are in many ways those with a clear traditional role in the development of foreign and defense policy. Clearly, there are additional considerations with respect to current and growing requirements for those with technical expertise, human resource management, finance/comptroller skills, etc. The development of personnel with such talents for these three agencies will not be the subject of this monograph.

Some critics might observe from the outset that the nation is at war and can ill-afford reorganizations or changes at this critical moment. The sad tragedy that has been the Iraq War would suggest otherwise. It became clear almost immediately following the invasion in 2003 that fundamental errors had been made in intelligence and policy analysis. From the very beginning the United States not only required additional troops for the occupation of Iraq but also enhanced civilian leadership and capacity to reconstruct Iraqi society. Without both these components, efforts to forestall the ensuing chaos as well as the resultant insurgency were doomed to failure.

Poor civilian leadership and mismanagement have been clearly documented in numerous studies, books, reports, and articles. Official reports provided by Stuart W. Bowen, Jr., Special Inspector General for Iraq Reconstruction (SIGIR), are particularly critical of American efforts in Iraq. In early 2007, SIGIR reported that despite nearly $108 billion budgeted for the reconstruction of Iraq since 2003, the country's electricity output and oil production were still below prewar levels. Stocks of gasoline and kerosene had actually plummeted to their lowest levels in at least 2 years. Consequently, Mr. Bowen testified before the Senate Judiciary Committee in March 2007 that his office planned to "aggressively pursue" the suspension and prosecution of contractors who are determined to have engaged in fraudulent contracting activities in Iraq. He further observed that the failure of the American-financed reconstruction program in Iraq threatened to be repeated elsewhere unless structural changes were made in the U.S. Government. Mr. Bowen compared his recommendations to the Congress as not dissimilar to proposals made in the 1980s that resulted in legislation strengthening the Joint Chiefs of Staff.

Prior to this, the Iraq Study Group (ISG) noted in its comprehensive report in late 2006 that "civilian agencies also have little experience with complex overseas interventions to restore and maintain order—stability operations—outside of the normal embassy setting." The ISG described the mission in Iraq as "unfamiliar and dangerous." As a result, the report observed that the United States had great difficulty filling civilian assignments in Iraq with sufficient qualified personnel. The ISG recommended that the constituent agencies (State, Defense, the U.S. Agency for International Development [USAID], Treasury, Justice, Intelligence community, etc.) train for and conduct joint operations across agency boundaries. It further suggested that the State Department expand its efforts to train personnel to carry out civilian tasks associated with such complex stability operations, concluding that a Foreign Service Reserve Corps with personnel and expertise to provide surge capacity for such operations be established. This effort should provide a model for other civilian agencies to include Treasury, Justice, and Agriculture. Such ideas, however, were hardly new. They had been recommended a year or more prior to the release of the ISG report by leading government experts and officials.

As American patience wears thin over the failure to achieve progress in Iraq the argument might be presented that this venture has been a tragic aberration. Once the United States withdraws from Iraq, it can simply avoid future efforts to rebuild societies torn apart by conflict. Unfortunately, this global conflict will not allow us that luxury. We are confronted by an enemy who would replace secular governments with theocratic regimes hostile to our national interests and values. Their strategy amounts to "a global series of insurgencies, competing for the right to govern" in many predominantly Muslim nations around the globe. State collapse will continue to challenge the national interests of the United States and its allies for decades to come. If we are to prevail, we must mobilize and synchronize all elements of our national power—diplomatic, military, economic, social, and informational—to confront these new and extremely dangerous adversaries. The key actions required in a counterinsurgency involve "work we associate with civilian skill sets and even agencies—but the uniformed military is often placed in the position of having to undertake such activities." Consequently, a rebalancing of roles between military and civilian leaders is required. Regardless of what the final outcome is in Iraq, that outcome may not be our past so much as our future. This new security environment requires better qualified civilian leaders to think in different patterns in order to accomplish these daunting tasks.

Terms

Understanding certain assumptions is crucial to this analysis. First, some observers may take exception to the distinction between the words "training" and "education." They may argue that they are synonymous, as we frequently use them interchangeably. They are *not* the same, there being a significant denotative difference. While training is more concerned with teaching *what* to think and what the *answers* ought to be, education is all about teaching *how* to think and what the *questions* ought to be: "Training is focused on the development and performance of specific tasks or skills, and education is oriented toward more generalized and abstract knowledge that may or may not be tied to specific tasks or action." Training is most frequently used when the goal is to prepare an individual or an organization to execute specified tasks. It often includes repetition of tasks, not unlike an athletic team learning to execute plays. Finally, it is normally the preferred method of learning when the goal is to perform operations in which success, failure, and completion can be clearly measured. Education has more to do with how to think about problems and how to deal with those things that may not lend themselves to categorical solutions. It becomes a matter of intellect, thought, indirect leadership, advice, and consensus building.

Second, we must also differentiate between "leadership" and "management." *Management is about coping with complexity.* It is a response to a significant development of the 20th century, namely, the emer-gence of large, complex organizations. Good management brings order to what would otherwise be chaos. *Leadership, by contrast, is about coping with change.* An expert in human development once wisely observed, "If you don't like change, you will like irrelevancy even less." American business recognized this phenomenon as competition in the market and volatility in business cycles became more intensive and jarring. Doing the same thing only slightly better was no longer good enough. *Management* remains important for the day-to-day success of any organization, focusing as it does on such issues as planning/budgeting, organizing/staffing, and controlling/problem solving. By contrast, *leadership* begins with setting directions, aligning people, and motivating them to achieve success. The successful development of government policy for the war on terrorism is wholly dependent upon developing leaders of substance at all levels of executive agencies. They must be able balance the pressing requirements of management with the critical need to provide leadership for their organizations and the collective effort.

These expanding requirements for improved leadership and management preceded 9/11, and remain an integral part of dealing with the rapid pace of change. In his widely acclaimed book, *The Lexus and the Olive Tree,* Thomas Friedman described the importance of change in the international system along with the corresponding demands placed on both organizations and individuals. He argued that "Globalization" had replaced the Cold War as the new defining international system. But "the globalization system, unlike the Cold War system, is not frozen, but a dynamic ongoing process." Friedman observed that "if the Cold War were a sport, it would be sumo wrestling." Quoting Professor Michael Mandelbaum, he continued: "It would be two big fat guys in a ring, with all sorts of posturing and rituals and stomping of feet, but actually very little contact, until the end of the match, when there is a brief moment of shoving and the loser gets pushed out of the ring, but nobody gets killed." Globalization, by contrast, "would be the 100meter dash, over and over and over. And no matter how many times you win, you have to race again the next day. And if you lose by just one-hundredth of a second, it can be as if you lost by an hour."

In this new environment, any program that places "the right people, in the right place, at the right time" must acknowledge that it seeks to develop policy substance as well as management and leadership in its workforce to confront the changes engendered by globalization and the new security environment. If the policy process is to be improved, it must have well-qualified policymakers who understand the issues. Many must also develop into leaders as they move through their careers. These future leaders must be able to set goals, inspire performance, and monitor progress for the success of their organizations and the overall process.

A BRIEF HISTORY OF THE PALESTINIAN STRUGGLE

The Holy Land, whose importance to several ideologues is analysed in this issue, has been a contentious place since Biblical times, whether named Canaan, *Eretz Yisrael* (the Land of Israel) or, as the Romans later called it, Palestine. The current conflict between Israelis and Palestinians can be traced back to the First World War (1914–1918) and the fall of the Ottoman Empire, which had at least nominally ruled the Middle East—including Palestine—for centuries, in the years that proceeded. The British and French colonial powers had long had a presence in the Middle East and had actually decided even before the collapse of the Ottoman Empire to carve up the region into spheres of influence in the famous Sykes-Picot Agreement (1916), drawn up by Sir Mark Sykes and Georges Picot, diplomats representing Britain and France respectively. In this agreement, Palestine fell under the British sphere of influence.

The different local actors—most importantly Zionists and Arab nationalists of various kinds—had started their quest for independence in Palestine even earlier. The Zionists, egged on by the rise of nationalist feelings across parts of Europe, persecution and anti-Semitism, and sometimes also a Biblically inspired longing for Jerusalem, had been active in Europe and the United States since the late 19th century. The Arab World, meanwhile, witnessed a similar sense of nationalist awakening and a renewed appreciation for the Arab literary and cultural heritage, although this did not always translate into direct opposition to the Ottoman Empire. The Zionists lobbied for (especially) British support for their goal of setting up a Jewish state in Palestine, which was eventually rewarded by the so-called Balfour Declaration (1917), an official British statement of support for "a Jewish national home" in Palestine, whose intent was later confirmed at the San Remo Conference (1920). In the meantime, the Arabs were also actively involved in efforts to achieve their independence. Most importantly, the Hashemite emir of Mecca, $usayn b. Al+ (c. 1853–1931), engaged in lobbying efforts of his own with the British official Sir Henry McMahon, promising to aid the allied war efforts against the Ottomans in return for Arab independence. This led to the infamous correspondence over the division of the Middle East between McMahon and $usayn in 1915, in which vague British promises were made and which caused the latter to launch the Arab Revolt against the Ottoman Empire in 1916.

The conflicting British promises to Zionists and Arabs not only contributed to the increased frustration and strife between the two rival parties in Palestine itself during the period of British rule (1917–1948), with both feeling betrayed by London, but it also pointed to a phenomenon that was to last for several decades after 1948: the relative lack of attention for what the Arabs of Palestine themselves wanted. Although the British presence and especially the huge waves of Jewish immigration were actively and repeatedly resisted by the country's Arab population, the latter seemed to play a very limited role at best in the international negotiations over their land. Instead, until the 1960s the major powers and the surrounding states were in control of what happened to Palestine.

Arab States

From the late 1940s to the late 1960s, the most important actors appropriating the question of Palestine on the diplomatic and military levels were not so much the Palestinians themselves but rather the leaders of Arab regimes. They were far from successful, however. The fact that the United Nations General Assembly voted in favour of Resolution 181, which divided British-controlled Palestine into an Arab and a Jewish state, showed that Arab diplomatic efforts ultimately came to naught. The same could be said about their military attempts to nip the newly founded state of Israel in the bud by entering the 1948 war for Palestine, which led to an increase in the territory controlled by Israel on the one hand and the Egyptian and Jordanian occupation of, respectively, the Gaza Strip and the West Bank (as they are now known) on the other.

Although the early Arab efforts to fight Israel in the 1940s clearly failed, the next decade saw several new Arab leaders rise to power whose ambitions did not stop at the borders of their own countries but who clearly also saw themselves as acting on behalf of the Palestinian cause. Foremost among them was the Egyptian President Gaml Abd al-Ncir (Nasser) (r. 1954–1970), who strove to unite the Arab world around his particular blend of Arab socialism and portrayed himself as the champion of the Palestinians as well. Through his powerful rhetoric, his staunch anti-colonialism and his pan-Arab discourse, Nasser was able to gain huge popularity in his own country and in the rest of the Arab world during his reign, and his defiance of France, Great Britain and Israel during the Suez Crisis of 1956 did nothing to diminish this. So much so, even, that historian William L. Cleveland refers to this period as "the age of Nasser". His popularity notwithstanding, the war between Israel and its Arab neighbours in 1967 led to a catastrophic defeat of the latter and caused a huge blow to Nasser's credibility and to his pan-Arab approach of the question of Palestine.

Perhaps less dramatic, but no less unsuccessful than Nasser, was the pursuit of the Hashemites, whose descendants still rule Jordan today, to represent the Palestinian cause. The precise nature of Hashemite ties with both the British and the Zionists has long been a subject of discussion. The controversies surrounding their ambivalent position towards Palestine in the first half of the 20 century include not only the correspondence between Sir Henry McMahon and $usayn b. Al+ mentioned above, but also the negotiations between the latter's son Faycal b. $usayn and the (later) first Israeli President Chaim Weizmann, as well as the deals that the first king of Jordan, Abdallh b. $usayn, tried to make with both Britain and the Zionists. Although King Abdallh (r. 1946–1951), like Nasser, managed to occupy part of Palestine in 1948, his grandson, King $usayn (r. 1953–1999), eventually lost this territory again in the same 1967 war that had so humiliated his Egyptian counterpart.

An essential difference between the Egyptian and Jordanian approach to the Palestinian cause was the latter's all-encompassing appropriation of the question of Palestine. Like Nasser, Jordan's rulers championed Palestinian rights for pan-Arab reasons of their own, but unlike the Egyptian president, they also viewed themselves as the true and sole representatives of the Palestinians for quite some time.

Several reasons accounted for this difference, such as the fact that many Palestinians had fled to Jordan during the 1948 war and that the country controlled the major part of what was left of Palestine—the West Bank, which included the historically and religiously significant old city of Jerusalem. As such, the Jordanian regime identified (or at least claimed to identify) with the Palestinian question in a way that no other non-Palestinian actor did.

Palestinian Nationalists

While the question of Palestine was a pan-Arab cause to Nasser and a national and religious issue to the Hashemite rulers of Jordan, to Palestinians themselves it was one of independence and self-determination. Although several small Palestinian guerrilla groups had been set up in the 1950s, of which Ysir Araft's nominally socialist Fata% movement was the most important, the main diplomatic vehicle used to further the Palestinian cause was the Palestine Liberation Organisation (PLO), founded in 1964. Born out of an idea to organise Palestinian resistance to Israel more formally, it enjoyed only reluctant support from some Arab leaders—notably King $usayn of Jordan, who feared the organisation would challenge his country's sovereignty over the West Bank and its inhabitants. As such, the PLO started as an Arab organisation dedicated to the Palestinian cause, rather than an organisation led by Palestinians themselves.

However, the mostly Arab character of the PLO did not last very long since the defeat of the Arab armies in the 1967 war not only dealt a blow to the rulers' credibility as champions of the Palestinian cause, but also caused them to lose the West Bank and the Gaza Strip—the only parts of Palestine still in Arab hands—to Israel. This, combined with the growing stature of Palestinian guerrilla fighters, eventually led to a "take-over" of the PLO by Palestinian groups in 1969. As such, the Arab loss in 1967 paved the way for a "Palestinisation" of the question of Palestine, which is something that the future Palestinian leader Ysir Araft seems to have realised quite well. However, the position of "true" representative of the Palestinian people remained contested for years, particularly between the PLO on the one hand and the Jordanian King $usayn on the other. It was not until the Palestinian intifada (1987–1992) began that the latter fully realised the important political standing of the PLO versus his own increasingly weak claims to Palestinian leadership, causing him to sever all administrative and financial ties between Jordan and the West

Bank in 1988. From that year onwards, the Palestinian cause was represented by Palestinians.

Palestinian Islamists

Our brief overview of Arab and Palestinian appropriations of the question of Palestine seems to suggest that, at least until 1988, Islam did not play much of a role in efforts to fight Israel. Although it is correct to state that large-scale organised Islamist action against Israel did not begin until the founding of the Palestinian Islamic Jihad in 1981, Islam has played a role in the Palestinian struggle for much longer. This is not surprising given the significance of Jerusalem in particular in Islam. The Prophet Muhammad is said to have used Jerusalem as the first direction of prayer (*qibla*), before using Mecca for this purpose. Moreover, Q. 17: 1 states (in Arberry's translation): "Glory be to Him, who carried His servant by night from the Holy Mosque (*al-masjid al-harm*) to the Further Mosque (*al-masjid al-aqc*)." The so-called "night journey" by the Prophet from Mecca to Jerusalem and his related journey to heaven are both connected with this verse and have come to signify the importance of Jerusalem in Islamic tradition, as embodied by the Al-Aqc Mosque and the Dome of the Rock, which were built in the early 8th and late 7th century AD, respectively. Considering the religious significance of Jerusalem, it is not surprising that this Islamic symbolism is regularly invoked by Palestinian Islamists.

It should be emphasised from the outset that pious Palestinian Muslims engaged in political or military action on behalf of the Palestinian cause need not necessarily do so out of religious conviction. It is not at all clear, for instance, whether early Palestinian Muslim scholars involved in the conflict with Israel should be seen as Islamists (i.e., as Muslims who believe their religion is also an ideology calling for political and social action), instead of simply as Palestinian nationalists who happen to be religious. In any case, the earliest well-known example of a Palestinian "Islamist" was Izz al-Din al-Qassm, a preacher from the coastal town of Haifa who is said to have started a revolt against the British in northern Palestine in the early 1930s. His death at the hands of the British in Jenin in 1935 caused huge crowds to attend his funeral, followed by a nation-wide strike several months later that, in turn, led to the Palestinian revolt of 1936–1939, suggesting that his ideals struck a chord among many Palestinians.

Another important Palestinian Muslim leader involved in the conflict was the erstwhile critic of al-Qassm, Muhammad Amin al-husayni (1895–1974), better known as al-Hajj Amin. A member of the prominent Jerusalemite al-husayni family, of which Ysir Araft was also part, al-Hajj Amin was closely involved in both dealing with the British and prominent Palestinian representatives of the day, including the rival Jerusalemite al-Nashshibi family. This wavering between two parties characterised the early part of his career as Mufti of Jerusalem, during which he became the most powerful leader of the Palestinian national movement. Although initially sceptical and reluctant to rise up against the British, the latter's ambivalent plans about Palestine and the revolt of 1936–1939 that swept through the country did not leave al-husayni untouched. He quickly became the (increasingly radical) leader of the revolt and was subsequently stripped of his duties and forced to go into exile, where he continued his efforts on behalf of Palestinian independence but ultimately had to leave it to the PLO to represent the Palestinian cause.

While al-Qassm and al-husayni can be said to have been individuals giving a more Islamic flavour to the Palestinian nationalist movement, the first half of the 20th century also witnessed a rise in organised Islamism in the form of the Muslim Brotherhood, which reached Palestine too. The organisation, founded in 1928 by the Egyptian Hasan al-Bann (1906–1949) to Islamise both state and society, came to Palestine in the 1930s, where a branch of the group was founded by alBann's son-in-law Saeed Raman in 1945. From that time onwards until 1947/1948, the Muslim Brotherhood became heavily involved in the Palestine question, even militarily. However, after the 1948 war the Palestinian Muslim Brotherhood in the West Bank became increasingly close to the Jordanian regime, much to the dismay of one of its members, Taqi al-Din al-Nabhni (1909–1977), who had studied at Al-Azhar University in Cairo. Al-Nabhni favoured a much more radical approach to Islamising state and society than the gradualism that his fellow Muslim

Brothers called for and broke away from the organisation to found the Islamic Liberation Party (Hizb al-Tahrir al-Islmi) in Jerusalem in 1953. His preferred solution to the Palestinian question was not so much nationalist but rather pan-Islamist, calling for an international Islamic effort to liberate Palestine and establishing a caliphate across the Muslim world, replacing the existing regimes there. Given this revolutionary position, the Islamic Liberation Party has often been suppressed throughout its history and has only a negligible presence in many Middle Eastern countries now. Little therefore appears to be left of al-Nabhni's legacy, although the organisation has a somewhat stronger presence in Western countries such as Great Britain.

A different Palestinian Islamist movement, though one that bore some striking ideological resemblances to al-Nabhni's ideas, was the Palestinian Islamic Jihad, founded by Fatmi al-Shiqqi (1951–1995) and Abd al-Aziz Awda (b. 1950) in 1981. Both men had studied in Egypt, where they came into contact with Islamist ideas. Like al-Nabhni, they grew increasingly frustrated with the Muslim Brotherhood's gradualist approach and preferred more radical action. This idea was further stimulated after the Islamic Revolution in Iran, which showed that an Islamic movement could not only overthrow a powerful regime but could even set up an Islamic state in its stead. Also like al-Nabhni, the Palestinian Islamic Jihad saw its fight as part of a greater Islamic struggle for a caliphate across the Middle East, although it placed more emphasis on the liberation of Palestine. The organisation developed a social infrastructure through its control of mosques, its founding of student associations and its publication of several periodicals. This aided the organisation in recruiting new members, which was complemented after a few years with armed struggle against Israel. Although the Islamic Jihad played a role in the intifada as well as in the Al-Aqc intifada (2000–2005) and is a force to be reckoned with even today, it could never reach the size, strength and popularity of its main Islamist challenger: Hamas.

The Islamic Resistance Movement (Harakat al-Muqwama allslmiyya), as Hamas is officially named, was initially a branch of the Muslim Brotherhood that had enough of only Islamisation from below, which had been the Brotherhood's policy until then, and also wanted to engage in armed struggle against Israel. This desire became particularly acute when the intifada broke out in 1987, during which elements within the Brotherhood did not want to be seen standing on the sidelines while the rest of the population resisted Israeli occupation. Thus, in December 1987, Hamas was founded. The organisation grew in size and popularity, eventually becoming perhaps the biggest Palestinian group in the occupied territories in terms of popular support, encompassing the Palestinian Muslim Brotherhood in its entirety. It participated not only in the uprising that started in 1987, but also played a major role in the al-Aqc intifada and has shown itself to be a staunch opponent of the peace process between Israel and the Palestinians through suicide-bombings and rocket attacks against Israeli civilians and soldiers. Incidentally, both the group's armed wing responsible for many of these attacks and Hamas's rockets have been named after Izz al-Din al-Qassm, further underlining the latter's stature in the historical imagination of Palestinian Islamists. Since 2006, the organisation has also attained political power after winning the parliamentary elections of that year, although subsequent conflicts with Fata% have lead to a split in power between the West Bank and the Gaza Strip, with only the latter being ruled by Hamas now.

Palestine and Transnational Islamism

The ideologues and groups mentioned above are Islamist, but also strongly Palestinian in nature. Yet the Palestinian question has always been an international one. However, the internationalisation of Palestine as an Islamic cause that Islamists all over the world claim as their own is of a more recent date, although its origins can perhaps be found in the pan-Islamist actions of Hajj Amin al-husayni, dating back to 1931. To understand this international Islamisation of the Palestinian question from the 1970s onwards—coinciding with the Middle Eastern rise of Islamism in general—two trends need to be taken into account: the spread of Salafism and the war in Afghanistan (1979–1989).

The rise of Salafism, often seen by both its adherents and uninformed outsiders as a pure and unadulterated form of Islam, coincided with the rise of Islamism as a whole since the Arab loss in 1967. Salafism can be defined as the branch of Sunni Islam whose adherents try to emulate the "pious predecessors" (*al-salaf al-clih*, hence the name Salafism), especially the first three generations of Muslims, as strictly and in as many spheres of life as possible. It is a much more scriptural and uncompromising trend than the relatively accommodating and doctrinally pragmatic Muslim Brotherhood and has different historical, theological and political roots. Perhaps partly because of its image as pure and devoid of cultural innovations (*bidah*), Salafism spread across the Muslim world, abetted by the writings of important mediaeval Salafi scholars such as Ibn Taymiyya (1263–1328), Ibn Qayyim al-Jawziyya (1292–1350) and Ibn Kathir (c. 1300–1373). A major factor in the promotion of Salafism was Saudi propaganda from the 1960s onwards, spreading a message of strict, yet regime-friendly Salafism to counter Nasser's socialist rhetoric, and, after 1979, the Shiite discourse of the Islamic Revolution in Iran. This process was stimulated even further by migrant workers in the Gulf region who often adopted Salafi customs there before returning to their home countries more conservative and more (overtly) pious than they had been before. This spread of Salafism had no direct link with the Palestine question, but it did mean that Islamism increasingly became Salafi in nature. This became more relevant in combination with the conflict in Afghanistan.

After the then Soviet Union had invaded Afghanistan to support the fledgling communist government there in 1979, many newly pious Muslims felt that it was their religious duty to help defend their fellow Afghan believers from the attacks by the Soviets and decided to travel to Afghanistan to fight them. This development was sometimes encouraged by Arab regimes, who often looked upon the greater religiosity of some of their citizens with concern and were therefore glad to get rid of them or were keen to support these "Afghan Arabs" in order to portray themselves as pious rulers. As such, a gathering of radical Islamists and pious Muslims—often of a Salafi persuasion—trained, studied and sometimes even fought together in Afghanistan. Their experiences not only forged ties between many of these men but also gave them military skills and in some cases led to a cross-fertilisation of ideas.

The combination of the increasing "Salafisation" of Islamism and the strengthened ties between its adherents forged on the battlefields of Afghanistan created not only a more or less ideologically coherent discourse on "Crusaders", "imperialism" and Arab "tyrants", but also an internationally supported Islamist message on Palestine. This discourse, represented most prominently by al-Qaida, is not only strongly pro-Palestinian, as we saw earlier, but also sometimes describes the question of Palestine as integral to its actions. Ayman al-'awhir+, for instance, bin Ldin's successor as the leader of al-Qaida, recently stated in relation to the political chaos in Egypt and Syria that "Cairo and Damascus are the two gates to Jerusalem" (*bawwbat bayt al-Maqdis*). This suggests that he sees the fight for overthrowing the rulers in Muslim countries at least partly as a step towards the "liberation" of Jerusalem, a belief he has expressed before.

The Rise of Salafism in Gaza

The spread of this international and much more Salafi form of Islamism championed by al-Qaida has not left Palestinians in the occupied territories untouched either. As Hroub has pointed out, Salafism of a peaceful and apolitical kind in the West Bank can be traced back to the 1970s and is related to Saudi efforts to counter the radical Shiite rhetoric coming from Iran after the Islamic Revolution took place there in 1979. The activities of such Palestinian Salafis have focussed on studying "pure" Islam, education and missionary activities. Similar Salafi groups exist in the Gaza Strip, where their activities started even before the Islamic Revolution, partly as a result of scholars returning from their studies in Saudi Arabia, but whose ideological focus is generally the same as that of their West Bank brethren. Issues such as the fight against Israel and the "liberation of Palestine", on the other hand, are seen by many Salafis from Gaza as "political", which should be avoided.

While most Palestinian Salafis do not fight the powers that be and focus on missionary activities instead, the past few years have witnessed the emergence of a radical Salafi minority that espouses a message that is much more akin to what al-Qaida stands for and engages in different types of violence. Although some of these groups seem to be rather tribal in nature without a coherent ideology, others are clearly Salafi in nature. In the Gaza Strip, groups such as Jund Ancr Allh and the Jamaat al-Tawhid wa-l-Jihd are the most prominent of a large cluster of small like-minded "organisations" that seem to have come into existence through frustration over Hamas's supposedly compromised and watered-down Jihad against Israel on the one hand and a susceptibility to the "purity" of the Salafi message—particularly that of al-Qaida—on the other. It is therefore not surprising that these groups pair a Salafi outlook with military activities against Israel. While such attacks— mostly rockets fired at Israeli towns like Sderot—are perhaps ideologically supported by Hamas, their activities may not always fit the latter's agenda of wanting to keep quiet in the Gaza Strip or maintaining a cease-fire with Israel. For this reason and others, Hamas has clashed with such radical Salafi organisations and has tried to suppress them, even going so far as killing some of their members.

Although the radical Salafi groups in the Gaza Strip are small and relatively insignificant, their conflicts with Hamas have garnered the attention of like-minded Salafi ideologues and activists across the world who were quick to condemn Hamas for its use of violence and its crackdown. The presence of such groups also shows that the Islamist concern for Palestine has, in a way, come full circle: having transcended the national level and having been adopted by international ideologues of different backgrounds in its new and more Salafi flavour, it has returned to Palestine and has been re-appropriated by some Palestinians themselves, who now use this radical Salafism as an ideology that inspires them to attack Israel and champion the Palestinian cause.

OUR FOCUS: TRANSNATIONAL JIHAD IDEOLOGUES OF PALESTINIAN ORIGIN

In this special issue, we focus on the *historical* dimension of the Palestineal-Qaida connection. Specifically, we ask whether the

Israeli-Palestinian conflict has fuelled transnational jihadism by producing activists predisposed—due to their exile and/or sense of grievance—to transnational militancy. Several analysts have proposed such an "agent production effect" of the Israeli-Palestinian conflict. The Israeli scholar of jihadism

Reuven Paz noted in 2002 that Palestinians appear to be overrepresented among ideologues associated with transnational forms of Islamism. Paz did not elaborate on the causal mechanism behind this overrepresentation, but listed a number of Palestinian ideologues of note, from Taq al-Dan al-Nabhn via Abdallh Azzm (the leader of the "Arab Afghan" movement) to Abk Qatda al-Filismini (the formerly UK-based radical preacher). More recently, the Lebanese journalist Hazim al-Amin has presented a more elaborate explanation for this phenomenon. In a book entitled "The Orphaned Salafi: The Palestinian Face of Global Jihad and al-Qaida" (2011), he argues that statelessness and exile led many Palestinian Islamists in the diaspora to focus on issues grander than national liberation. The Palestinian-Jordanian author Marwn Shahda has made a similar argument, though in less depth.

There is much anecdotal evidence to support this hypothesis. A good example is the diary of the former al-Qaida facilitator Zayn al-Abidin Muhammad $usayn (Abk Zubayda), a Palestinian who grew up in Saudi Arabia. In 1990—before radicalizing—he wrote "[I am a Palestinian] with no homeland, no passport and no identity... while the Jews are running loose in my country." Abk Zubayda was forced to attend university in India because only Saudi nationals were allowed to study computer science (his preferred subject) in the Kingdom. Only after arriving in India did he decide to explore jihadi training camps in Peshawar, Pakistan.

The main purpose of this special issue is to assess al-Amin's proposition that exile has made Palestinians predisposed to transnational activism. It is perhaps useful to start by surveying some of the available quantitative evidence on the presence of Palestinians in the world of transnational jihadism. In so doing, it is important to bear in mind that, numbering around 10 million, Palestinian Muslims make up no more than 0.6 % of the world's Muslim population. If transnational jihads were a cross-section of the Muslim population we should expect 1 in every 170 jihads to be of Palestinian descent.

As it happens, the available data suggests that Palestinians are not overrepresented in the movement as a whole. They are present, but not in particularly large numbers. The cross-national sample of 172 al-Qaida associates presented in Marc Sageman's book *Understanding Terrorist Networks* contains only two Palestinians. Available data on Jihad foreign fighters suggest the same. One of us (Hegghammer) collected a preliminary list of names of Arab fighters who appear in the main sources on the Afghan Jihad in the 1980s. Only 8 of around 250 named individuals in the sample are Palestinians (although the list is non-representative and potentially biased). In the so-called "Sinjar Records", which provide the self-reported national origin of 595 foreign fighters with al-Qaida in Iraq around the year 2006, there are no Palestinians. Even in the current war in Syria, which is right next door to Israel, Palestinians appear to be only slightly overrepresented among the pro-rebel foreign fighters: A recent study found that only 7 of 280 individuals hailed as fallen martyrs on Jihad websites were Palestinian. There are all kinds of problems with the above-mentioned data, but what exists suggests that Palestinians are not strongly overrepresented in transnational Jihad networks.

To be sure, al-Amin and Paz were not talking about foot soldiers. Indeed, if we look at lists of Jihad ideologues, Palestinians appear to be slightly better represented, although the numbers are less striking than al-Amin's argument seems to suggest. For example, the *Militant Ideology Atlas* produced by the Combating Terrorism Centre at West Point in 2006 included 132 ideologues, only 3 of whom we could identify as Palestinian. Another list circulated on Jihad websites in 2009 under the title "Mujahid's bookbag", includes some 53 names, four of which appear to be Palestinian. On both these lists, Saudis and Egyptians outnumber the Palestinians.

However, not all Jihad ideologues are equally influential. If we take into consideration the "weight" of the Palestinian presence in the Jihad ideological pantheon, then the picture changes completely. Palestine is represented on the above-mentioned lists with three veritable giants of Jihad ideology: Abdallh Azzm, Abk Muhammad al-Maqdisi, and Abk Qatda al-Filismini. Azzm (d. 1989) has been called the "Godfather of Jihad" due to his crucial role in bringing foreign fighters to Afghanistan in the 1980s. He also wrote several seminal works of Jihad literature that continue to be widely read today, such as *The Defence of Muslim Lands* and *Join the Caravan*. Al-Maqdisi, who lives in Jordan, is widely recognized as one of the most influential Jihad clerics alive today. Al-Filisyini is also a very prolific and influential author, and was long considered one of the most prominent Jihad clerics residing in the West. (He was based in the UK from 1993 until his deportation to Jordan in 2013.)

It is difficult to reliably quantify the influence of these figures, but one indicator is download counts from Jihad literature repositories. According to data from 2006, the 20 most accessed texts on any topic on the website *Minbar al-Tawhid wa-l-Jihd* included ten by al-Maqdisi (including the top one) and two by al-Filisyini. Of the 20 most downloaded texts on any topic, 11 were by al-Maqdisi and one was by Azzm. Another indicator is recommendations and reading lists. We have already mentioned that these three men are among the 53 names in the "Mujahid's Bookbag". We also find them on a more exclusive list of the top five authors any budding Jihad should read. The list appears in a popular manual titled "39 Ways to Serve Jihad and Take Part in It", written in 2003 by a Saudi militant named Muhammad al-Slim, Abdallh Azzm [Palestinian-Jordanian], 2) Yksuf al-Uyayri [Saudi], 3) Abk Muhammad al-Maqdisi [Palestinian-Jordanian], 4) Abk Qatda al-Filisyini [Palestinian-Jordanian], and 5) Abd al-Qdir b. Abd al-Aziz [Egyptian]. All of this is anecdotal evidence, of course, but our basic claim—that Azzm, al-Maqdis, and al-Filisyini are prominent voices in the transnational Jihad movement—should not be particularly controversial.

Given that Palestinian ideologues have been few, but very influential, it is not possible to assess the historical effect of the Palestinian issue on the evolution of jihadism by looking merely at the overall proportion of Palestinian ideologues. Instead we need a research design that digs deep into these few individuals' biographies and traces the Palestinian factor, if any, in their trajectory toward transnationalism. That is why the four articles in this special issue are all in-depth biographical studies based on new primary sources. Each of the four main articles that make up this special issue examines a prominent Palestinian Islamist who engaged in or advocated some form of transnational militancy. Mark Sanagan first examines the early 20 century figure Izz al-Din al-Qassm (1882–1935), who is included here partly because he is a very prominent and understudied figure in the history of Palestinian Islamism, and partly because he engaged in what today we would call "foreign fighter activism" against the Italians in Libya and the French in Syria.

The biographies vary slightly in their focus and approach, reflecting author preferences and subject specificities, but all articles set out to explore the relationship between nationalism and transnationalism in the lives of these figures. Key questions include: What are the objective details of their biography relating to Palestine? How Palestinian did (or do) they consider themselves? What was (or is) their view of the Palestinian issue and its significance relative to other problems in the world? Why did they choose transnational activism instead of a career focused narrowly on Palestine? Did they "go global" despite or because of their Palestinian heritage?

Before we let the contributors answer these questions, it may be useful to review, briefly, the history of the Palestinian resistance. Biographies constitute rather narrow windows into history, and our case studies cover partially distinct periods. Al-Qassm's prime time (1910s to 30s) was very different from that of Azzm (1960s to 80s), and even more so from that of al-Maqdisi and al-Filisyini (1990s and 2000s). The following section therefore draws out the historical lines that allow us to connect and contextualise the biographies we are about to read.

ISI & FOMENTING OF GLOBAL TERROR

In the post 9/11 decade, ISI's involvement in fomenting terror modules in different parts of the world, using proxy outfits like the LeT or the HUJI has been exposed, be it through the arrest of

Virgil Brigitte in Australia (2003) or the failed terror plots in the UK and the US in more recent times.

This global terrorist networks with linkages to ISI us shown in the diagram that follows. Outfits inside Pakistan which have had links with or were spawned by the ISI include the LeT, the Jaish e Mohd (JeM), Lashkar e Jhangvi (LeJ – more into sectarian terrorism), Harkat ul Mujahideen (HuM) which morphed into HUJI, and the Dawood underworld mafia. On the periphery ring are outfits with presence in countries like Bangladesh-the Ahle Hadis al Bangladesh (AHAB), HUJI-BD, Jamiyatul Mujahideen Bangladesh (JMB) and Jagrata Muslim Janata Bangladesh (JMJB). In recent years though, security agencies of the new government in Bangladesh havedone much to dismantle these outfits. Nevertheless, linkages persist between ISI and Pakistan based religious or ideologically motivated terrorism outfits like LeT, Jaish and HUJI in countries like Afghanistan. Modules have also been found in Europe or USA.

Decision makers in army/views and orientation of senior officers in Army/ISI on matters of geo-strategic import.

A career or a posting in the ISI has now emerged as a desirable option, with young officers of the rank of captain, major or colonel enjoying far greater power, perks and privileges in the ISI than many of their peers in more routine army field assignments. At any given time, the decision makers in the ISI are the army chief and the DG, ISI. At the second rung of ISI are major generals, one or the other of them could be personally close to the COAS, in which case they may be able influence policy decisions but this may be the exception than the rule. As in the army itself, a collegiate or consensus decision making pattern is usually the norm and prevails in decision making and operational initiatives undertaken by ISI.

Army/ISI & Politicization

With regard to military-civilian interaction, all ISI officers believe in the primacy of the army and its status as the vanguard institution of state. There is a general contempt for all manner of politicians and political parties. This is compounded by the fact that there are no politicians of individually high popularity or charismain Pakistan at present.

Though the lustre attaching to ISI was somewhat tarnished by the US sealsmission to take out Osama bin Laden in Abbotabad in Ma,2011, as well asthe opprobrium following the Saleem Shehzad murder post the attack on theMehran Naval Base. But by and large, all army officers, especially those in ISI,even at middle or relatively junior levels believe that the army's dominant rolein taking vital foreign policy decisions has only been good for the country andcannot be questioned. They would not readily countenance any erosion in thisdominance, unless the army chief himself and the collegiate leadership group of Corps Commanders acquiesce in such a role re-definition. This is not likely to happen in the foreseeable future.

FUTURE ENGAGEMENT WITH THE ISI

When interviewed about the relationship between the West and Pakistan and the ongoing conflict in Afghanistan, the bestselling author Steven Coll stated:

This could not be a more complicated war. If you think about it, the United States is essentially waging a war against its own ally. The Taliban are a proxy of the government of Pakistan [orchestrated by the ISI]. We are an ally of the government of Pakistan. We are fighting the Taliban. In the end, the Taliban will be defeated strategically when the government of Pakistan makes a strategic decision that its future does not lie in partnership with Islamic extremists. (2009)

Coll pinpoints the root of current and future problems in dealing with the ISI and their clandestine terrorist support networks. In 2009, the U.S. provided close to $6.5 billion dollars in aid to the Pakistani government; $300 million of that was dedicated to military spending (Mohammad). The West is figuratively caught between a rock and a hard place. It requires the assistance of Pakistan to successfully prosecute counter-terrorism campaigns in Southwest Asia. Yet, the ISI has infiltrated all ranks of Pakistan's military structure and leverages sympathizers and supporters throughout the Pakistani population. A large amount of that military aid is falling into the hands of the sponsors of the exact networks the West is attempting to defeat. On February 16, 2010 the Taliban's second in command, Mullah Baradar, was captured in a raid conducted jointly by the ISI and the U.S. Western leaders hoped that this would be a catalyst for strengthening the cooperation between the ISI and Western intelligence agencies and serve as an indication that the ISI would begin dismissing its historical involvement with militants. However, after a close examination into the raid, the New York Times provided: Relations between the intelligence services, [CIA and ISI], of the United States and Pakistan have long been marred by suspicions that Pakistan has sheltered the Afghan Taliban. The Pakistanis have long denied it. New details of the raid indicate that the arrest of the No. 2 Taliban leader was not necessarily the result of a new determination by Pakistan to go after the Taliban, or a bid to improve its strategic position in the region. Rather, it may be something more prosaic: "a lucky accident..." (Shane and Schmitt) Upon Baradar's capture, ISI officers delayed allowing U.S. intelligence officers to question him and were hesitant in sharing news and information about his detention with the Pakistani press (in fear of casting themselves in a pro-Western light).

The ISI will continue to act out of its own interest. It has grown in size from its inception and now forms a state within the Pakistani state. While it serves as an intelligence agency of the Pakistani government, the Pakistani government is largely unable to control its actions or relationships with terrorist organizations, both domestic and abroad. Ongoing operations to defeat extremists and terrorists places the ISI at a crossroads with Western intelligence agencies and irregular warfare personnel. Without a complete transformation of the ISI's motivations, allegiances, extremist slant, and structure, it will continue to exist as more of an enemy to the West than an ally.

Conclusion

The historic actions of the ISI in sponsoring organizations like al-Qaeda, JEM, LET and HUM, as well as their utilization of the Taliban as a proxy for foreign policy, signals that the ISI is a significant state sponsor of terrorism. "Since Pakistan has terrorism, nuclear weapons, religious extremism, economic instability, and political volatility, easy [foreign policy] answers provide little guidance in a dangerous, fluid environment. If, due to ISI sins of omission or commission, terrorists acquire Pakistani nuclear weapons and there is a nuclear incident or nuclear war, the consequences will be unthinkable" (Roberts 109). These variables set the ISI's sponsorship apart from other international sponsors and make it definitively the most dangerous.

A careful policy of continued engagement with the ISI and accountability of Western funding to Pakistan will be essential to secure future stability in the region.

The ISI will continue to be a clandestine sponsor of worldwide extremism and transnational terrorism. The fragile nature of Pakistani politics, the existence of deeply entrenched Islamic foundations, and insecurity surrounding the Pakistani nuclear arsenal make the ISI the foremost terrorist threat and non-state sponsor of terrorism in the international community. The ISI masquerades as a controllable tool of the Pakistani government while covertly supporting enemies of the international community – conclusively acting as a threat to international stability and as a fifth column within the Pakistani state.

Bibliography

Alam, Aftab : *US Policy Towards South Asia: Special Reference to Indo-Pak Relations*, Raj, Delhi, 1998.

Allana, G.: *Pakistan Movement: Historic Documents*, Karachi, Department of International Relations, University of Karachi, 1967.

Allison, Graham, *Nuclear Terrorism: The Ultimate Preventable Catastrophe*, New York: Times Books, 2004.

Ayesha Siddiqa-Agha: *Military Inc.: Inside Pakistan's Military Economy*, London: Pluto, 2007.

Azad, Maulana Abul Kalam: *India Wins Freedom*, New Delhi, Orient Longman, 1959.

Behera, Navnita : *State, identity and violence : Jammu, Kashmir and Laddakh*, New Delhi: Manohar, 2000.

Benjamin, Joseph : *Indo-Pak Relations : Prospect and Retrospect*, Reference Press, Delhi, 2004.

Chaudhary, M.: *Partition and the Curse of Rehabilitation*. Calcutta: Bengal Rehabilitation Organization, 1964.

Chitkara, M.G. : *Indo-Pak Relations Challenges Before New Millennium*, APH, Delhi, 2001.

Das, Bharti : *Irritants in Indo-Pak Relations*, Kilaso, Delhi, 2005.

Das. P.K.: *Jihad : Terrorist Strategies Against the West*, Sumit Enterprises, Delhi, 2009.

Dilip H. Mohite : *Rise of Islamic Fundamentalism and the Grand American Strategy* : Kalinga, Delhi, 2002.

Ghosh, Abhijit : *Indian Political Thought and Movement : New Interpretations and Emerging Issues*, Kolkata, K.P. Bagchi and Company, 2007.

Gupta, J.B. Das : *Islamic Fundamentalism and India* : Hope India Publications, Delhi, 2002.

Hassan, Lt Gen Gul, *Memoirs of Lt Gen Gul Hassan*, Oxford University Press, 1993.

Hoffman, Bruce, *Inside Terrorism*, New York: Columbia University Press, 1998.

Khan, Major General Sher Ali: *The Story of Soldiering and Politics in India and Pakistan*, Wajidalis, 1978.

Laquer, Walter, *The New Terrorism: Fanaticism and the Arms of Mass Destruction*, Oxford: Oxford University Press, 1999.

Lohia, Ram Manohar: *Guilty Men of India's Partition*. Allahabad: Navahind, 1960.

Multani, R K P : *Islamic Fundamentalism in South Asia* : Sumit Enterprises, Delhi, 2007.

Noorani, A.G.: *Islam and Jihad*, Leftword, Delhi, 2002.

Rizvi, Hassan Askari: *The Military and Politics in Pakistan: 1947 - 86*, Progressive Publishers 1986.

Shahid Javed: *Pakistan: The Continuing Search for Nationhood*, Westview Press, 1991.

Shuja Nawaz: *Crossed Swords: Pakistan, Its Army, and the Wars Within*, Karachi: Oxford University Press, 2008.

Stephen P. Cohen: *The Idea of Pakistan*, Washington, DC: Brookings Institution Press, 2004.

Thomas R. Metcalf : *A Concise History of India and Pakistan*, New York: Cambridge University Press, 2002).

William R. Thompson: *The Grievances of Military Coup-makers*, Beverly Hills: Sage Publications, 1973.

Index

❑❑❑